INDUSTRIAL PSYCHOLOGY

INDUSTRIAL PSYCHOLOGY

Dr. Asha Rani

CENTRUM PRESS
NEW DELHI-110002 (INDIA)

CENTRUM PRESS

H.O.: 4360/4, Ansari Road, Daryaganj,
New Delhi-110002 (India)
Tel: 23278000, 23261597, 23255577, 23286875

B.O.: No. 1015, Ist Main Road, BSK IIIrd Stage,
IIIrd Phase, IIIrd Block, Bangalore-560085 (INDIA)
Tel: 080-41723429

Email: centrumpress@gmail.com
Visit us at: www.centrumpress.com

Industrial Psychology

First Edition, 2011

ISBN 978-93-80921-58-7

PRINTED IN INDIA

Printed at Tarun Offset Printers, Delhi-110053

Contents

Preface

Industrial psychology is a relatively new branch of psychology that was created for corporations and organizations that needed more structure. Industrial psychology is able to provide this structure by evaluating employee behaviour for the good of the company. It is often referred to as *organizational psychology* because of its emphasis on analysing individuals who work for various organizations. Essentially, industrial psychologists study the behaviour of employees in a work setting. Although industrial psychology didn't begin until the 1920's, the discipline has evolved rapidly and revolutionized the workplace within the last century. Because the workplace is a social system, the application of industrial psychology is useful in understanding its complexity. For years, psychologists have studied how human beings have interacted with their environments and each other, but industrial psychology begins to evaluate the interaction between people and their jobs. Industrial psychologists can be used to improve job satisfaction as well as company productivity and is becoming vital to the success of many organizations.

There are certain things that industrial psychologists focus on when evaluating the relationship a person has with their work. They analyse the way a person works, their skills, duties, obligations, and general satisfaction with their job on a day-to-day basis. This information is extremely helpful to human resources departments and company overseers who must create training programs, feedback and rewards systems, and make hiring decisions as well as engage in recruitment practices. Most companies use industrial psychologists to train their own staff so that the organizations can run smoothly and at peak capacity. One of the most interesting aspects of industrial psychology is how employee behaviour affects others individuals on the job and organization in general. Industrial psychology can be used to reduce counterproductive behaviour, enhance team effectiveness, and boost morale. It is also vital in conflict resolution. Many individuals find the brunt of their work dissatisfaction rooted in their relationships with managers and colleagues. Fortunately, industrial psychology provides solutions for this. Although industrial psychology is a mixture of anthropology, counselling, sociology and industrial management, there are key components used in this type of psychology. Some of the key components include the evaluation of employee's personalities, perceptions, as well the biological side of their behaviour. By documenting these key points, industrial psychologists have the ability to help organizations improve their functionality and set up a system that promotes growth for the company and employees.

Industrial psychology also helps CEOs and executives adjust their way of thinking and their management style, which can impact the stress levels of the employees that they manage. By using psychology, many companies are able to retain their employees because they understand how to keep them happy. Organizations with a low retention rate and employee dissatisfaction benefit from the work and assessment of industrial psychologists.

It is an approachable and readable text for students at all levels, from undergraduates to professionals retraining.

1

Introduction

Industrial psychology is a relatively new branch of psychology that was created for corporations and organizations that needed more structure. Industrial psychology is able to provide this structure by evaluating employee behaviour for the good of the company. It is often referred to as *organizational psychology* because of its emphasis on analysing individuals who work for various organizations.

Essentially, industrial psychologists study the behaviour of employees in a work setting. Although industrial psychology didn't begin until the 1920's, the discipline has evolved rapidly and revolutionized the workplace within the last century. Because the workplace is a social system, the application of industrial psychology is useful in understanding its complexity.

For years, psychologists have studied how human beings have interacted with their environments and each other, but industrial psychology begins to evaluate the interaction between people and their jobs. Industrial psychologists can be used to improve job satisfaction as well as company productivity and is becoming vital to the success of many organizations.

There are certain things that industrial psychologists focus on when evaluating the relationship a person has with their work. They analyse the way a person works, their skills, duties, obligations, and general satisfaction with their job on a day-to-day basis. This information is extremely helpful to human resources departments and company overseers who must create training programs, feedback and rewards systems, and make hiring decisions as well as engage in recruitment practices. Most companies use industrial psychologists to train their own staff so that the organizations can run smoothly and at peak capacity.

One of the most interesting aspects of industrial psychology is how employee behaviour affects others individuals on the job and organization in general. Industrial psychology can be used to reduce counterproductive behaviour, enhance team effectiveness, and boost morale. It is also vital in conflict resolution. Many individuals find the brunt of their work dissatisfaction rooted in their relationships with managers and colleagues. Fortunately, industrial psychology provides solutions for this.

Although industrial psychology is a mixture of anthropology, counselling, sociology and industrial management, there are key components used in this type of psychology. Some of the key components include the evaluation of employee's personalities, perceptions, as well the biological side of their behaviour. By documenting these key points, industrial psychologists have the ability to help organizations improve their functionality and set up a system that promotes growth for the company and employees.

Industrial psychology also helps CEOs and executives adjust their way of thinking and their management style, which can impact the stress levels of the employees that they manage. By using psychology, many companies are able to retain their employees because they understand how to keep them happy. Organizations with a low retention rate and employee dissatisfaction benefit from the work and assessment of industrial psychologists.

Impact of Industrialization

Industrialisatioon (British English) or Industrialization (Canadian & American English) is the process of social and economic change that transforms a human group from a pre-industrial society into an industrial one. It is a part of a wider modernisation process, where social change and economic development are closely related with technological innovation, particularly with the development of large-scale energy and metallurgy production. It is the extensive organisation of an economy for the purpose of manufacturing.

Industrialisation also introduces a form of philosophical change where people obtain a different attitude towards their perception of nature, and a sociological process of ubiquitous rationalisation. There is considerable literature on the factors facilitating industrial modernisation and enterprise development. Key positive factors identified by researchers have ranged from favourable political-legal environments for industry and commerce, through abundant natural resources of various kinds, to plentiful supplies of relatively low-cost, skilled and adaptable labour.

One survey of countries in Africa, Latin America, the Caribbean, and the Middle East and the rest of Asia in the late 20th century found that high levels of structural differentiation, functional specialisation, and autonomy of economic systems from government were likely to contribute greatly to industrial-commercial growth and prosperity. Amongst other things, relatively open trading systems with zero or low duties on imported goods tended to stimulate industrial cost-efficiency and innovation across the board. Free and flexible labour and other markets also helped raise general business-economic performance levels, as did rapid popular learning capabilities.

Positive work ethics in populations at large combined with skills in quickly utilising new technologies and scientific discoveries were likely to boost production and income levels – and as the latter rose, markets for consumer goods and services of all kinds tended to expand and provide a further stimulus to industrial investment and economic growth. By the end of the century, East Asia was one of the most economically successful regions of the world – with free market countries such as Hong Kong being widely seen as models for other, less developed countries around the world to emulate. The first country to industrialise was Great Britain during the Industrial Revolution.

According to the original sector classification of Jean Fourastié, an economy consists of a "Primary sector" of commodity production (farming, livestock breeding, exploitation of mineral resources), a "secondary sector" of manufacturing and processing, and a "Tertiary Sector" of service industries. The industrialisation process is historically based on the expansion of the secondary sector in an economy dominated by primary activities.

The first ever transformation to an industrial economy from an agrarian one was called the Industrial Revolution and this took place in the late 18th and early 19th centuries in a few countries of Western Europe and North America, beginning in Great Britain. This was the first industrialization in the world's history.

The Second Industrial Revolution describes a later, somewhat less dramatic change that came about in the late 19th century with the widespread availability of electric power, internal combustion engines, and assembly lines to the already industrialised nations.

The lack of an industrial sector in a country is widely seen as a major handicap in improving a country's economy, and power, pushing many governments to encourage or enforce industrialisation.

History of Industrialisation

Most pre-industrial economies had standards of living not much above subsistence, aming that the majority of the population were focused on producing their means of survival. For example, in medieval Europe, 80% of the labour force was employed in subsistence agriculture.

Some pre-industrial economies, such as classical Athens, had trade and commerce as significant factors, so native Greeks could enjoy wealth far beyond a sustenance standard of living through the use of slavery. Famines were frequent in most pre-industrial societies, although some, such as the Netherlands and England of the seventeenth and eighteenth centuries, the Italian city states of the fifteenth century, the medieval Islamic Caliphate, and the ancient Greek and Roman civilisations were able to escape the famine cycle through increasing trade and commercialisation of the agricultural sector. It is estimated that during the seventeenth century Netherlands imported nearly 70% of its grain supply and in the fifth century BC Athens imported three quarters of its total food supply.

Industrialisation through innovation in manufacturing processes first started with the Industrial Revolution in the northwest and Midlands of England in the eighteenth century. It spread to Europe and North America in the nineteenth century, and to the rest of the world in the twentieth.

Industrial Revolution in Western Europe

In the eighteenth and nineteenth centuries, Great Britain experienced a massive increase in agricultural productivity known as the British Agricultural Revolution, which enabled an unprecedented population growth, freeing a significant percentage of the workforce from farming, and helping to drive the Industrial Revolution.

Due to the limited amount of arable land and the overwhelming efficiency of mechanised farming, the increased population could not be dedicated to agriculture. New agricultural techniques allowed a single peasant to feed more workers than previously; however, these techniques also increased the demand for machines and other hardwares, which had traditionally been provided by the urban artisans. Artisans, collectively called bourgeoisie, employed rural exodus workers to increase their output and meet the country's needs.

The growth of their business coupled with the lack of experience of the new workers pushed a rationalisation and standardisation of the duties the in workshops, thus leading to a division of labour, that is, a primitive form of Fordism. The process of creating a good was divided into simple tasks, each one of them being gradually mechanized in order to boost productivity and thus increase income.

The accumulation of capital allowed investments in the conception and application of new technologies, enabling the industrialisation process to continue to evolve. The industrialisation process formed a class of industrial workers who had more money to spend than their agricultural cousins. They spent this on items such as tobacco and sugar, creating new mass markets that stimulated more investment as merchants sought to exploit them.

The mechanisation of production spread to the countries surrounding England in western and northern Europe and to British settler colonies, helping to make those areas the wealthiest, and shaping what is now known as the Western world.

Some economic historians argue that the possession of so-called 'exploitation colonies' eased the accumulation of capital to the countries that possessed them, speeding up their development. The consequence was that the subject country integrated a bigger economic system in a subaltern position, emulating the countryside, which demands manufactured goods and offers raw materials, while the colonial power stressed its urban posture, providing goods and importing food. A classical example of this mechanism is said to be the triangular trade, which involved England, southern United States and western Africa. Critics argue that this polarity still affects the world, and has deeply retarded industrialisation of what is now known as the Third World.

Some have stressed the importance of natural or financial resources that Britain received from its many overseas colonies or that profits from the British slave trade between Africa and the Caribbean helped fuel industrial investment.

Early Industrialisation in other Countries

After the Convention of Kanagawa issued by Commodore Matthew C. Perry forced Japan to open the ports of Shimoda and Hakodate to American trade, the Japanese government realised that drastic reforms were necessary to stave off Western influence. The Tokugawa shogunate abolished the feudal system. The government instituted military reforms to modernise the Japanese army and also constructed the base for industrialisation. In the 1870s, the Meiji government vigorously promoted technological and industrial development that eventually changed Japan to a powerful modern country.

In a similar way, Russia suffered during the Allied intervention in the Russian Civil War. The Soviet Union's centrally controlled economy decided to invest a big part of its resources to enhance its industrial production and infrastructures to assure its survival, thus becoming a world superpower. During the Cold war, the other European socialist countries, organised under the Comecon framework, followed the same developing scheme, albeit with a less emphasis on heavy industry.

Southern European countries saw a moderate industrialisation during the 1950s-1970s, caused by a healthy integration of the European economy, though their level of development, as well as those of eastern countries, doesn't match the western standards.

The Third World

A similar state-led developing programme was pursued in virtually all the Third World countries during the Cold War, including the socialist ones, but especially in Sub-Saharan Africa after the decolonisation period. The primary scope of those projects was to achieve self-sufficiency through the local production of previously imported goods, the mechanisation of agriculture and the spread of education and health care. However, all those experiences failed bitterly due to a lack of realism: most countries didn't have a pre-industrial bourgeoisie able to carry on a capitalistic development or even a stable and peaceful state. Those aborted experiences left huge debts toward western countries and fuelled public corruption.

Petrol Producing Countries

Oil-rich countries saw similar failures in their economic choices. An EIA report stated that OPEC member nations were projected to earn a net amount of $1.251 trillion in 2008 from their oil exports. Because oil is both important and expensive, regions that had big reserves of oil had huge liquidity incomes. However, this was rarely followed by economic development. Experience shows that local elites were unable to re-invest the petrodollars obtained through oil export, and currency is wasted in luxury goods.

This is particularly evident in the Persian Gulf states, where the per capita income is comparable to those of western nations, but where no industrialisation has started. Apart from two little countries (Bahrain and the United Arab Emirates), Arab states have not diversified their economies, and no replacement for the upcoming end of oil reserves is envisaged.

Industrialisation in Asia

Apart from Japan, where industrialisation began in the late 19th century, a different pattern of industrialisation followed in East Asia. One of the fastest rates of industrialisation occurred in the late 20th century across four countries known as the Asian tigers thanks to the existence of stable governments and well structured societies, strategic locations, heavy foreign investments, a low cost skilled and motivated workforce, a competitive exchange rate, and low custom duties.

In the case of South Korea, the largest of the four Asian tigers, a very fast paced industrialisation took place as it quickly moved away from the manufacturing of value added goods in the 1950s and 60s into the more advanced steel, shipbuilding and automobile industry in the 1970s and 80s, focusing on the high-tech and service industry in the 1990s and 2000s. As a result, South Korea became a major economic power and today is one of the wealthiest countries in Asia.

This starting model was afterwards successfully copied in other larger Eastern and Southern Asian countries, including communist ones. The success of this phenomenon led to a huge wave of offshoring – i.e., Western factories or Tertiary Sector corporations choosing to move their activities to countries where the workforce was less expensive and less collectively organised.

China and India, while roughly following this development pattern, made adaptations in line with their own histories and cultures, their major size and importance in the world, and the geo-political ambitions of their governments (etc.).

Currently, China's government is actively investing in expanding its own infrastructures and securing the required energy and raw materials supply channels, is supporting its exports by financing the United States balance payment deficit through the purchase of US treasury bonds, and is strengthening its military in order to endorse a major geopolitical role.

Meanwhile, India's government is investing in specific vanguard economic sectors such as bioengineering, nuclear technology, pharmaceutics, informatics, and technologically-oriented higher education, openly overpassing its needs, with the goal of creating several specialisation poles able to conquer foreign markets.

Both Chinese and Indian corporations have also started to make huge investments in Third World countries, making them significant players in today's world economy.

Newly Industrialised Countries

In recent decades, a few countries in Latin America, Asia, and Africa, such as Turkey, South Africa, Malaysia, Philippines and Mexico have experienced substantial industrial growth, fuelled by exportations going to countries that have bigger economies: the United States, Japan, China, India and the EU. They are sometimes called newly-industrialised countries. Despite this trend being artificially influenced by the oil price increases since 2003, the phenomenon is not entirely new nor totally speculative. Most analysts conclude in the next few decades the whole world will experience industrialisation, and international inequality will be replaced with worldwide social inequality.

Other Outcomes

Urbanisation

Urbanization, Urbanisation or Urban Drift is the physical growth of urban areas as a result of global change. Urbanization is also defined by the United Nations as movement of people from rural to urban areas with population growth equating to urban migration. The United Nations projected that half of the world's population would live in urban areas at the end of 2008.

Urbanization is closely linked to modernization, industrialization, and the sociological process of rationalization.

Movement

As more and more people leave villages and farms to live in cities, urban growth results. The rapid growth of cities like

Chicago in the late 19th century and Mumbai a century later can be attributed largely to rural-urban migration. This kind of growth is especially commonplace in developing countries.

The rapid urbanization of the world's population over the twentieth century is described in the 2005 Revision of the UN World Urbanization Prospects report. The global proportion of urban population rose dramatically from 13% (220 million) in 1900, to 29% (732 million) in 1950, to 49% (3.2 billion) in 2005. The same report projected that the figure is likely to rise to 60% (4.9 billion) by 2030. However, French economist Philippe Bocquier, writing in THE FUTURIST magazine, has calculated that "the proportion of the world population living in cities and towns in the year 2030 would be roughly 50%, substantially less than the 60% forecast by the United Nations (UN), because the messiness of rapid urbanization is unsustainable. Both Bocquier and the UN see more people flocking to cities, but Bocquier sees many of them likely to leave upon discovering that there's no work for them and no place to live."

According to the UN State of the World Population 2007 report, sometime in the middle of 2007, the majority of people worldwide will be living in towns or cities, for the first time in history; this is referred to as the arrival of the "Urban Millennium" or the 'tipping point'. In regard to future trends, it is estimated 93% of urban growth will occur in developing nations, with 80% of urban growth occurring in Asia and Africa.

Urbanization rates vary between countries. The United States and United Kingdom have a far higher urbanization level than China, India, Swaziland or Niger, but a far slower annual urbanization rate, since much less of the population is living in a rural area.

- Urbanization in the United States never reached the Rocky Mountains in locations such as Jackson Hole, Wyoming; Telluride, Colorado; Taos, New Mexico; Douglas County, Colorado and Aspen, Colorado. The state of Vermont has also been affected, as has the coast of Florida, the Birmingham-Jefferson County, AL area, the Pacific Northwest and the barrier islands of North Carolina.

- In the United Kingdom, two major examples of new urbanization can be seen in Swindon, Wiltshire and Milton Keynes, Buckinghamshire. These two towns show some of the quickest growth rates in Europe.

Urbanization occurs naturally from individual and corporate efforts to reduce time and expense in commuting and transportation while improving opportunities for jobs, education, housing, and transportation. Living in cities permits individuals and families to take advantage of the opportunities of proximity, diversity, and marketplace competition.

People move into cities to seek economic opportunities. A major contributing factor is known as "rural flight". In rural areas, often on small family farms, it is difficult to improve one's standard of living beyond basic sustenance. Farm living is dependent on unpredictable environmental conditions, and in times of drought, flood or pestilence, survival becomes extremely problematic. In modern times, industrialization of agriculture has negatively affected the economy of small and middle-sized farms and strongly reduced the size of the rural labour market.

Cities, in contrast, are known to be places where money, services and wealth are centralized. Cities are where fortunes are made and where social mobility is possible. Businesses, which generate jobs and capital, are usually located in urban areas. Whether the source is trade or tourism, it is also through the cities that foreign money flows into a country. It is easy to see why someone living on a farm might wish to take their chance moving to the city and trying to make enough money to send back home to their struggling family.

There are better basic services as well as other specialist services that aren't found in rural areas. There are more job opportunities and a greater variety of jobs. Health is another major factor. People, especially the elderly are often forced to move to cities where there are doctors and hospitals that can cater for their health needs. Other factors include a greater variety of entertainment (restaurants, movie theaters, theme parks, etc.) and a better quality of education, namely universities. Due to their high populations, urban areas can also have much more diverse social communities allowing others to find people like them when they might not be able to in rural areas.

These conditions are heightened during times of change from a pre-industrial society to an industrial one. It is at this time that many new commercial enterprises are made possible, thus creating new jobs in cities. It is also a result of industrialization that farms become more mechanized, putting many labourers out of work. This is currently occurring fastest in India.

Economic Effects

In recent years, urbanization of rural areas has increased. As agriculture, more traditional local services, and small-scale industry give way to modern industry the urban and related commerce with the city drawing on the resources of an ever-widening area for its own sustenance and goods to be traded or processed into manufactures.

Research in urban ecology finds that larger cities provide more specialized goods and services to the local market and surrounding areas, function as a transportation and wholesale hub for smaller places, and accumulate more capital, financial service provision, and an educated labour force, as well as often concentrating administrative functions for the area in which they lie. This relation among places of different sizes is called the urban hierarchy.

As cities develop, effects can include a dramatic increase in costs, often pricing the local working class out of the market, including such functionaries as employees of the local municipalities. The almost universal European division into a 'good' west end and a 'poor' east end of large cities developed in this period." This is likely due the prevailing southwest wind which carries coal smoke and other airborne pollutants downwind, making the western edges of towns preferable to the eastern ones. Similar problems now affect the developing world, rising inequality resulting from rapid urbanisation trends. The drive for rapid urban growth and often efficiency can lead to less equitable urban development, think tanks such as the

Overseas Development Institute have even proposed policies that encourage labour intensive growth as a means of absorbing the influx of low skilled and unskilled labour.

Urbanization is often viewed as a negative trend, but can in fact, be perceived simply as a natural occurrence from individual and corporate efforts to reduce expense in commuting and transportation while improving opportunities for jobs, education, housing, and transportation. Living in cities permits individuals and families to take advantage of the opportunities of proximity, diversity, and marketplace competition.

Environmental Effects

The urban heat island has become a growing concern and is increasing over the years. The urban heat island is formed when industrial and urban areas are developed and heat becomes more abundant. In rural areas, a large part of the incoming solar energy is used to evaporate water from vegetation and soil. In cities, where less vegetation and exposed soil exists, the majority of the sun's energy is absorbed by urban structures and asphalt. Hence, during warm daylight hours, less evaporative cooling in cities allows surface temperatures to rise higher than in rural areas. Additional city heat is given off by vehicles and factories, as well as by industrial and domestic heating and cooling units. This effect causes the city to become 2 to 10° F (1 to 6° C) warmer than surrounding landscapes.. Impacts also include reducing soil moisture and intensification of carbon dioxide emissions.

In his book *Whole Earth Discipline*, Stewart Brand argues that the effects of urbanization are on the overall positive for the environment. Firstly, the birth rate of new urban dwellers falls immediately to replacement rate, and keeps falling. This can prevent overpopulation in the future. Secondly, it puts a stop to destructive subsistence farming techniques, like slash and burn agriculture. Finally, it minimizes land use by humans, leaving more for nature.

Changing Forms

Different forms of urbanization can be classified depending on the style of architecture and planning methods as well as historic growth of areas. In cities of the developed world urbanization traditionally exhibited a concentration of human activities and settlements around the downtown area, the so-called *in-migration*. In-migration refers to migration from former colonies and similar places. The fact that many immigrants settle in impoverished city centres led to the notion of the "peripheralization of the core", which simply describes that people who used to be at the periphery of the former empires now live right in the centre.

Recent developments, such as inner-city redevelopment schemes, mean that new arrivals in cities no longer necessarily settle in the centre. In some developed regions, the reverse effect, originally called counter urbanisation has occurred, with cities losing population to rural areas, and is particularly common for richer families. This has been possible because of improved communications, and has been caused by factors such as the fear of crime and poor urban environments. Later termed *"white flight"*, the effect is not restricted to cities with a high ethnic minority population.

When the residential area shifts outward, this is called suburbanization. A number of researchers and writers suggest that suburbanization has gone so far to form new points of concentration outside the downtown both in developed and developing countries such as India. This networked, poly-centric form of concentration is considered by some an emerging pattern of urbanization. It is called variously exurbia, edge city (Garreau, 1991), network city (Batten, 1995), or postmodern city (Dear, 2000). Los Angeles is the best-known example of this type of urbanization.

Rural migrants are attracted by the possibilities that cities can offer, but often settle in shanty towns and experience extreme poverty. In the 1980s, this was attempted to be tackled with the urban bias theory which was promoted by Michael Lipton who wrote: "...the most important class conflict in the poor countries of the world today is not between labour and capital. Nor is it between foreign and national interests. It is between rural classes and urban classes. The rural sector contains most of the poverty and most of the low-cost sources of potential advance; but the urban sector contains most of the articulateness, organization and power. So the urban classes have been able to win most of the rounds of the struggle with the countryside...". Most of the urban poor in developing countries able to find work can spend their lives in insecure, poorly paid jobs. According to research by the Overseas Development Institute pro-poor urbanisation will require labour intensive growth, supported by labour protection, flexible land use regulation and investments in basic services.'

Urbanization can be planned urbanization or organic. Planned urbanization, i.e. planned community or the garden city movement, is based on an advance plan, which can be prepared for military, aesthetic, economic or urban design reasons. Examples can be seen in many ancient cities; although with exploration came the collision of nations, which meant that many invaded cities took on the desired planned characteristics of their occupiers. Many ancient organic cities experienced redevelopment for military and economic purposes, new roads carved through the cities, and new parcels of land were cordoned off serving various planned purposes giving cities distinctive geometric designs. UN agencies prefer to see urban infrastructure installed before urbanization occurs. Landscape planners are responsible for landscape infrastructure (public parks, sustainable urban drainage systems, greenways etc.) which can be planned before urbanization takes place, or afterward to revitalize an area and create greater livability within a region. Concepts of control of the urban expansion are considered in the American Institute of Planners.

Exploitation

Most often, the word *exploitation* is used to refer to economic exploitation; that is, the act of using another person's labour without offering them an adequate compensation. There are two major perspectives on economic exploitation:

- Organizational or "micro-level" exploitation: in the broad tradition of liberal economic thinking, most theories of exploitation centre on the market power of economic *organizations* within a market setting. Some neoclassical theory points to exploitation not based on market power.

- Structural or "macro-level" exploitation: "new liberal" theories focus on exploitation by large sections of society even (or *especially*) in the context of free markets. Marxist theory points to the entire capitalist class as an exploitative entity, and to capitalism as a system based on exploitation.

Developing nations (commonly called "third world countries" or "poor countries") are the focus of much debate over the issue of exploitation, particularly in the context of the global economy.

Critics of foreign companies allege, for instance, that firms such as Nike and Gap Inc. resort to child labour and sweatshops in developing nations, paying their workers wages far lower than those that prevail in developed nations (where the products are sold). This, it is argued, is insufficient to allow workers to attain the local subsistence standard of living if working hours common in the first world are observed, so that working hours much longer than in the first world are necessary. It is also argued that work conditions in these developing-world factories are much less safe and much more unhealthy than in the first world. For example, observers point to cases where employees were unable to escape factories burning down—and thus dying—because of locked doors, a common signal that sweatshop conditions exist. The Triangle Shirtwaist Factory fire of 1911 was another example, but it occurred in the US, so the first world of then is the equivalent of the third world of today.

Others argue that, in the absence of compulsion, the only way that corporations are able to secure adequate supplies of labour is to offer wages and benefits superior to preexisting options, and that the presence of workers in corporate factories indicates that the factories present options which are seen as better—by the workers themselves—than the other options available to them.

A common response is that this is disingenuous, as the companies are in fact *exploiting* people by the terms of unequal human standards (applying lower standards to their third world workers than to their first world ones). Furthermore, the argument goes, if people choose to work for low wages and in unsafe conditions because it is their only alternative to starvation or scavenging from garbage dumps (the "preexisting options"), this cannot be seen as any kind of "free choice" on their part. It also argued that if a company intends to sell its products in the first world, it should pay its workers by first world standards.

Following such a view, some in the United States propose that the U.S. government should mandate that businesses in foreign countries adhere to the same labour, environmental, health, and safety standards as the U.S. before they are allowed to trade with businesses in the U.S. (this has been advocated by Howard Dean, for example). They believe that such standards would improve the quality of life in less developed nations. According to others, however, this would harm the economies of less developed nations by discouraging the U.S. from trading with them. Milton Friedman is an economist who thinks that such a policy would have that effect.

However, the common response to the argument that corporations exploit poor labourers by lowering working standards, wages, etc. is that the corporation only has an incentive to do business in these nations if there is this alleged "exploitation." If activists were to achieve their goal of raising work standards, it is likely that the corporation would no longer have a profit incentive to invest in that nation. The result would probably the corporation pulling back to its developed nation, leaving their former workers out of the job.

Groups who see themselves as fighting against global exploitation also point to secondary effects such as the dumping of government-subsidized corn on developing world markets which forces subsistence farmers off of their lands, sending them into the cities or across borders in order to survive. More generally, some sort of international regulation of transnational corporations is called for, such as the enforcement of the International Labour Organization's labour standards.

Exploitation of Natural Resources

Some exploitation of natural resources is an essential condition of the human existence. This refers primarily to food production and necessities. The exploitation of nature is often done unsustainably and is of increasing concern as the depletion of natural resources from economic growth and population growth ultimately threatens human existence.

Why Resources are under Pressure

- Increase in sophistication of technology enabling natural resources to be extracted quickly and efficiently. *For Example*: In the past, it could take long hours just to cut down one tree only using saws. Due to increased technology, rates of deforestation have greatly increased
- A rapidly increasing population. This leads to greater demand for natural resources.
- Cultures of consumerism. Materialistic views lead to gold and diamonds mined and used for jewellery—something unnecessary for human life or advancement.
- Excessive demand often leads to conflicts due to intense competition. Organizations, such as Global Witness and the United Nations have documented the connections.
- Another reason maybe because of non-equitable distribution of resources.

Problems arising from exploitation of natural resources;

- Deforestation
- Desertification
- Extinction of species
- Soil erosion
- Oil depletion
- Ozone depletion
- Greenhouse gas increase
- Butt Depletion.

Workers have to leave their family in order to come to work in the towns and cities where the industries are found..

Change to Family Structure

The family structure changes with industrialisation. The sociologist Talcott Parsons noted that in pre-industrial societies there is an extended family structure spanning many generations who robably remained in the same location for generations. In industrialised societies the nuclear family, consisting of only of parents and their growing children, predominates. Families and children reaching adulthood are more mobile and tend to relocate to where jobs exist. Extended family bonds become more tenuous.

Environment

Industrialisation has spawned its own health problems. Modern stressors include noise, air, water pollution, poor nutrition, dangerous machinery, impersonal work, isolation, poverty, homelessness, and substance abuse. Health problems in industrial nations are as much caused by economic, social, political, and cultural factors as by pathogens. Industrialisation has become a major medical issue world wide.

Current Situation

In 2005, the USA was the largest producer of industrial output followed by Japan and China, according to International Monetary Fund.

Currently the "international development community" (World Bank, OECD, many United Nations departments, and some other organisations) endorses development policies like water purification or primary education. The community does not recognise traditional industrialisation policies as being adequate to the Third World or beneficial in the longer term, with the perception that it could only create inefficient local industries unable to compete in a free-trade dominated world.

Methodology

Psychometrics

Psychometrics is the field of study concerned with the theory and technique of educational and psychological measurement, which includes the measurement of knowledge, abilities, attitudes, and personality traits. The field is primarily concerned with the construction and validation of measurement instruments, such as questionnaires, tests, and personality assessments.

It involves two major research tasks, namely: (i) the construction of instruments and procedures for measurement; and (ii) the development and refinement of theoretical approaches to measurement. Those who practice psychometrics are known as psychometricians and although they may also be clinical psychologists, they are not obliged to be so and could instead be (for example) human resources or learning and development professionals. Either way specific, separate, qualifications in psychometrics are required.

Origins and Background

Much of the early theoretical and applied work in psychometrics was undertaken in an attempt to measure intelligence. Francis Galton, often referred to as "the father of psychometrics", devised and included mental tests among his anthropometric measures. However, the origin of psychometrics also has connections to the related field of psychophysics. Two other pioneers of psychometrics obtained doctorates in the Leipzig Psychophysics Laboratory under Wilhelm Wundt: James McKeen Cattell in 1886 and Charles Spearman in 1906.

The psychometrician L. L. Thurstone, founder and first president of the Psychometric Society in 1936, developed and applied a theoretical approach to measurement referred to as the law of comparative judgment, an approach that has close connections to the psychophysical theory of Ernst Heinrich Weber and Gustav Fechner. In addition, Spearman and Thurstone both made important contributions to the theory and application of factor analysis, a statistical method developed and used extensively in psychometrics.

More recently, psychometric theory has been applied in the measurement of personality, attitudes, and beliefs, and academic achievement. Measurement of these unobservable phenomena is difficult, and much of the research and accumulated science in this discipline has been developed in an attempt to properly define and quantify such phenomena. Critics, including practitioners in the physical sciences and social activists, have argued that such definition and quantification is impossibly difficult, and that such measurements are often misused, such as with psychometric personality tests used in employment procedures:

> *"For example, an employer wanting someone for a role requiring consistent attention to repetitive detail will probably not want to give that job to someone who is very creative and gets bored easily."*

Definition of Measurement in the Social Sciences

The definition of measurement in the social sciences has a long history. A currently widespread definition, proposed by Stanley Smith Stevens (1946), is that measurement is "the assignment of numerals to objects or events according to some rule". This definition was introduced in the paper in which Stevens proposed four levels of measurement. Although widely adopted, this definition differs in important respects from the more classical definition of measurement adopted in the physical sciences, which is that *measurement is the numerical estimation and expression of the magnitude of one quantity relative to another.*

Indeed, Stevens's definition of measurement was put forward in response to the British Ferguson Committee, whose chair, A. Ferguson, was a physicist. The committee was appointed in 1932 by the British Association for the Advancement of Science to investigate the possibility of quantitatively estimating sensory events. Although its chair and other members were physicists, the committee also included several psychologists. The committee's report highlighted the importance of the definition of measurement. While Stevens's response was to propose a new definition, which has had considerable influence in the field, this was by no means the only response to the report. Another, notably different, response was to accept the classical definition, as reflected in the following statement:

> *"Measurement in psychology and physics are in no sense different. Physicists can measure when they can find the operations by which they may meet the necessary criteria; psychologists have but to do the same. They need not worry about the mysterious*

differences between the meaning of measurement in the two sciences."

These divergent responses are reflected in alternative approaches to measurement. For example, methods based on covariance matrices are typically employed on the premise that numbers, such as raw scores derived from assessments, are measurements. Such approaches implicitly entail Stevens's definition of measurement, which requires only that numbers are *assigned* according to some rule. The main research task, then, is generally considered to be the discovery of associations between scores, and of factors posited to underlie such associations.

On the other hand, when measurement models such as the Rasch model are employed, numbers are not assigned based on a rule. Instead, in keeping with Reese's statement above, specific criteria for measurement are stated, and the goal is to construct procedures or operations that provide data that meet the relevant criteria. Measurements are estimated based on the models, and tests are conducted to ascertain whether the relevant criteria have been met.

Instruments and Procedures

The first psychometric instruments were designed to measure the concept of intelligence. The best known historical approach involved the Stanford-Binet IQ test, developed originally by the French psychologist Alfred Binet. Contrary to a fairly widespread misconception, there is no compelling evidence that it is possible to measure innate intelligence through such instruments, in the sense of an innate learning capacity unaffected by experience, nor was this the original intention when they were developed. Nevertheless, intelligence tests are useful tools for various purposes. An alternative conception of intelligence is that cognitive capacities within individuals are a manifestation of a general component, or general intelligence factor, as well as cognitive capacity specific to a given domain.

Psychometrics is applied widely in educational assessment to measure abilities in domains such as reading, writing, and mathematics. The main approaches in applying tests in these domains have been Classical Test Theory and the more recent Item Response Theory and Rasch measurement models. These latter approaches permit joint scaling of persons and assessment items, which provides a basis for mapping of developmental continua by allowing descriptions of the skills displayed at various points along a continuum. Such approaches provide powerful information regarding the nature of developmental growth within various domains.

Another major focus in psychometrics has been on personality testing. There have been a range of theoretical approaches to conceptualizing and measuring personality. Some of the better known instruments include the Minnesota Multiphasic Personality Inventory, the Five-Factor Model (or "Big 5") and tools such as Personality and Preference Inventory and the Myers-Briggs Type Indicator. Attitudes have also been studied extensively using psychometric approaches. A common method in the measurement of attitudes is the use of the Likert scale. An alternative method involves the application of unfolding measurement models, the most general being the Hyperbolic Cosine Model.

Theoretical Approaches

Psychometricians have developed a number of different measurement theories. These include classical test theory (CTT) and item response theory (IRT) An approach which seems mathematically to be similar to IRT but also quite distinctive, in terms of its origins and features, is represented by the Rasch model for measurement. The development of the Rasch model, and the broader class of models to which it belongs, was explicitly founded on requirements of measurement in the physical sciences.

Psychometricians have also developed methods for working with large matrices of correlations and covariances. Techniques in this general tradition include: factor analysis, a method of determining the underlying dimensions of data; multidimensional scaling, a method for finding a simple representation for data with a large number of latent dimensions; and data clustering, an approach to finding objects that are like each other. All these multivariate descriptive methods try to distill large amounts of data into simpler structures. More recently, structural equation modeling and path analysis represent more sophisticated approaches to working with large covariance matrices. These methods allow statistically sophisticated models to be fitted to data and tested to determine if they are adequate fits.

One of the main deficiencies in various factor analysis is a lack of consensus in cutting points for determining the number of latent factors. A usual procedure is to stop factoring when eigenvalues drop below one because the original sphere shrinks. The lack of the cutting points concerns other multivariate methods, also.

Key Concepts

Key concepts in classical test theory are reliability and validity. A reliable measure is one that measures a construct consistently across time, individuals, and situations. A valid measure is one that measures what it is intended to measure. A measure may be reliable without being valid. However, reliability is necessary, but not sufficient, for validity. Both reliability and validity can be assessed statistically. Consistency over repeated measures of the same test can be assessed with the Pearson correlation coefficient, and is often called *test-retest reliability*. Similarly, the equivalence of different versions of the same measure can be indexed by a Pearson correlation, and is called *equivalent forms reliability* or a similar term.

Internal consistency, which addresses the homogeneity of a single test form, may be assessed by correlating performance on two halves of a test, which is termed *split-half reliability*; the value of this Pearson product-moment correlation coefficient for two half-tests is adjusted with the Spearman-Brown prediction formula to correspond to the correlation between two full-length tests. Perhaps the most commonly used index of reliability is Cronbach's á, which is equivalent to the mean of all possible split-half coefficients. Other approaches include the intra-class correlation, which is the ratio of variance of measurements of a given target to the variance of all targets.

There are a number of different forms of validity. Criterion-related validity can be assessed by correlating a measure with a criterion measure known to be valid. When the criterion measure is collected at the same time as the measure being validated the goal is to establish *concurrent validity*; when the criterion is collected later the goal is to establish *predictive validity*. A measure has *construct validity* if it is related to measures of other constructs as required by theory. *Content validity* is a demonstration that the items of a test are drawn from the domain being measured. In a personnel selection example, test content is based on a defined statement or set of statements of knowledge, skill, ability, or other characteristics obtained from a *job analysis*.

Item response theory models the relationship between latent traits and responses to test items. Among other advantages, IRT provides a basis for obtaining an estimate of the location of a test-taker on a given latent trait as well as the standard error of measurement of that location. For example, a university student's knowledge of history can be deduced from his or her score on a university test and then be compared reliably with a high school student's knowledge deduced from a less difficult test. Scores derived by classical test theory do not have this characteristic, and assessment of actual ability (rather than ability relative to other test-takers) must be assessed by comparing scores to those of a "norm group" randomly selected from the population. In fact, all measures derived from classical test theory are dependent on the sample tested, while, in principle, those derived from item response theory are not.

Standards of Quality

The considerations of validity and reliability typically are viewed as essential elements for determining the quality of any test. However, professional and practitioner associations frequently have placed these concerns within broader contexts when developing standards and making overall judgments about the quality of any test as a whole within a given context. A consideration of concern in many applied research settings is whether or not the metric of a given psychological inventory is meaningful or arbitrary.

Testing Standards

In this field, the *Standards for Educational and Psychological Testing* place standards about validity and reliability, along with errors of measurement and related considerations under the general topic of test construction, evaluation and documentation. The second major topic covers standards related to fairness in testing, including fairness in testing and test use, the rights and responsibilities of test takers, testing individuals of diverse linguistic backgrounds, and testing individuals with disabilities. The third and final major topic covers standards related to testing applications, including the responsibilities of test users, psychological testing and assessment, educational testing and assessment, testing in employment and credentialing, plus testing in program evaluation and public policy.

Evaluation Standards

In the field of evaluation, and in particular educational evaluation, the Joint Committee on Standards for Educational Evaluation has published three sets of standards for evaluations. *The Personnel Evaluation Standards* was published in 1988, *The Program Evaluation Standards* (2nd edition) was published in 1994, and *The Student Evaluation Standards* was published in 2003.

Each publication presents and elaborates a set of standards for use in a variety of educational settings. The standards provide guidelines for designing, implementing, assessing and improving the identified form of evaluation. Each of the standards has been placed in one of four fundamental categories to promote educational evaluations that are proper, useful, feasible, and accurate. In these sets of standards, validity and reliability considerations are covered under the accuracy topic. For example, the student accuracy standards help ensure that student evaluations will provide sound, accurate, and credible information about student learning and performance.

Public Relations

Public relations (PR) is a field concerned with maintaining public image for businesses, non-profit organizations or high-profile people, such as celebrities and politicians. An earlier definition of public relations, by The first World Assembly of Public Relations Associations held in Mexico City in August 1978, was "the art and social science of analysing trends, predicting their consequences, counselling organizational leaders, and implementing planned programs of action, which will serve both the organization and the public interest."

Others define it as the practice of managing communication between an organization and its publics. Public relations provides an organization or individual exposure to their audiences using topics of public interest and news items that provide a third-party endorsement and do not direct payment. Once common activities include speaking at conferences, working with the media, crisis communications and social media engagement, and employee communication.

The European view of public relations notes that besides a relational form of interactivity there is also a reflective paradigm that is concerned with publics and the public sphere; not only with relational, which can in principle be private, but also with public consequences of organizational behaviour. A much broader view of neo-ubiquitous interactive communication using the Internet, as outlined by Phillips and Young in Online Public Relations Second Edition (2009), describes the form and nature of Internet-mediated public relations. It encompasses social media and other channels for communication and many platforms for communication such as personal computers (PCs), mobile phones and video game consoles with Internet access.

Public relations is used to build rapport with employees, customers, investors, voters, or the general public. Almost any organization that has a stake in how it is portrayed in the public arena employs some level of public relations. There are a number of public relations disciplines falling under the banner of corporate communications, such as analyst relations, media relations, investor relations, internal communications and labour relations.

Other public relations disciplines include:

- Financial public relations-providing information mainly to business reporters

- Consumer/lifestyle public relations-gaining publicity for a particular product or service, rather than using advertising
- Crisis public relations-responding to negative accusations or information
- Industry relations-providing information to trade bodies
- Government relations-engaging government departments to influence policymaking.

In the United States of America, Edward L. Bernays, nephew of Sigmund Freud, is widely recognized as the father of public relations. In Europe and in antiquity there are many more contenders as the founders of the practice. Most notably, according to Bournemouth academic, Dr Kevin Moloney, Georgiana Cavendish, Duchess of Devonshire with her political activism, use of printed news outlets, events management and social gatherings in the late 18th century in favour of her, predominantly, political clients, has a claim to be an early practitioner.

Two hundred years after the death of the Duchess, Bernays graduated from Cornell University in 1912 and opened the first recognized public-relations firm with Doris Fleischman in 1919. As Harold Lasswell explained in 1928, "public relations" was a term used as a way of shielding the profession from the ill repute increasingly associated with the word "propaganda": "Propaganda has become an epithet of contempt and hate, and the propagandists have sought protective coloration in such names 'public relations council,' 'specialist in public education,' 'public relations adviser.'

Global Alliance for Public Relations and Communication Management

Globally, the profession is represented by The Global Alliance for Public Relations and Communication Management, which is the umbrella organisation linking public relations professional associations worldwide. At its World Public Relations Forum in 2010, the Alliance accepted the Stockholm Accord for public relations. These accords present the practice of public relations in the following terms:

The Communicative Organisation

The concept of the communicative organisation was conceived as a result of the five-year research programme "Business Effective Communication" a collaboration between the Swedish Public Relations Association, Mälardalen University and the Stockholm School of Economics. During the project a number of cases were studied to define how information and communication can be used in the leadership of organisations in order to achieve a higher degree of external effectiveness.

The Value-creation Networks

The world is no longer a straight line from company to consumer. The organization holds a position in a network full of different stakeholders, and the network decides if you are valuable enough to keep your position. You can be replaced anytime. Your organization needs to find the perfect position where it is so valuable that the network cannot do without you. The key to this is to develop the organisation's communicative skills. This is where the communicator comes in to save the day.

The Contextual Leadership

The communicator needs to take on leadership in the communicative organization. It is his or her task to put the ideological leadership (i.e. the business idea or purpose) into the correct context. However the saying goes, perhaps selling sand in Sahara is not the best of ideas. The leadership can take different forms; as system building, mediation, coaching or influencing. The important thing is, communication is an organizational quality, rather than a function.

The Industry Today

The need for public relations personnel is growing at a fast pace. The types of clients for whom public relations people work include the government, educational institutions, nonprofit organizations, specific industries, corporations, athletic teams, entertainment companies, and even countries. The title public relations is a broad description of the field because careers that one can have in the public relations field include a publicist, media specialist, analyst, and communications specialist.

The practice of public relations is spread widely. On the professional level, there is an organization called Public Relations Society of America (PRSA), the world's largest public relations organization. PRSA is a community of more than 21,000 professionals that work to advance the skill set of public relations. PRSA also fosters a national student organization called Public Relations Student Society of America (PRSSA).

In the USA, public relations professionals earn an average annual salary of $49,800 which compares with £40,000 for a practitioner with a similar job in the UK. Top earners bring home around $89,220 annually, while entry-level public relations specialists earn around $28,080.

In the industry today, it is very critical for public relations professionals to learn and know the importance of new media outlets. New media outlets include blogs, social networking sites, as well as Internet radio. Public relations professionals must know that using these new media outlets are ways to directly send messages to their key publicians, also known as target audiences.

Methods, Tools and Tactics

Public relations and publicity are not synonymous, but many public relations campaigns include provisions for publicity. Publicity is the spreading of information to gain public awareness for a product, person, service, cause or organization, and can be seen as a result of effective public relations planning. More recently in public relations, professionals are using technology as their main tool to get their messages to target audiences. With the creation of social networks, blogs, and even Internet radio public relations professionals are able to send direct messages through these mediums that attract the target audiences. Methods used to find out what is appealing to target audiences include the use of surveys, conducting research or even focus groups. Tactics are the ways to attract target audiences by using the information gathered about that audience and directing a message to them using tools such as social mediums or other technology. Another emerging theme is the application of psychological theories of impression management.

Tools

There are various tools that can be used in the practice of public relations. Traditional tools include press releases and media kits which are sent out to generate positive press on behalf of the organization. Other widely-used tools include brochures, newsletters and annual reports. Increasingly, companies are utilizing interactive social media outlets, such as blogs, Twitter and Facebook, as tools in their public relations campaigns. Unlike the traditional tools which allowed for only one-way communication, social media outlets allow the organization to engage in two-way communication, and receive immediate feedback from their various stakeholders and publics.

One of the most popular and traditional tools used by public relations professionals is a press kit, also known as a media kit. A press kit is usually a folder that consists of promotional materials that give information about an event, organization, business, or even a person. What are included would be backgrounders or biographies, fact sheets, press releases (or media releases), media alerts, brochures, newsletters, photographs with captions, copies of any media clips, and social mediums. With the way that the industry has changed, many organizations may have a website with a link, "Press Room" which would have online versions of these pieces.

Targeting Publics

A fundamental technique used in public relations is to identify the target audience, and to tailor every message to appeal to that audience. It can be a general, nationwide or worldwide audience, but it is more often a segment of a population. A good elevator pitch can help tailor messaging to each target audience. Marketers often refer to socio-economically-driven "demographics", such as "black males 18-49". However, in public relations an audience is more fluid, being whoever someone wants to reach. Or, in the new paradigm of value based networked social groups, the values based social segment could be a trending audience. For example, recent political audiences seduce such buzzword monikers as "soccer moms" and "NASCAR dads."

An alternative and less flexible, more simplistic, approach uses stakeholders theory to identify people who have a stake in a given institution or issue. All audiences are stakeholders (or presumptive stakeholders), but not all stakeholders are audiences. For example, if a charity commissions a public relations agency to create an advertising campaign to raise money to find a cure for a disease, the charity and the people with the disease are stakeholders, but the audience is anyone who is likely to donate money.

Sometimes the interests of differing audiences and stakeholders common to a public relations effort necessitate the creation of several distinct but complementary messages. This is not always easy to do, and sometimes, especially in politics, a spokesperson or client says something to one audience that creates dissonance with another audience or group of stakeholders.

Lobby Groups

Lobby groups are established to influence government policy, corporate policy, or public opinion. An example of this is the American Israel Public Affairs Committee (AIPAC), which influences American foreign policy. Such groups claim to represent a particular interest and in fact are dedicated to doing so. When a lobby group hides its true purpose and support base, it is known as a front group. Moreover, governments may also lobby public relations firms in order to sway public opinion. A well illustrated example of this is the way civil war in Yugoslavia was portrayed. Governments of newly succeeded republics of Croatia and Bosnia invested heavily with American public relations firms, so that they would give them a positive war image in the USA.

Spin

In public relations, spin is sometimes a pejorative term signifying a heavily biased portrayal in specific favour of an event or situation. While traditional public relations may also rely on creative presentation of the facts, spin often, though not always, implies disingenuous, deceptive and/or highly manipulative tactics. Politicians are often accused of spin by commentators and political opponents when they produce a counterargument or position.

The techniques of spin include selectively presenting facts and quotes that support ideal positions (cherry picking), the so-called "non-denial denial", phrasing that in a way presumes unproven truths, euphemisms for drawing attention away from items considered distasteful, and ambiguity in public statements.

Another spin technique involves careful choice of timing in the release of certain news so it can take advantage of prominent events in the news. A famous reference to this practice occurred when British Government press officer Jo Moore used the phrase "It's now a very good day to get out anything we want to bury", (widely paraphrased or misquoted as "It's a good day to bury bad news"), in an email sent on the day of the September 11, 2001 attacks. The furor caused when this email was reported in the press eventually caused her to resign.

Spin Doctors

Skilled practitioners of spin are sometimes called "spin doctors", despite the negative connotation associated with the term. Perhaps the best-known person in the UK often described as a "spin doctor" is Alastair Campbell, who was involved with Tony Blair's public relations between 1994 and 2003, and also played a controversial role as press relations officer to the British and Irish Lions rugby union side during their 2005 tour of New Zealand.

State-run media in many countries also engage in spin by selectively allowing news stories that are favorable to the government while censoring anything that could be considered critical. They may also use propaganda to indoctrinate or actively influence citizens' opinions. Privately run media may also use the same techniques of "issue" versus "non-issue" to spin its particular political viewpoints.

Other

- Publicity events, pseudo-events, photo ops or publicity stunts
- Talk show circuit: a public relations spokesperson, or the client, "does the circuit" by being interviewed on television and radio talk shows with audiences that the client wishes to reach
- Books and other writings
- Blogs
- After a public relations practitioner has been working in the field for a while, he or she accumulates a list of contacts in the media and elsewhere in the public affairs sphere. This "Rolodex" becomes a prized asset, and job announcements sometimes even ask for candidates with an existing Rolodex, especially those in the media relations area of public relations.
- Direct communication (carrying messages directly to constituents, rather than through the mass media) with, e.g., newsletters – in print and e-letters
- Collateral literature, traditionally in print and now predominantly as web sites
- Speeches to constituent groups and professional organizations; receptions; seminars, and other events; personal appearances
- The slang term for a public relations practitioner or publicist is a "flack" (sometimes spelled "flak")
- A desk visit is where the public relations person literally takes their product to the desk of the journalist in order to show them emerging promotions
- Astroturfing is the act of public relations agencies placing blog and online forum messages for their clients, in the guise of a normal "grassroots" user or comment (an illegal practice across the larger practice areas such as the European Union)
- Online social media and Internet mediated public relations practices.

Politics and Civil Society

Defining the Opponent

In the USA, but not in the larger public relations markets, the tactic known as "defining one's opponent" is used in political campaigns. Opponents can be candidates, organizations and other groups of people.

In the 2004 US presidential campaign, Howard Dean defined John Kerry as a "flip-flopper," which was widely reported and repeated by the media, particularly the conservative media. Similarly, George H.W. Bush characterized Michael Dukakis as weak on crime (the Willie Horton ad) and hopelessly liberal ("a card-carrying member of the ACLU"). In 1996, President Bill Clinton seized upon opponent Bob Dole's promise to take America back to a simpler time, promising in contrast to "build a bridge to the 21st century." This painted Dole as a person who was somehow opposed to progress.

In the debate over abortion, self-titled pro-choice groups, by virtue of their name, defined their opponents as "anti-choice", while self-titled pro-life groups refer to their opponents as "pro-abortion" or "anti-life".

Managing Language

If, in the USA, a politician or organization can use an apt phrase in relation to an issue in interviews or news releases, the news media will often repeat it verbatim, without questioning its aptness. This perpetuates both the message and whatever preconceptions might underlie it. Often, something that sounds innocuous can stand in for something greater; a "culture of life" sounds like general goodwill to most people, but will evoke opposition to abortion for many pro-life advocates. The phrase "States' rights" was used as a code for anti-civil rights legislation in the United States in the 1960s, and allegedly in the 1970s and 1980s.

Conveying the Message

The means by which a message is communicated can be as important as the message itself. Direct mail, robocalling, advertising and public speaking are commonly used depending upon the intended audience and the message that is conveyed. Press releases are also used, but since many newspapers are folding in the USA, they have become a less reliable way of communicating for American practitioners, and other methods have become more popular. In the USA and India, news organizations have begun to rely more on their own websites and have developed a variety of unique approaches to publicity and public relations, on and off the web.

Long after many initiatives across the world by more advanced nations; the use of online communication by al-Qaida dating back to 2001, the country of Israel has employed a series of Web 2.0 initiatives and are indicative of how a small nation can use internet mediated communication. Israel's initiative in 2008 included a blog, MySpace page, YouTube channel, Facebook page and a political blog to reach different audiences. The Israeli Ministry of Foreign Affairs started the country's video blog as well as its political blog. The Foreign Ministry held the first microblogging press conference via Twitter about its war with Hamas, with Consul David Saranga answering live questions from a worldwide public in common text-messaging abbreviations. The questions and answers were later posted on IsraelPolitik, the country's official political blog.

Front Groups

One of the most controversial practices in public relations is the use of front groups, organizations that purport to serve a public cause while actually serving the interests of a client whose sponsorship may be obscured or concealed. Critics of the public relations industry, such as PR Watch, contend that some public relations firms involve a "multi-billion dollar propaganda-for-hire industry" that "concocts and spins the news, organizes phony grassroots front groups, spies on citizens, and conspires with lobbyists and politicians to thwart democracy."

Instances with the use of front groups as a public relations technique have been documented in many industries. Coal mining corporations have created "environmental groups" that contend that increased carbon dioxide emissions and global warming will contribute to plant growth and will be beneficial, trade groups for bars have created and funded citizens' groups to attack anti-alcohol groups, tobacco companies have created and funded citizens' groups to advocate for tort reform and to attack personal injury lawyers, while trial lawyers have created "consumer advocacy" front groups to oppose tort reform.

Industrial Bureaucracy

Industrial bureaucracy is the hierarchical arrangement of managements seen in the industrial world. Industrial bureaucracy represents complete control of the management, and this control may suppress the needs of the individual for the benefit of everyone. An industrial bureaucracy is run by rules and regulations. The functions it performs are clear and concise, and are performed in a mechanistic way. The owner of the organization may not necessarily be the highest ranking official; leadership depends upon the qualifications of the person.

Organizational Structure

An organizational structure is a description of the types of coordination used to organize the actions of individuals and departments that contribute to achieving a common aim. Many organizations have hierarchical structures, but not all.

Organizations are a variant of clustered entities. An organization can be structured in many different ways, depending on their objectives. The structure of an organization will determine the modes in which it operates and performs.

Organizational structure allows the expressed allocation of responsibilities for different functions and processes to different entities such as the branch, department, workgroup and individual. Individuals in an organizational structure are normally hired under time-limited work contracts or work orders, or under permanent employment contracts or program orders.

Operational Organizations and Informal Organizations

The set organizational structure may not coincide with facts, evolving in operational action. Such divergence decreases performance, when growing. E.g. a wrong organizational structure may hamper cooperation and thus hinder the completion of orders in due time and within limits of resources and budgets. Organizational structures shall be adaptive to process requirements, aiming to optimize the ratio of effort and input to output.

An effective organizational structure shall facilitate working relationships between various entities in the organization and may improve the working efficiency within the organizational units. Organization shall retain a set order and control to enable monitoring the processes. Organization shall support command for coping with a mix of orders and a change of conditions while performing work. Organization shall allow for application of individual skills to enable high flexibility and apply creativity. When a business expands, the chain of command will lengthen and the spans of control will widen. When an organization comes to age, the flexibility will decrease and the creativity will fatigue. Therefore organizational structures shall be altered from time to time to enable recovery. If such alteration is prevented internally, the final escape is to turn down the organization to prepare for a re-launch in an entirely new set up.

Success Factors

Common success criteria for organizational structures are:

- Decentralized reporting
- Flat hierarchy
- High transient speed
- High transparency
- Low residual mass
- Permanent monitoring
- Rapid response
- Shared reliability
- Matrix hierarchy.

History

Organizational structures developed from the ancient times of hunters and collectors in tribal organizations through highly royal and clerical power structures to industrial structures and today's post-industrial structures.

Organizational Structure Types

Pre-bureaucratic Structures

Pre-bureaucratic (entrepreneurial) structures lack standardization of tasks. This structure is most common in smaller organizations and is best used to solve simple tasks. The structure is totally centralized. The strategic leader makes all key decisions and most communication is done by one on one conversations. It is particularly useful for new (entrepreneurial) business as it enables the founder to control growth and development.

They are usually based on traditional domination or charismatic domination in the sense of Max Weber's tripartite classification of authority.

Bureaucratic Structures

Bureaucratic structures have a certain degree of standardization. They are better suited for more complex or larger scale organizations. They usually adopt a tall structure. Then tension between bureaucratic structures and non-bureaucratic is echoed in Burns and Stalker distinction between mechanistic and organic structures. It is not the entire thing about bureaucratic structure. It is very much complex and useful for hierarchical structures organization, mostly in tall organizations.

Post-bureaucratic

The term of post bureaucratic is used in two senses in the organizational literature: one generic and one much more specific. In the generic sense the term post bureaucratic is often used to describe a range of ideas developed since the 1980s that specifically contrast themselves with Weber's ideal type bureaucracy. This may include total quality management, culture management and matrix management, amongst others. None of these however has left behind the core tenets of Bureaucracy. Hierarchies still exist, authority is still Weber's rational, legal type, and the organization is still rule bound. Heckscher, arguing along these lines, describes them as cleaned up bureaucracies, rather than a fundamental shift away from bureaucracy. Gideon Kunda, in his classic study of culture management at 'Tech' argued that 'the essence of bureaucratic control-the formalisation, codification and enforcement of rules and regulations-does not change in principle.....it shifts focus from organizational structure to the organization's culture'.

Another smaller group of theorists have developed the theory of the Post-Bureaucratic Organization., provide a detailed discussion which attempts to describe an organization that is fundamentally not bureaucratic. Charles Heckscher has developed an ideal type, the post-bureaucratic organization, in which decisions are based on dialogue and consensus rather than authority and command, the organization is a network rather than a hierarchy, open at the boundaries (in direct contrast to culture management); there is an emphasis on meta-decision making rules rather than decision making rules. This sort of horizontal decision making by consensus model is often used in housing cooperatives, other cooperatives and when running a non-profit or community organization. It is used in order to encourage participation and help to empower people who normally experience oppression in groups.

Still other theorists are developing a resurgence of interest in complexity theory and organizations, and have focused on how simple structures can be used to engender organizational adaptations. For instance, Miner *et al.* (2000) studied how simple structures could be used to generate improvisational outcomes in product development. Their study makes links to simple structures and improviseal learning. Other scholars such as Jan Rivkin and Sigglekow, and Nelson Repenning revive an older interest in how structure and strategy relate in dynamic environments.

Functional Structure

Employees within the functional divisions of an organization tend to perform a specialized set of tasks, for instance the engineering department would be staffed only with software engineers. This leads to operational efficiencies within that group. However it could also lead to a lack of communication between the functional groups within an organization, making the organization slow and inflexible.

As a whole, a functional organization is best suited as a producer of standardized goods and services at large volume and low cost. Coordination and specialization of tasks are centralized in a functional structure, which makes producing a limited amount of products or services efficient and predictable. Moreover, efficiencies can further be realized as functional organizations integrate their activities vertically so that products are sold and distributed quickly and at low cost. For instance, a small business could start making the components it requires for production of its products instead of procuring it from an external organization.But not only beneficial for organization but also for employees faiths.

Divisional Structure

Also called a "product structure", the divisional structure groups each organizational function into a division. Each division within a divisional structure contains all the necessary resources and functions within it. Divisions can be categorized from different points of view. There can be made a distinction on geographical basis (a US division and an EU division) or on product/service basis (different products for different customers: households or companies). Another example, an automobile company with a divisional structure might have one division for SUVs, another division for subcompact cars, and another division for sedans. Each division would have its own sales, engineering and marketing departments.

Matrix Structure

The matrix structure groups employees by both function and product. This structure can combine the best of both separate structures. A matrix organization frequently uses teams of employees to accomplish work, in order to take advantage of the strengths, as well as make up for the weaknesses, of functional and decentralized forms. An example would be a company that produces two products, "product a" and "product b". Using the matrix structure, this company would organize functions within the company as follows: "product a" sales department, "product a" customer service department, "product a" accounting, "product b" sales department, "product b" customer service department, "product b" accounting department. Matrix structure is amongst the purest of organizational structures, a simple lattice emulating order and regularity demonstrated in nature.

- Weak/Functional Matrix: A project manager with only limited authority is assigned to oversee the cross-functional aspects of the project. The functional managers maintain control over their resources and project areas.
- Balanced/Functional Matrix: A project manager is assigned to oversee the project. Power is shared equally between the project manager and the functional managers. It brings the best aspects of functional and projectized organizations. However, this is the most difficult system to maintain as the sharing power is delicate proposition.
- Strong/Project Matrix: A project manager is primarily responsible for the project. Functional managers provide technical expertise and assign resources as needed.

Among these matrixes, there is no best format; implementation success always depends on organization's purpose and function.

Organizational Circle: Moving back to Flat

The flat structure is common in enterpreneriaI start-ups, university spin offs or small companies in general. As the company grows, however, it becomes more complex and hierarchical, which leads to an expanded structure, with more levels and departments.

Often, it would result in bureaucracy, the most prevalent structure in the past. It is still, however, relevant in former Soviet Republics and China, as well as in most governmental organizations all over the world. Shell Group used to represent the typical bureaucracy: top-heavy and hierarchical. It featured multiple levels of command and duplicate service companies existing in different regions. All this made Shell apprehensive to market changes, leading to its incapacity to grow and develop further. The failure of this structure became the main reason for the company restructuring into a matrix.

Starbucks is one of the numerous large organizations that successfully developed the matrix structure supporting their focused strategy. Its design combines functional and product based divisions, with employees reporting to two heads. Creating a team spirit, the company empowers employees to make their own decisions and train them to develop both hard and soft skills. That makes Starbucks one of the best at customer service.

Some experts also mention the multinational design, common in global companies, such as Procter & Gamble, Toyota and Unilever. This structure can be seen as a complex form of the matrix, as it maintains coordination among products, functions and geographic areas.

In general, over the last decade, it has become increasingly clear that through the forces of globalization, competition and more demanding customers, the structure of many companies has become flatter, less hierarchical, more fluid and even virtual.

Team

One of the newest organizational structures developed in the 20th century is *team*. In small businesses, the team structure can define the entire organization. Teams can be both horizontal and vertical. While an organization is constituted as a set of people who synergize individual competencies to achieve newer dimensions, the quality of organizational structure revolves around the competencies of teams in totality.

For example, every one of the Whole Foods Market stores, the largest natural-foods grocer in the US developing a focused strategy, is an autonomous profit centre composed of an average of 10 self-managed teams, while team leaders in each store and each region are also a team. Larger bureaucratic organizations can benefit from the flexibility of teams as well. Xerox, Motorola, and DaimlerChrysler are all among the companies that actively use teams to perform tasks.

Network

Another modern structure is network. While business giants risk becoming *too clumsy to proact (such as), act and react efficiently*, the new network organizations contract out any business function, that can be done better or more cheaply. In essence, managers in network structures spend most of their time coordinating and controlling external relations, usually by electronic means. H&M is outsourcing its clothing to a network of 700 suppliers, more than two-thirds of which are based in low-cost Asian countries. Not owning any factories, H&M can be more flexible than many other retailers in lowering its costs, which aligns with its low-cost strategy. The potential management opportunities offered by recent advances in complex networks theory have been demonstrated including applications to product design and development, and innovation problem in markets and industries.

Virtual

A special form of boundaryless organization is *virtual.* It works in a network of external alliances, using the Internet. This means while the core of the organization can be small but still the company can operate globally be a market leader in its niche. According to Anderson, because of the unlimited shelf space of the Web, the cost of reaching niche goods is falling dramatically. Although none sell in huge numbers, there are so many niche products that collectively they make a significant profit, and that is what made highly innovative Amazon.com so successful.

2

Industrial Leadership

Leadership has been described as the "process of social influence in which one person can enlist the aid and support of others in the accomplishment of a common task." Definitions more inclusive of followers have also emerged. Alan Keith stated that, "Leadership is ultimately about creating a way for people to contribute to making something extraordinary happen." Tom DeMarco says that leadership needs to be distinguished from posturing.

The following sections discuss several important aspects of leadership including a description of what leadership is and a description of several popular theories and styles of leadership. This article also discusses topics such as the role of emotions and vision, as well as leadership effectiveness and performance, leadership in different contexts, how it may differ from related concepts (i.e., management), and some critiques of leadership as generally conceived.

Leadership is "organizing a group of people to achieve a common goal." The leader may or may not have any formal authority. Students of leadership have produced theories involving traits, situational interaction, function, behaviour, power, vision and values, charisma, and intelligence among others.

Early History

The search for the characteristics or traits of leaders has been ongoing for centuries. History's greatest philosophical writings from Plato's *Republic* to Plutarch's *Lives* have explored the question of "What qualities distinguish an individual as a leader?" Underlying this search was the early recognition of the importance of leadership and the assumption that leadership is rooted in the characteristics that certain individuals possess. This idea that leadership is based on individual attributes is known as the "trait theory of leadership."

This view of leadership, the trait theory, was explored at length in a number of works in the previous century. Most notable are the writings of Thomas Carlyle and Francis Galton, whose works have prompted decades of research. In *Heroes and Hero Worship* (1841), Carlyle identified the talents, skills, and physical characteristics of men who rose to power. In Galton's (1869) *Hereditary Genius*, he examined leadership qualities in the families of powerful men. After showing that the numbers of eminent relatives dropped off when moving from first degree to second degree relatives, Galton concluded that leadership was inherited. In other words, leaders were born, not developed. Both of these notable works lent great initial support for the notion that leadership is rooted in characteristics of the leader.

For decades, this trait-based perspective dominated empirical and theoretical work in leadership. Using early research techniques, researchers conducted over a hundred studies proposing a number of characteristics that distinguished leaders from nonleaders: intelligence, dominance, adaptability, persistence, integrity, socioeconomic status, and self-confidence just to name a few.

Rise of Alternative Theories

In the late 1940s and early 1950s, however, a series of qualitative reviews of these studies prompted researchers to take a drastically different view of the driving forces behind leadership. In reviewing the extant literature, Stogdill and Mann found that while some traits were common across a number of studies, the overall evidence suggested that persons who are leaders in one situation may not necessarily be leaders in other situations. Subsequently, leadership was no longer characterized as an enduring individual trait, as situational approaches posited that individuals can be effective in certain situations, but not others. This approach dominated much of the leadership theory and research for the next few decades.

Reemergence of Trait Theory

New methods and measurements were developed after these influential reviews that would ultimately reestablish the trait theory as a viable approach to the study of leadership. For example, improvements in researchers' use of the round robin research design methodology allowed researchers to see that individuals can and do emerge as leaders across a variety of situations and tasks. Additionally, during the 1980s statistical advances allowed researchers to conduct meta-analyses, in which they could quantitatively analyse and summarize the findings from a wide array of studies. This advent allowed trait theorists to create a comprehensive and parsimonious picture of previous leadership research rather than rely on the qualitative reviews of the past. Equipped with new methods, leadership researchers revealed the following:

- Individuals can and do emerge as leaders across a variety of situations and tasks
- Significant relationships exist between leadership and such individual traits as:
- intelligence
- adjustment
- extraversion
- conscientiousness
- openness to experience
- general self-efficacy.

While the trait theory of leadership has certainly regained popularity, its reemergence has not been accompanied by a corresponding increase in sophisticated conceptual frameworks.

Specifically, Zaccaro (2007) noted that trait theories still:

1. Focus on a small set of individual attributes such as Big Five personality traits, to the neglect of cognitive abilities, motives, values, social skills, expertise, and problem-solving skills

2. Fail to consider patterns or integrations of multiple attributes
3. Do not distinguish between those leader attributes that are generally not malleable over time and those that are shaped by, and bound to, situational influences
4. Do not consider how stable leader attributes account for the behavioural diversity necessary for effective leadership.

Attribute Pattern Approach

Considering the criticisms of the trait theory outlined above, several researchers have begun to adopt a different perspective of leader individual differences-the leader attribute pattern approach. In contrast to the traditional approach, the leader attribute pattern approach is based on theorists' arguments that the influence of individual characteristics on outcomes is best understood by considering the person as an integrated totality rather than a summation of individual variables. In other words, the leader attribute pattern approach argues that integrated constellations or combinations of individual differences may explain substantial variance in both leader emergence and leader effectiveness beyond that explained by single attributes, or by additive combinations of multiple attributes.

Behavioural and Style Theories

In response to the early criticisms of the trait approach, theorists began to research leadership as a set of behaviours, evaluating the behaviour of 'successful' leaders, determining a behaviour taxonomy and identifying broad leadership styles. David McClelland, for example, Leadership takes a strong personality with a well developed positive ego. Not so much as a pattern of motives, but a set of traits is crucial.

Kurt Lewin, Ronald Lipitt, and Ralph White developed in 1939 the seminal work on the influence of leadership styles and performance. The researchers evaluated the performance of groups of eleven-year-old boys under different types of work climate. In each, the leader exercised his influence regarding the type of group decision making, praise and criticism and the management of the group tasks (project management) according to three styles: (1) authoritarian, (2) democratic and (3) laissez-faire. *Authoritarian climates* were characterized by leaders who make decisions alone, demand strict compliance to his orders, and dictate each step taken; future steps were uncertain to a large degree.

The leader is not necessarily hostile but is aloof from participation in work and commonly offers personal praise and criticism for the work done. *Democratic climates* were characterized by collective decision processes, assisted by the leader. Before accomplishing tasks, perspectives are gained from group discussion and technical advice from a leader. Members are given choices and collectively decide the division of labour. Praise and criticism in such an environment are objective, fact minded and given by a group member without necessarily having participated extensively in the actual work. *Laissez faire climates* gave freedom to the group for policy determination without any participation from the leader. The leader remains uninvolved in work decisions unless asked, does not participate in the division of labour, and very infrequently gives praise. The results seemed to confirm that the democratic climate was preferred.

The managerial grid model is also based on a behavioural theory. The model was developed by Robert Blake and Jane Mouton in 1964 and suggests five different leadership styles, based on the leaders' concern for people and their concern for goal achievement.

B.F. Skinner is the father of Behaviour Modification and developed the concept of positive reinforcement. Positive reinforcement occurs when a positive stimulus is presented in response to a behaviour, increasing the likelihood of that behaviour in the future. The following is an example of how positive reinforcement can be used in a business setting. Assume praise is a positive reinforcer for a particular employee. This employee does not show up to work on time every day. The manager of this employee decides to praise the employee for showing up on time every day the employee actually shows up to work on time. As a result, the employee comes to work on time more often because the employee likes to be praised. In this example, praise (i.e. stimulus) is a positive reinforcer for this employee because the employee arrives (i.e. behaviour) to work on time more frequently after being praised for showing up to work on time.

The use of positive reinforcement is a successful and growing technique used by leaders to motivate and attain desired behaviours from subordinates. Organizations such as Frito-Lay, 3M, Goodrich, Michigan Bell, and Emery Air Freight have all used reinforcement to increase productivity. Empirical research covering the last 20 years suggests that reinforcement theory has a 17 percent increase in performance. Additionally, many reinforcement techniques such as the use of praise are inexpensive, providing higher performance for lower costs.

Situational and Contingency Theories

Situational theory also appeared as a reaction to the trait theory of leadership. Social scientists argued that history was more than the result of intervention of great men as Carlyle suggested. Herbert Spencer (1884) said that the times produce the person and not the other way around. This theory assumes that different situations call for different characteristics; according to this group of theories, no single optimal psychographic profile of a leader exists. According to the theory, "what an individual actually does when acting as a leader is in large part dependent upon characteristics of the situation in which he functions."

Some theorists started to synthesize the trait and situational approaches. Building upon the research of Lewin et al., academics began to normatize the descriptive models of leadership climates, defining three leadership styles and identifying which situations each style works better in. The *authoritarian leadership style*, for example, is approved in periods of crisis but fails to win the "hearts and minds" of their followers in the day-to-day management; the *democratic leadership style* is more adequate in situations that require consensus building; finally, the *laissez faire leadership style* is appreciated by the degree of freedom it provides, but as the leader does not "take charge", he can be perceived as a failure in protracted or thorny organizational problems. Thus, theorists defined the style of leadership as contingent to the situation, which is sometimes classified as contingency theory. Four contingency leadership theories appear more prominently in the recent years: Fiedler contingency model, Vroom-Yetton decision model, the path-goal theory, and the Hersey-Blanchard situational theory.

The Fiedler contingency model bases the leader's effectiveness on what Fred Fiedler called *situational contingency*. This results from the interaction of leadership style and situational favorableness (later called "situational control"). The theory defined two types of leader: those who tend to accomplish the task by developing good-relationships with the group (*relationship-oriented*), and those who have as their prime concern carrying out the task itself (*task-oriented*). According to Fiedler, there is no ideal leader. Both task-oriented and relationship-oriented leaders can be effective if their leadership orientation fits the situation. When there is a good leader-member relation, a highly structured task, and high leader position power, the situation is considered a "favorable situation". Fiedler found that task-oriented leaders are more effective in extremely favourable or unfavourable situations, whereas relationship-oriented leaders perform best in situations with intermediate favourability.

Victor Vroom, in collaboration with Phillip Yetton (1973) and later with Arthur Jago (1988), developed a taxonomy for describing leadership situations, taxonomy that was used in a normative decision model where leadership styles were connected to situational variables, defining which approach was more suitable to which situation. This approach was novel because it supported the idea that the same manager could rely on different group decision making approaches depending on the attributes of each situation. This model was later referred as situational contingency theory.

The path-goal theory of leadership was developed by Robert House (1971) and was based on the expectancy theory of Victor Vroom. According to House, the essence of the theory is "the meta proposition that leaders, to be effective, engage in behaviours that complement subordinates' environments and abilities in a manner that compensates for deficiencies and is instrumental to subordinate satisfaction and individual and work unit performance.

The theory identifies four leader behaviours, *achievement-oriented*, *directive*, *participative*, and *supportive*, that are contingent to the environment factors and follower characteristics. In contrast to the Fiedler contingency model, the path-goal model states that the four leadership behaviours are fluid, and that leaders can adopt any of the four depending on what the situation demands. The path-goal model can be classified both as a contingency theory, as it depends on the circumstances, but also as a transactional leadership theory, as the theory emphasizes the reciprocity behaviour between the leader and the followers.

The situational leadership model proposed by Hersey and Blanchard suggests four leadership-styles and four levels of follower-development. For effectiveness, the model posits that the leadership-style must match the appropriate level of followership-development. In this model, leadership behaviour becomes a function not only of the characteristics of the leader, but of the characteristics of followers as well.

Functional Theory

Functional leadership theory is a particularly useful theory for addressing specific leader behaviours expected to contribute to organizational or unit effectiveness. This theory argues that the leader's main job is to see that whatever is necessary to group needs is taken care of; thus, a leader can be said to have done their job well when they have contributed to group effectiveness and cohesion. While functional leadership theory has most often been applied to team leadership it has also been effectively applied to broader organizational leadership as well. In summarizing literature on functional leadership, Klein, Zeigert, Knight, and Xiao (2006) observed five broad functions a leader performs when promoting organisation's effectiveness. These functions include: (1) environmental monitoring, (2) organizing subordinate activities, (3) teaching and coaching subordinates, (4) motivating others, and (5) intervening actively in the group's work.

A variety of leadership behaviours are expected to facilitate these functions. In initial work identifying leader behaviour, Fleishman (1953) observed that subordinates perceived their supervisors' behaviour in terms of two broad categories referred to as consideration and initiating structure. Consideration includes behaviour involved in fostering effective relationships. Examples of such behaviour would include showing concern for a subordinate or acting in a supportive manner towards others. Initiating structure involves the actions of the leader focused specifically on task accomplishment. This could include role clarification, setting performance standards, and holding subordinates accountable to those standards.

Transactional and Transformational Theories

The transactional leader is given power to perform certain tasks and reward or punish for the team's performance. It gives the opportunity to the manager to lead the group and the group agrees to follow his lead to accomplish a predetermined goal in exchange for something else. Power is given to the leader to evaluate, correct and train subordinates when productivity is not up to the desired level and reward effectiveness when expected outcome is reached.

The transformational leader motivates its team to be effective and efficient. Communication is the base for goal achievement focusing the group on the final desired outcome or goal attainment. This leader is highly visible and uses chain of command to get the job done. Transformational leaders focus on the big picture, needing to be surrounded by people who take care of the details. The leader is always looking for ideas that move the organization to reach the company's vision.

Emotions

Leadership can be perceived as a particularly emotion-laden process, with emotions entwined with the social influence process. In an organization, the leader's mood has some effects on his/her group. These effects can be described in 3 levels:

1. The mood of individual group members. Group members with leaders in a positive mood experience more positive mood than do group members with leaders in a negative mood. The leaders transmit their moods to other group members through the mechanism of emotional contagion. Mood contagion may be one of the psychological mechanisms by which charismatic leaders influence followers.
2. The affective tone of the group. Group affective tone represents the consistent or homogeneous affective reactions within a group. Group affective tone is an aggregate of the moods of the individual members of the group and refers to mood at the group level of analysis. Groups with leaders in a positive mood have a more positive affective tone than do groups with leaders in a negative mood.
3. Group processes like coordination, effort expenditure, and task strategy. Public expressions of mood impact how group members think and act. When people experience and express mood, they send signals to others. Leaders signal their goals, intentions, and attitudes through their expressions of moods. For example, expressions of positive moods by leaders signal that leaders deem progress toward goals to be good. The group members respond to those signals cognitively and behaviourally in ways that are reflected in the group processes.

In research about client service, it was found that expressions of positive mood by the leader improve the performance of the group, although in other sectors there were other findings.

Beyond the leader's mood, her/his behaviour is a source for employee positive and negative emotions at work. The leader creates situations and events that lead to emotional response. Certain leader behaviours displayed during interactions with their employees are the sources of these affective events. Leaders shape workplace affective events. Examples – feedback giving, allocating tasks, resource distribution. Since employee behaviour and productivity are directly affected by their emotional states, it is imperative to consider employee emotional responses to organizational leaders. Emotional intelligence, the ability to understand and manage moods and emotions in the self and others, contributes to effective leadership in organizations. Leadership is about being responsible.

Neo-emergent Theory

The Neo-emergent leadership theory (from the Oxford school of leadership) espouses that leadership is created through the emergence of information by the leader or other stakeholders, not through the true actions of the leader himself. In other words, the reproduction of information or stories form the basis of the perception of leadership by the majority. It is well known that the great naval hero Lord Nelson often wrote his own versions of battles he was involved in, so that when he arrived home in England he would receive a true hero's welcome. In modern society, the press, blogs and other sources report their own views of a leader, which may be based on reality, but may also be based on a political command, a payment, or an inherent interest of the author, media or leader. Therefore, it can be contended that the perception of all leaders is created and in fact does not reflect their true leadership qualities at all.

Environmental Leadership Theory

The Environmental leadership model (Carmazzi) describes leadership from a Group dynamics perspective incorporating group psychology and self awareness to nurture "Environments" that promote self sustaining group leadership based on personal emotional gratification from the activities of the group. The Environmental Leader creates the psychological structure by which employees can find and attain this gratification through work or activity.

It stems from the idea that each individual has various environments that bring out different facets from their own Identity, and each facet is driven by emotionally charged perceptions within each environment... The Environmental Leader creates a platform through education and awareness where individuals fill each others emotional needs and become more conscious of when, and how they affect personal and team emotional gratifications. This is accomplished by knowing why people "react" to their environment instead of act intelligently.

"Environmental Leadership is not about changing the mindset of the group or individual, but in the cultivation of an environment that brings out the best and inspires the individuals in that group. It is not the ability to influence others to do something they are not committed to, but rather to nurture a culture that motivates and even excites individuals to do what is required for the benefit of all. It is not carrying others to the end result, but setting the surrounding for developing qualities in them to so they may carry each other."

Carmazzi

The role of an Environmental Leader is to instill passion and direction to a group and the dynamics of that group. This leader implements a psychological support system within a group that fills the emotional and developmental needs of the group.

Styles

Leadership style refers to a leader's behaviour. It is the result of the philosophy, personality and experience of the leader.

Kurt Lewin

Kurt Lewin and colleagues identified different styles of leadership:

- Autocratic
- Participative
- Laissez-Faire.

Autocratic or Authoritarian Style

Under the autocratic leadership style, all decision-making powers are centralized in the leader, as with dictator leaders.

They do not entertain any suggestions or initiatives from subordinates. The autocratic management has been successful as it provides strong motivation to the manager. It permits quick decision-making, as only one person decides for the whole group and keeps each decision to himself until he feels it is needed to be shared with the rest of the group.

Participative or Democratic Style

The democratic leadership style favors decision-making by the group as shown, such as leader gives instruction after consulting the group. They can win the co-operation of their group and can motivate them effectively and positively. The decisions of the democratic leader are not unilateral as with the autocrat because they arise from consultation with the group members and participation by them.

Laissez-faire or Free Rein Style

A free rein leader does not lead, but leaves the group entirely to itself as shown; such a leader allows maximum freedom to subordinates, i.e., they are given a free hand in deciding their own policies and methods.

Different situations call for different leadership styles. In an emergency when there is little time to converge on an agreement and where a designated authority has significantly more experience or expertise than the rest of the team, an autocratic leadership style may be most effective; however, in a highly motivated and aligned team with a homogeneous level of expertise, a more democratic or laissez-faire style may be more effective. The style adopted should be the one that most effectively achieves the objectives of the group while balancing the interests of its individual members.

Performance

In the past, some researchers have argued that the actual influence of leaders on organizational outcomes is overrated and romanticized as a result of biased attributions about leaders. Despite these assertions however, it is largely recognized and accepted by practitioners and researchers that leadership is important, and research supports the notion that leaders do contribute to key organizational outcomes. To facilitate successful performance it is important to understand and accurately measure leadership performance.

Job performance generally refers to behaviour that is expected to contribute to organizational success. Campbell identified a number of specific types of performance dimensions; leadership was one of the dimensions that he identified. There is no consistent, overall definition of leadership performance (Yukl, 2006). Many distinct conceptualizations are often lumped together under the umbrella of leadership performance, including outcomes such as leader effectiveness, leader advancement, and leader emergence. For instance, leadership performance may be used to refer to the career success of the individual leader, performance of the group or organization, or even leader emergence. Each of these measures can be considered conceptually distinct. While these aspects may be related, they are different outcomes and their inclusion should depend on the applied/research focus.

Contexts—Organizations

An organization that is established as an instrument or means for achieving defined objectives has been referred to as a formal organization. Its design specifies how goals are subdivided and reflected in subdivisions of the organization. Divisions, departments, sections, positions, jobs, and tasks make up this work structure. Thus, the formal organization is expected to behave impersonally in regard to relationships with clients or with its members. According to Weber's definition, entry and subsequent advancement is by merit or seniority. Each employee receives a salary and enjoys a degree of tenure that safeguards her/him from the arbitrary influence of superiors or of powerful clients. The higher his position in the hierarchy, the greater his presumed expertise in adjudicating problems that may arise in the course of the work carried out at lower levels of the organization. It is this bureaucratic structure that forms the basis for the appointment of heads or chiefs of administrative subdivisions in the organization and endows them with the authority attached to their position.

In contrast to the appointed head or chief of an administrative unit, a leader emerges within the context of the informal organization that underlies the formal structure. The informal organization expresses the personal objectives and goals of the individual membership. Their objectives and goals may or may not coincide with those of the formal organization. The informal organization represents an extension of the social structures that generally characterize human life — the spontaneous emergence of groups and organizations as ends in themselves.

In prehistoric times, humanity was preoccupied with personal security, maintenance, protection, and survival. Now humanity spends a major portion of waking hours working for organizations. Her/His need to identify with a community that provides security, protection, maintenance, and a feeling of belonging continues unchanged from prehistoric times. This need is met by the informal organization and its emergent, or unofficial, leaders.

Leaders emerge from within the structure of the informal organization. Their personal qualities, the demands of the situation, or a combination of these and other factors attract followers who accept their leadership within one or several overlay structures. Instead of the authority of position held by an appointed head or chief, the emergent leader wields influence or power. Influence is the ability of a person to gain co-operation from others by means of persuasion or control over rewards. Power is a stronger form of influence because it reflects a person's ability to enforce action through the control of a means of punishment.

A leader is a person who influences a group of people towards a specific result. It is not dependent on title or formal authority. (elevos, paraphrased from Leaders, Bennis, and Leadership Presence, Halpern & Lubar). Leaders are recognized by their capacity for caring for others, clear communication, and a commitment to persist. An individual who is appointed to a managerial position has the right to command and enforce obedience by virtue of the authority of his position. However, she or he must possess adequate personal attributes to match his authority, because authority is only potentially available to him. In the absence of sufficient personal competence, a manager may be confronted by an emergent leader who can challenge her/his role in the organization and reduce it to that of a figurehead. However, only authority of position has the backing of formal sanctions. It follows that whoever wields personal influence and power can legitimize this only by gaining a formal position in the hierarchy, with commensurate authority. Leadership can be defined as one's ability to get others to willingly follow. Every organization needs leaders at every level.

Management

Over the years the philosophical terminology of "management" and "leadership" have, in the organisational context, been used both as synonyms and with clearly differentiated meanings. Debate is fairly common about whether the use of these terms should be restricted, and generally reflects an awareness of the distinction made by Burns (1978) between "transactional" leadership (characterised by e.g. emphasis on procedures, contingent reward, management by exception) and "transformational" leadership (characterised by e.g. charisma, personal relationships, creativity).

Group Leadership

In contrast to individual leadership, some organizations have adopted group leadership. In this situation, more than one person provides direction to the group as a whole. Some organizations have taken this approach in hopes of increasing creativity, reducing costs, or downsizing. Others may see the traditional leadership of a boss as costing too much in team performance. In some situations, the maintenance of the boss becomes too expensive-either by draining the resources of the group as a whole, or by impeding the creativity within the team, even unintentionally.

A common example of group leadership involves cross-functional teams. A team of people with diverse skills and from all parts of an organization assembles to lead a project. A team structure can involve sharing power equally on all issues, but more commonly uses *rotating leadership*. The team member(s) best able to handle any given phase of the project become(s) the temporary leader(s). Additionally, as each team member has the opportunity to experience the elevated level of empowerment, it energizes staff and feeds the cycle of success. Leaders who demonstrate persistence, tenacity, determination and synergistic communication skills will bring out the same qualities in their groups. Good leaders use their own inner mentors to energize their team and organizations and lead a team to achieve success.

According to the National School Boards Association (USA): These Group Leadership or Leadership Teams have specific characteristics:

Characteristics of a Team

- There must be an awareness of unity on the part of all its members.
- There must be interpersonal relationship. Members must have a chance to contribute, learn from and work with others.
- The member must have the ability to act together toward a common goal.

Ten characteristics of well-functioning teams:

- Purpose: Members proudly share a sense of why the team exists and are invested in accomplishing its mission and goals.
- Priorities: Members know what needs to be done next, by whom, and by when to achieve team goals.
- Roles: Members know their roles in getting tasks done and when to allow a more skilful member to do a certain task.
- Decisions: Authority and decision-making lines are clearly understood.
- Conflict: Conflict is dealt with openly and is considered important to decision-making and personal growth.
- Personal traits: members feel their unique personalities are appreciated and well utilized.
- Norms: Group norms for working together are set and seen as standards for every one in the groups.
- Effectiveness: Members find team meetings efficient and productive and look forward to this time together.

- Success: Members know clearly when the team has met with success and share in this equally and proudly.
- Training: Opportunities for feedback and updating skills are provided and taken advantage of by team members.

Primates

Richard Wrangham and Dale Peterson, in *Demonic Males: Apes and the Origins of Human Violence* present evidence that only humans and chimpanzees, among all the animals living on earth, share a similar tendency for a cluster of behaviours: violence, territoriality, and competition for uniting behind the one chief male of the land. This position is contentious. Many animals beyond apes are territorial, compete, exhibit violence, and have a social structure controlled by a dominant male (lions, wolves, etc.), suggesting Wrangham and Peterson's evidence is not empirical. However, we must examine other species as well, including elephants (which are matriarchal and follow an alpha female), meerkats (who are likewise matriarchal), and many others.

It would be beneficial, to examine that most accounts of leadership over the past few millennia (since the creation of Christian religions) are through the perspective of a patriarchal society, founded on Christian literature. If one looks before these times, it is noticed that Pagan and Earth-based tribes in fact had female leaders. It is important also to note that the peculiarities of one tribe cannot necessarily be ascribed to another, as even our modern-day customs differ. The current day patrilineal custom is only a recent invention in human history and our original method of familial practices were matrilineal (Dr. Christopher Shelley and Bianca Rus, UBC). The fundamental assumption that has been built into 90% of the world's countries is that patriarchy is the 'natural' biological predisposition of homo sapiens. Unfortunately, this belief has led to the widespread oppression of women in all of those countries, but in varying degrees. (Whole Earth Review, Winter, 1995 by Thomas Laird, Michael Victor). The Iroquoian First Nations tribes are an example of a matrilineal tribe, along with Mayan tribes, and also the society of Meghalaya, India. (Laird and Victor,).

By comparison, bonobos, the second-closest species-relatives of man, do *not* unite behind the chief male of the land. The bonobos show deference to an alpha or top-ranking female that, with the support of her coalition of other females, can prove as strong as the strongest male in the land. Thus, if leadership amounts to getting the greatest number of followers, then among the bonobos, a female almost always exerts the strongest and most effective leadership. However, not all scientists agree on the allegedly "peaceful" nature of the bonobo or its reputation as a "hippie chimp".

Historical Views

Sanskrit literature identifies ten types of leaders. Defining characteristics of the ten types of leaders are explained with examples from history and mythology.

Aristocratic thinkers have postulated that leadership depends on one's blue blood or genes: monarchy takes an extreme view of the same idea, and may prop up its assertions against the claims of mere aristocrats by invoking divine sanction: see the divine right of kings. Contrariwise, more democratically-inclined theorists have pointed to examples of meritocratic leaders, such as the Napoleonic marshals profiting from careers open to talent.

In the autocratic/paternalistic strain of thought, traditionalists recall the role of leadership of the Roman *pater familias*. Feminist thinking, on the other hand, may object to such models as patriarchal and posit against them emotionally-attuned, responsive, and consensual empathetic guidance, which is sometimes associated with matriarchies.

Comparable to the Roman tradition, the views of Confucianism on "right living" relate very much to the ideal of the (male) scholar-leader and his benevolent rule, buttressed by a tradition of filial piety.

Leadership is a matter of intelligence, trustworthiness, humaneness, courage, and discipline... Reliance on intelligence alone results in rebelliousness. Exercise of humaneness alone results in weakness. Fixation on trust results in folly. Dependence on the strength of courage results in violence.

Excessive discipline and sternness in command result in cruelty. When one has all five virtues together, each appropriate to its function, then one can be a leader. — Sun Tzu

In the 19th century, the elaboration of anarchist thought called the whole concept of leadership into question. (Note that the *Oxford English Dictionary* traces the word "leadership" in English only as far back as the 19th century.) One response to this denial of élitism came with Leninism, which demanded an élite group of disciplined cadres to act as the vanguard of a socialist revolution, bringing into existence the dictatorship of the proletariat.

Other historical views of leadership have addressed the seeming contrasts between secular and religious leadership. The doctrines of Caesaro-papism have recurred and had their detractors over several centuries. Christian thinking on leadership has often emphasized stewardship of divinely-provided resources-human and material-and their deployment in accordance with a Divine plan. Compare servant leadership.

Action Oriented Environments

This is a unique approach to team leadership that is aimed at action oriented environments where effective functional leadership is required to achieve critical or reactive tasks by small teams deployed into the field. In other words leadership of small groups often created to respond to a situation or critical incident.

In most cases these teams are tasked to operate in remote and changeable environments with limited support or backup (action environments). Leadership of people in these environments requires a different set of skills to that of front line management. These leaders must effectively operate remotely and negotiate both the needs of the individual, team and task within a changeable environment. This has been termed Action Oriented Leadership. Some example action oriented leadership is demonstrated in the following ways: extinguishing a rural fire, locating a missing person, leading a team on an outdoor expedition or rescuing a person from a potentially hazardous environment.

Titles Emphasizing Authority

At certain stages in their development, the hierarchies of social ranks implied different degrees or ranks of leadership in society. Thus a knight led fewer men in general than did a duke; a baronet might in theory control less land than an earl.

In the course of the 18th and 20th centuries, several political operators took non-traditional paths to become dominant in their societies. They or their systems often expressed a belief in strong individual leadership, but existing titles and labels ("King", "Emperor", "President" and so on) often seemed inappropriate, insufficient or downright inaccurate in some circumstances. The formal or informal titles or descriptions they or their flunkies employ express and foster a general veneration for leadership of the inspired and autocratic variety. The definite article when used as part of the title (in languages that use definite articles) emphasizes the existence of a sole "true" leader.

Critical Thought

Noam Chomsky and others have brought critical thinking to the very concept of leadership and have provided an analysis that asserts that people abrogate their responsibility to think and will actions for themselves.

While the conventional view of leadership is rather satisfying to people who "want to be told what to do", these critics say that one should question why they are being subjected to a will or intellect other than their own if the leader is not a Subject Matter Expert (SME).

The fundamentally anti-democratic nature of the leadership principle is challenged by the introduction of concepts such as autogestion, employeeship, common civic virtue, etc., which stress individual responsibility and/or group authority in the work place and elsewhere by focusing on the skills and attitudes that a person needs in general rather than separating out leadership as the basis of a special class of individuals.

Similarly, various historical calamities are attributed to a misplaced reliance on the principle of leadership.

Varieties of Individual Power

According to Patrick J. Montana and Bruce H. Charnov, the ability to attain these unique powers is what enables leadership to influence subordinates and peers by controlling organizational resources. The successful leader effectively uses these power(s) to influence employees, and it is important for the leader to understand the uses of power to strengthen the leadership functioning.

The authors distinguish the following types of organizational power:

- Legitimate Power refers to the different types of professional positions within an organization structure that inherent such power. E.g. Manager, Vice President, Director, Supervisor, et cetera. These levels of power commands to the hierarchical executive levels within the organization itself. The higher position such as President of the company has a higher power than the rest of professional positions in the hierarchical executive levels.
- Reward Power given the power to managers that attain administrative power over a range of rewards. Employees whom work for managers desire the reward from the manager, they will be influenced by receiving them as the product of work performance. The rewards may be the obvious—pay raise or promotions.
- Coercive Power given the manager's ability to punish an employee whom did not follow the company policy, loss of profit, et cetera. Punishment can be determined range of mild to serious punishment... a mild punishment is a suspension and serious punishment is actual termination.
- Expert Power an expert power attained by the manager by their own talents such as skills, knowledge, abilities, or previous experience. Any of these manager has the power within the organization will be very valuable and important manager in the company.
- Charisma Power a manager has a charisma that will

positively influence on workers, and admired manager that creates the opportunity for interpersonal influence. A person has charisma, and this will confer great power as a manager.

- Referent Power a power that gained by association. This person with whom he or she is associated or has a relationship, often referred to assistant or deputy.
- Information Power a person who has possession of important information at a important time when such information is needed to organizational functioning. Someone who has this information knowledge has genuine power. Manager's secretary would be in a powerful position if a secretary has information power.

Human Resource Management

Human resource management (HRM) is the strategic and coherent approach to the management of an organization's most valued assets-the people working there who individually and collectively contribute to the achievement of the objectives of the business. The terms "human resource management" and "human resources" (HR) have largely replaced the term "personnel management" as a description of the processes involved in managing people in organizations. In simple words, HRM means employing people, developing their capacities, utilizing, maintaining and compensating their services in tune with the job and organizational requirement.

Features

Its features include:

- Organizational management
- Personnel administration
- Manpower management
- Industrial management.

But these traditional expressions are becoming less common for the theoretical discipline. Sometimes even employee and industrial relations are confusingly listed as synonyms, although these normally refer to the relationship between management and workers and the behaviour of workers in companies. The theoretical discipline is based primarily on the assumption that employees are individuals with varying goals and needs, and as such should not be thought of as basic business resources, such as trucks and filing cabinets.

The field takes a positive view of workers, assuming that virtually all wish to contribute to the enterprise productively, and that the main obstacles to their endeavors are lack of knowledge, insufficient training, and failures of process.

Human Resource Management (HRM) is seen by practitioners in the field as a more innovative view of workplace management than the traditional approach. Its techniques force the managers of an enterprise to express their goals with specificity so that they can be understood and undertaken by the workforce, and to provide the resources needed for them to successfully accomplish their assignments. As such, HRM techniques, when properly practiced, are expressive of the goals and operating practices of the enterprise overall. HRM is also seen by many to have a key role in risk reduction within organisations.

Synonyms such as *personnel management* are often used in a more restricted sense to describe activities that are necessary in the recruiting of a workforce, providing its members with payroll and benefits, and administrating their work-life needs. So if we move to actual definitions, Torrington and Hall (1987) define personnel management as being:

> *"a series of activities which: first enable working people and their employing organisations to agree about the objectives and nature of their working relationship and, secondly, ensures that the agreement is fulfilled".*

While Miller (1987) suggests that HRM relates to:

> *".......those decisions and actions which concern the management of employees at all levels in the business and which are related to the implementation of strategies directed towards creating and sustaining competitive advantage".*

Academic Theory

Research in the area of HRM has much to contribute to the organisational practice of HRM. For the last 20 years, empirical work has paid particular attention to the link between the practice of HRM and organisational performance, evident in improved employee commitment, lower levels of absenteeism and turnover, higher levels of skills and therefore higher productivity, enhanced quality and efficiency. This area of work is sometimes referred to as 'Strategic HRM' or SHRM. The notion of best practice-sometimes called 'high commitment' HRM-proposes that the adoption of certain best practices in HRM will result in better organisational performance. Perhaps the most popular work in this area is that of Pfeffer who argued that there were seven best practices for achieving competitive advantage through people and 'building profits by putting people first'. These practices included: providing employment security, selective hiring, extensive training, sharing information, self-managed teams, high pay based on company performance and the reduction of status differentials.

Best fit, or the contingency approach to HRM, argues that HRM improves performance where there is a close vertical fit between the HRM practices and the company's strategy. This link ensures close coherence between the HR people processes and policies and the external market or business strategy. There are a range of theories about the nature of this vertical integration. For example, a set of 'lifecycle' models argue that HR policies and practices can be mapped onto the stage of an organisation's development or lifecycle. Competitive advantage models take Porter's (1985) ideas about strategic choice and map a range of HR practices onto the organisation's choice of competitive strategy. Finally 'configurational models' provide a more sophisticated approach which advocates a close examination of the organisation's strategy in order to determine the appropriate HR policies and practices. However, this approach assumes that the strategy of the organisation can be identified-many organisations exist in a state of flux and development.

The Resource Based View (RBV), argued by some to be at the foundation of modern HRM, focusses on the internal resources of the organisation and how they contribute to competitive advantage. The uniqueness of these resources is preferred to homogeneity and HRM has a central role in developing human resources that are valuable, rare, difficult to copy or substitute and that are effectively organised. Overall, the theory of HRM argues that the goal of human resource management is to help an organization to meet strategic goals by attracting, and maintaining employees and also to manage them effectively. The key word here perhaps is "fit", i.e. a HRM approach seeks to ensure a fit between the management of an organisation's employees, and the overall strategic direction of the company (Miller, 1989). The basic premise of the academic theory of HRM is that humans are not machines, therefore we need to have an interdisciplinary examination of people in the workplace. Fields such as psychology, industrial relations, industrial engineering, sociology, economics, and critical theories: postmodernism, post-structuralism play a major role. Many colleges and universities offer bachelor and master degrees in Human Resources Management or in Human Resources and Industrial Relations. One widely used scheme to describe the role of HRM, developed by Dave Ulrich, defines 4 fields for the HRM function:

- Strategic business partner
- Change management
- Employee champion
- Administration.

However, many HR functions these days struggle to get beyond the roles of administration and employee champion, and are seen as reactive rather than strategically proactive partners for the top management. In addition, HR organisations also have difficulty in proving how their activities and processes add value to the company. Only in recent years have HR scholars and professionals focused on developing models that can measure the value added by HR.

Business Practice

Human resources management involves several processes. Together they are supposed to achieve the above mentioned goal. These processes can be performed in an HR department, but some tasks can also be outsourced or performed by line-managers or other departments. When effectively integrated they provide significant economic benefit to the company.

- Workforce planning
- Recruitment (sometimes separated into attraction and selection)
- Induction, Orientation and Onboarding
- Skills management
- Training and development
- Personnel administration
- Compensation in wage or salary
- Time management
- Travel management (sometimes assigned to accounting rather than HRM)
- Payroll (sometimes assigned to accounting rather than HRM)
- Employee benefits administration
- Personnel cost planning
- Performance appraisal
- Labour relations.

HRM Strategy

An HRM strategy pertains to the means as to how to implement the specific functions of HRM. An organization's HR function may possess recruitment and selection policies, disciplinary procedures, reward/recognition policies, an HR plan, or learning and development policies, however all of these functional areas of HRM need to be aligned and correlated, in order to correspond with the overall business strategy. An HRM strategy thus is an overall plan, concerning the implementation of specific HRM functional areas.

An HRM strategy typically consists of the following factors:

- "Best fit" and "best practice"-meaning that there is correlation between the HRM strategy and the overall corporate strategy. As HRM as a field seeks to manage human resources in order to achieve properly organizational goals, an organization's HRM strategy seeks to accomplish such management by applying a firm's personnel needs with the goals/objectives of the organisation. As an example, a firm selling cars could have a corporate strategy of increasing car sales by 10% over a five year period. Accordingly, the HRM strategy would seek to facilitate how exactly to manage personnel in order to achieve the 10% figure. Specific HRM functions, such as recruitment and selection, reward/recognition, an HR plan, or learning and development policies, would be tailored to achieve the corporate objectives.

- Close co-operation (at least in theory) between HR and the top/senior management, in the development of the corporate strategy. Theoretically, a senior HR representative should be present when an organization's corporate objectives are devised. This is so, since it is a firm's personnel who actually construct a good, or provide a service. The personnel's proper management is vital in the firm being successful, or even existing as a going concern. Thus, HR can be seen as one of the critical departments within the functional area of an organization.
- Continual monitoring of the strategy, via employee feedback, surveys, etc.

The implementation of an HR strategy is not always required, and may depend on a number of factors, namely the size of the firm, the organizational culture within the firm or the industry that the firm operates in and also the people in the firm.

An HRM strategy can be divided, in general, into two facets-the people strategy and the HR functional strategy. The people strategy pertains to the point listed in the first paragraph, namely the careful correlation of HRM policies/actions to attain the goals laid down in the corporate strategy. The HR functional strategy relates to the policies employed within the HR functional area itself, regarding the management of persons internal to it, to ensure its own departmental goals are met.

Functions

The Human Resources Management (HRM) function includes a variety of activities, and key among them is deciding what staffing needs you have and whether to use independent contractors or hire employees to fill these needs, recruiting and training the best employees, ensuring they are high performers, dealing with performance issues, and ensuring your personnel and management practices conform to various regulations. Activities also include managing your approach to employee benefits and compensation, employee records and personnel policies. Usually small businesses (for-profit or nonprofit) have to carry out these activities themselves because they can't yet afford part-or full-time help. However, they should always ensure that employees have—and are aware of—personnel policies which conform to current regulations. These policies are often in the form of employee manuals, which all employees have.

Note that some people distinguish a difference between HRM (a major management activity) and HRD (Human Resource Development, a profession). Those people might include HRM in HRD, explaining that HRD includes the broader range of activities to develop personnel inside of organizations, including, e.g., career development, training, organization development, etc.

There is a long-standing argument about where HR-related functions should be organized into large organizations, e.g., "should HR be in the Organization Development department or the other way around?"

The HRM function and HRD profession have undergone major changes over the past 20–30 years. Many years ago, large organizations looked to the "Personnel Department," mostly to manage the paperwork around hiring and paying people. More recently, organizations consider the "HR Department" as playing an important role in staffing, training and helping to manage people so that people and the organization are performing at maximum capability in a highly fulfilling manner.

Professional Industrial Management in India

India has a people and leadership crisis despite its huge population. Corporates whine that the Indian education system does not produce 'employable human resources.' Engineers need to be re-skilled before they can write software and face clients confidently. Graduates need extensive training before they can turn call specialists, sales staff or store managers. B-school graduates go through companies as management trainees to become functional managers...

In the midst of a high growth era, where Indian companies have been consumed by the challenge of base level hiring, have enough and competent leaders been groomed? Most Indian companies, I suspect, have been woefully myopic on that count. Thus, one sees expatriates being hired at astronomical salaries or 'the good line manager' from a well-regarded breeding ground bagging a leadership position.

Neither of the two approaches can yield results. The expatriate is hamstrung by the lack of experience with a diverse population: India, as a country, is arguably more diverse than Europe is, as a continent. The good line manager — newly crowned and eager to flag his/her arrival — is unable to come to terms right away with his/her newfound power. Most attempt to run away like racing stock and fail to understand that putting together ambitious yet happy teams is the sustainable way to build businesses.

There is no short cut to building one's own leadership. Besides business skills, leadership needs to be steeped in the culture of the company and aligned to its goals. To my mind, this is India Inc's biggest challenge, in its march forward. If one looks at the dominance of the American corporate on the world stage, one can single out leadership as the most important factor. To cite an example, GE had groomed three strong leaders to take over from Jack Welch. Within days of Jeffrey Immelt being appointed as the successor, 3M and Home Depot snapped up the other two incumbents James McNerney and Robert

Nardelli, respectively. GE filled three top positions from within its ranks. With ease. Here are a few haves in leadership, in the Indian context:

Importance of Continuity and Assertiveness

Successive, strong leadership can alone produce good results in India, with all its diversity (read, myriad opinions and fractured consensus). To illustrate the point: Good leadership in the past has intermittently elevated the offices of the President, the Chief Justice of India, the Central Vigilance Commissioner and the Sebi chairman. However, when leadership has had some continuity and strength of character, the results have been better than good. The office of the Chief Election Commissioner and the relative fairness in the electoral system today versus that which prevailed a couple of decades ago is a case in point. Similarly, compare the fortunes of a Reliance or a Wipro today vis a vis the heavyweight business groups that dotted the Indian corporate world as more than their equals in 1991.

Cultural and Class Inclusiveness

In a nation as diverse as ours, it pays to build culturally inclusive leadership. A lot of Indian corporates, including the so-called professional ones, have relied on family, friends and community to build the circle of leadership. For example, one software company is grappling with the situation of having close to 60 vice presidents from a single community. How did it happen? What does it portend for the hundreds of employees the company has? Such situations abound in India. And, unfortunately, it does not build an environment of trust. Nor does a situation where young men and women from elitist backgrounds filled up the management and top rungs of an organisation. Some large MNCs in India (regarded as breeding grounds) are guilty of having fostered an environment of 'thinking Brahmanism.'

But that was in the last millennium. That is dead. Here is a new India that is emerging as much from its vibrant, small towns as from its growing cities.

3

Industrial Supervision

Supervision means the act of watching over the work or tasks of another who may lack full knowledge of the concept at hand. Supervision does not mean control of another but guidance in a work, professional or personal context.

There are several interpretations of the term "supervision", but typically supervision is the activity carried out by supervisors to oversee the productivity and progress of employees who report directly to the supervisors. For example, first-level supervisors supervise entry-level employees. Depending on the size of the organization, middle-managers supervise first-level supervisors, chief executives supervise middle-managers, etc. Supervision is a management activity and supervisors have a management role in the organization.

Typical Experience of a First-Time Supervisor

Rarely have Adequate Training

Often, employees are promoted to supervision because of their strong technical expertise — expertise in building a product or providing a service. Suddenly, the new supervisor is now charged with a whole new range of responsibilities, many of which have little to do with technical expertise.

Managers often deal with great deal of paperwork and people. Although paperwork is usually the most tedious, it's often the most predictable. People aren't predictable. They have moods, illnesses, career expectations, crises in their family lives, etc. The supervisor's technical expertise is often useless when it comes to supervising people.

Sometimes Intimidated by Wide Range of Policies and Procedures

The new supervisor is suddenly faced with a wide range of rules and regulations — each of which the supervisor is responsible to enforce. The supervisor is responsible for signing time cards, authorizing overtime, granting compensation time, dealing with performance problems, developing job descriptions, following hiring procedures, dealing with grievances, conforming to a complicated pay system, and the list goes on. It can be quite difficult to conform to today's wide range of employee laws, rules and regulations — and at the same time, produce a product or service.

New Supervisors Rarely have Enough Time

No matter how many courses or degrees a new supervisor has completed, they're often surprised that management activities are so hectic and demanding. No matter how thorough the planning, managers rarely get to spend much time on any one activity. The role of most managers, whether new supervisors or executives, is interspersed with frequent interruptions. Any surprise in the work or lives of employees is a sudden demand on supervisors.

New supervisors often expect to have complete knowledge of everything that goes on in their group. They don't want to encounter any surprises. So they spend more time reading, thinking, planning, communicating with employees — new supervisors often spend 60 hours a week on the job. Still, they don't feel they have enough time to do the job right.

New Supervisors often Feel very Alone

Each manager has a unique role in the organization. Each organization is unique. Usually there are no clear procedures for dealing with the numerous challenges that suddenly face management. Ultimately, it's up to each manager to get through the day. Faced with a great deal of pressure, little time and continuing demands from other people, the new supervisor can feel quite alone. The supervisor is responsible to be an advocate for the organization and an advocate for the employee. For example, if the organization implements an unpopular new policy, the supervisor is often responsible to communicate and justify that new policy to the employee. In this case, management expects the supervisor to present and support the new policy, and the employee vents his or her frustration to the supervisor. However, if the supervisor wants to promote the employee or present some other reward, he or she is now representing the employee's case to the rest of management. The supervisor is often alone, stuck in the middle. The new supervisor wants to come across as having deserved their promotion, as being in control of the situation. It's difficult to seek help from others in the organization. Even when there is someone there to talk to, it's difficult to fully explain the situation — the new supervisor sometimes doesn't know how things got so hectic and confusing.

New Supervisors often Feel Overwhelmed, Stressed Out

The new supervisor is responsible, often for the first time, for the activities of another employee. The supervisor must ensure the employee knows his or her job, has the resources to do the job and does the job as effectively as possible. Until a new supervisor develops a "feeling for the territory", they often deal with the stresses of supervision by working harder, rather than smarter. They miss the comfort and predictability of their previous job. The stress and loneliness in the role of new supervisor can bring out the worst in a person. If they deal with stress by retreating, they'll retreat to their offices and close the door. If they deal with frustration, they'll become angry and unreasonable with their employees. If they are used to getting strong praise and high grades, they'll work harder and harder until their jobs become their lives.

Support and Development are Critical for New Supervisors

Courses in supervision, delegation, time management, stress management, etc., are not enough. New supervisors need ongoing coaching and support. They need someone whom they can confide in. Ideally, they have a mentor in the organization who remembers what it's like to be a first-time supervisor, someone who makes themselves available.

If the experience of first-time supervision is successful — it's challenging, but fulfilling — the supervisor goes on to become a progressive, supportive manager.

Impact of Individual Differences

Individual differences — the ways in which people differ from one another.

Personality — the pattern of relatively enduring ways that a person feels, thinks, and behaves.

Nature — biological heritage, genetic makeup.

Nurture — life experiences.

Attraction-selection-attrition (ASA) framework — the idea that an organization attracts and selects individuals with similar personalities and loses individuals with other types of personalities.

Trait — a specific component of personality.

The Big Five Personality Profile

Extraversion — the tendency to experience positive emotional states and feel good about oneself in the world around them, also called positive affectivity.

Neuroticism — the tendency to experience negative emotional states in the oneself in the world around one negatively, also called negative affectivity.

Agreeableness — the tendency to get along well with others.

Conscientiousness — the extent to which a person is careful, scrupulous, and preserving.

Openness to experience — the extent to which a person is original, has broad interests, and is willing to take risks.

Locus of Control

External locus of control — describes people who believe

that fate, lot, or outside forces are responsible for happens to them.

Internal locus of control — describes people who believe that ability, effort, or their own actions determine what happens to them.

Self-monitoring — the extent to which people try to control the way they present themselves to others.

Self-esteem — the extent to which people have pride in themselves and their capabilities.

Personality Types

Type a-a person who has an intense desire to achieve, is extremely competitive, it has a strong sense of urgency.

Type b-a person who tends to be easy-going and relaxed.

Need for achievement — the desire to perform challenging tasks well and to meet ones own high standards.

Need for affiliation — the desire to establish and maintain good relations with others.

Need for power — the desire to exert emotional and behavioural control or influence over other.

How personality is measured.

Ability — the mental or physical capacity to do something.

Cognitive Abilities

Verbal ability — ability to understand and use written and spoken language.

Numerical ability — ability to solve arithmetic problems and deal with numbers.

Reasoning ability — ability to come up with solutions for problems and understand the principles by which different problems can be solved.

Deductive ability — ability to reach of appropriate conclusions from an array of observations or evaluate the implications of a series of facts.

Ability to see relationships — the ability to see how two

things are related to each other and then apply this knowledge to other relationships and situations.

Ability to remember — abilities to recall things ranging from simple associations to complex groups of statements or sentences.

Spatial ability — ability to determine the location or arrangement of two objects in relation to one's own position and to imagine how an object would appear if its position in space were altered.

Perceptual — ability to uncover visual patterns and see relationships within and across patterns.

Physical Ability

motor skills — the ability to physically manipulate objects in an environment physical skills — a person's fitness and strength.

Emotional intelligence — the ability to understand and manage one's own feelings and emotions and the feelings and emotions and other people.

Summary

The two main types of individual differences are personality differences and ability differences. Understanding the nature, determinants, and consequences of individual differences is essential for managing organizational behaviour. Because people differ so much from each other, an appreciation of the nature of individual differences is necessary to understand why people act the way they do in organizations.

Personality is the pattern of relatively enduring ways that a person feels, things, and behaves. Personality is determined both by nature (biological heritage) and nurture (situational factors). Organizational outcomes that have been shown to be predicted by personality include job satisfaction, work stress, and leadership effectiveness. Personality is not a useful predictor of organizational outcomes when there are strong situational constraints. Because personality tends to be stable over time, managers should not expect to change personality in the short run. Managers should except employees personalities as they are and develop effective ways to deal with people.

Feelings, thoughts, attitudes, and behaviours in an organization are determined by the interaction of personality and the situation.

The big five personality traits are extraversion, neuroticism, agreeableness, conscientiousness, and openness to experience. Other personality traits particularly relevant to organizational behaviour include locus of control, self-monitoring, self-esteem, type a & type b personalities, and the needs for achievement, affiliation, and power.

In addition to possessing different personalities, employees also differ in their abilities, or what they are capable of doing. The two major types of ability are cognitive ability and physical ability.

Types of cognitive ability can be arranged in a hierarchy with General intelligence at the top. Specific types of cognitive abilities are verbal ability, numerical ability, reasoning ability, deductive ability, ability to see relationships, ability to remember, spatial ability, and perceptual ability.

There are two types of physical ability, motor skills and physical skills.

Both nature and nurture contribute to determining physical ability and cognitive ability. A third, recently identified, ability is emotional intelligence.

In organizations, ability can be measured by selecting individuals who have the abilities needed to compost tasks, placing employees in jobs that capitalize on their abilities, and training employees to enhance their ability levels.

Consistency vs. Individual Differences

Generally, human behaviour is not random. People behave in a particular way that they believe is in their best interest Following a systematic approach to the study of human behaviour will bring to light important facts and relationships that will, in turn, serve as a basis for more accurate predictions of behaviour.

Happy Workers need not be Productive

According to traditional theories in the study of organizational psychology and organizational behaviour, happy workers are more productive. These theories suggest that organizations should create a good work environment, offer fringe benefits and provide such facilities as to make the workers happy. However, a research study by psychologist, Dr. Robert Sinclair, along with his student, Carrie Lavis, at the University of Alberta refuted the traditional theories and proved the reverse: hard workers are more productive than happy workers.

Sinclair and Lavis created feelings of happiness and sadness in employees working on circuit boards. They observed that both sad and happy employees produced the same number of circuit boards, but the boards produced by happy employees bore more defects than those produced by sad employees. Sinclair and Lavis gave the following reason: Happy people did not want to disturb their pleasant feelings by being serious at work. They did not pay much attention to the task at hand as they were more concerned about their own happiness. But, sad people concentrated on their work and tried to perform their level best to overcome their somberness. In fact, recent studies in social psychology have also indicated that sad employees tend to reflect more deeper than do happy employees and thus are more rational and accurate in their judgments.

Though these findings are contrary to the popular belief that happy workers are better workers, it does not imply that organizations should cease to provide amenities and employee benefits to make their employees sad and therefore more productive. The sad and happy moods observed in the employees in the above studies had nothing to do with the work or workplace. In their studies, Sinclair and Lavis found that people were dedicated to their job in the belief that their grievances would subside. Hence, organizations should strive to create such work environment (depending on the employee's nature and emotions) where people feel good by performing the task given to them. According to Sinclair, this practice will help organizations motivate employees and enhance their performance.

It may be interpreted that the organizations should take more care in making the task and its impact on the employee a pleasant experience rather than only focusing on improving the work/office environment in general.

Adapted from "Sad Workers May Make Better Workers," Science Daily, University of Alberta, June 14, 2001.

The knowledge about how a person perceives a particular situation can help predict his behaviour. Though a person's behaviour may appear rather irrational to others, it may seem perfectly rational to him This difference in perception arises because an outsider may not have access to the same information or may not perceive a given situation in the same way as the person whose behaviour is in consideration. However, certain consistencies can be identified in the behaviour of every individual. These consistencies are significant since they make room for accurate prediction of other's behaviour in specific situations.

For example, while driving a car, people make certain predictions regarding other drivers. The rules of driving give certain inputs that help people predict rather accurately that all drivers will stop at red signals, drive on the left side of the road, overtake from the right and never cross the solid double line on mountain roads. However, same cannot be said about the behaviour of people at work in an organization. For instance, consider a situation in which a manager lias passed inter-departmental transfer orders to a few employees to adjust the excess and under capacities existing in these departments. He may observe that some employees willingly accept the Liter-unit transfer and begin to receive training for the new job while some employees strongly resist the change and resort to strikes and violence. In this case, systematic study of the behaviour of employees would have helped the manager to make reasonably accurate predictions about their behaviour.

By systematic study, we mean a study based on viewing relationships, attributing causes and effects, and drawing conclusions on the basis of scientific evidence. For this, data should be gathered under controlled conditions and measured and interpreted rigorously.

Generalization about behaviour may be based on intuition. And intuition is a feeling that is not necessarily supported by research. Therefore, one of the challenges to the study of OB is to overcome the belief that behaviour is either the outcome of intuition or is based on common sense. Moreover, what might be common sense to one person may not be so to another. Thus, OB specialists seek to move away from intuitive views of behaviour to a systematic analysis that is essential for improving one's accuracy in the prediction and explanation of organizational behaviour.

You are interviewing a candidate for a position as a cashier in a supermarket. You need someone polite, courteous, patient, and dependable. The candidate you are talking to seems nice. But how do you know who is the right person for the job? Will the job candidate like the job or get bored? Will they have a lot of accidents on the job or be fired for misconduct? Don't you wish you knew before hiring? One company approaches this problem scientifically, saving companies time and money on hiring hourly wage employees.

Retail employers do a lot of hiring, given their growth and high turnover rate. According to one estimate, replacing an employee who leaves in retail costs companies around $4,000. High turnover also endangers customer service. Therefore, retail employers have an incentive to screen people carefully so that they hire people with the best chance of being successful and happy on the job. Unicru, an employee selection company, developed software that quickly became a market leader in screening of hourly workers. The company was acquired by Massachusetts-based Kronos Inc. in 2006.

The idea behind the software is simple: If you have a lot of employees and keep track of your data over time, you have access to an enormous resource. By analysing this data, you can specify the profile of the "ideal" employee. The software captures the profile of the potential high performers, and applicants are screened to assess their fit with this particular profile. More important, the profile is continuously updated as new employees are hired. As the database gets larger, the software does a better job of identifying the right people for the job. If you applied for a job in retail, you may have already been a part of this database: The users of this system include giants such as Albertsons, Universal Studios, Costco Wholesale Corporation, Macy's, Blockbuster Inc., Target Brands Inc., and other retailers and chain restaurants. In companies such as Target or Blockbuster, applicants use a kiosk in the store to answer a list of questions and to enter their background, salary history, and other information. In other companies, such as some in the trucking industry, candidates enter the data through the Web site of the company they are applying to. The software screens people on basic criteria such as availability in scheduling as well as personality traits.

Candidates are asked to agree or disagree with statements such as "slow people irritate me" or "I don't act polite when I don't want to." After the candidates complete the questions, hiring managers are sent a report complete with a color-coded suggested course of action. Red means the candidate does not fit the job, yellow means proceed with caution, and green means the candidate can be hired on the spot. Interestingly, the company contends that faking answers to the questions of the software is not easy because it is difficult for candidates to predict the desired profile. For example, according to their research, being a successful salesman has less to do with being an extraverted and sociable person and more to do with a passion for the company's product.

Matching candidates to jobs has long been viewed as a key way of ensuring high performance and low turnover in the workplace, and advances in computer technology are making it easier and more efficient to assess candidate-job fit. Companies using such technology are cutting down the time it takes to hire people, and it is estimated that using such techniques lowers their turnover by 10%–30%.

Individuals bring a number of differences to work, such as unique personalities, values, emotions, and moods. When new employees enter organizations, their stable or transient characteristics affect how they behave and perform. Moreover, companies hire people with the expectation that those individuals have certain skills, abilities, personalities, and values. Therefore, it is important to understand individual characteristics that matter for employee behaviours at work.

Psychological Testing and Measurement in Personnel Selection

Personality Tests: *A selection procedure measure the personality characteristics of applicants that are related to future job performance.* Personality tests typically measure one or more of five personality dimensions: extroversion, emotional stability, agreeableness, conscientiousness, and openness to experience.

Advantages;

- can result in lower turnover due if applicants are selected for traits that are highly correlated with employees who have high longevity within the organization
- can reveal more information about applicant's abilities and interests can identify interpersonal traits that may be needed for certain jobs.

Disadvantages;

- difficult to measure personality traits that may not be well defined
- applicant's training and experience may have greater impact on job performance than applicant's personality
- responses by applicant may may be altered by applicant's desire to respond in a way they feel would result in their selection
- lack of diversity if all selected applicants have same personality traits
- cost may be prohibitive for both the test and interpretation of results
- lack of evidence to support validity of use of personality tests.

Tips

Select traits carefully An employer that selects applicants with high degree of 'assertiveness', 'independence', and 'self-confidence' may end up excluding females significantly more than males which would result in *adverse impact.* Select tests carefully Any tests should have been analysed for (high) reliability and (low) adverse impact. Not used exclusively Personality tests should not be the sole instrument used for selecting applicants. Rather, they should be used in conjunction with other procedures as one element of the selection process. Applicants should not be selected on the basis of personality tests alone.

Summary of Personality Tests

1. Since there is not a correct answer to personality tests, the scoring of the procedure could be questioned.
2. Recent litigation has suggested that some items for these types of tests may be too intrusive.
3. This technique lacks face validity. In other words, it would be difficult to show how individual questions on certain personality measures are job related even if the overall personality scale is a valid predictor of job performance.
4. Hooke and Krauss (1971) administered three (3) tests to sergeant candidates; the Minnesota Multiphasic Personality Inventory, the Allport-Vemon-Lindzey Study of Values, and the Gough Adjective Check List. These tests did not differentiate candidates rated as good sergeant material from those rates as poorer candidates. The researchers concluded that the groups may have been so similar that these tests were not sensitive enough to differentiate them.

Types of Personality Tests

1. Personal Attribute Inventory. An interpersonal assessment instrument which consists of 50 positive and 50 negative adjectives from Gough's Adjective Check List. The subject is to select 30 which are most descriptive of the taregt group or person in question. This instrument was specifically designed to tap affective reactions and may be used in either assessing attitudes toward others or as a self-concept scale.

2. Personality Adjective Checklist A comprehensive, objective measure of eight personality styles (which are closely aligned with DSM-III-R Axis II constructs). These eight personality styles are: introversive, inhibited, cooperative, sociable, confident, forceful, respectful, and sensitive. This instrument is designed for use with nonpsychiatric patients and normal adults who read minimally at the eighth grade level. Test reports are computer-generated and are intended for use by qualified professionals only. Interpretive statements are based on empirical data and theoretical inference. They are considered probabilistic in nature and cannot be considered definitive. (2K)
3. Cross-Cultural Adaptability Inventory Self-scoring six-point rating scale is a training instrument designed to provide feedback to individuals about their potential for cross-cultural effectiveness. It is most effective when used as part of a training program. It can also be used as a team-building tool for culturally diverse work groups and as a counselling tool for people in the process of cross-cultural adjustment. The inventory contains 50 items, distributed among 4 subscales: emotional resilience, flexibility/openness, perceptual acuity, personal autonomy.

Materials

4. California Psychological Inventory Multipurpose questionnaire designed to assess normal personality characteristics important in everyday life that individuals make use of to understand, classify, and predict their own behaviours and that of others. In this revision, two new scales, empathy and independence, have been added; semantic changes were made in 29 items; and 18 items were eliminated. The inventory is applicable for use in a variety of settings, including business and industry, schools and colleges, clinics and counselling agencies, and for cross cultural and other research. May be used to advise employees/applicants about their vocational plans.

Personnel Selection Tests and Interviews

Personnel selection is the process used to hire (or, less commonly, promote) individuals. Although the term can apply to all aspects of the process (recruitment, selection, hiring, acculturation, etc.) the most common meaning focuses on the selection of workers.

Overview

The professional standards of industrial psychologists require that any selection system be based on a job analysis to ensure that the selection criteria are job-related. The requirements for a selection system are knowledge, skills, ability, and other characteristics, known as *KSAO's*. U.S. law also recognizes *bona fide occupational qualifications* (BFOQs), which are requirements for a job which would be discriminatory were they not necessary — such as only employing men as wardens of maximum-security male prisons, or enforcing a mandatory retirement age for airline pilots, or a religious college only employing professors of its religion to teach its theology.

The goal of personnel selection, as all business processes, is to ensure an adequate return on investment. In the case of selection, this entails assurances that the productivity of the new hires produce more value than the costs of recruiting, selecting, and training them. Within industrial psychology, the area of utility analysis specifically addresses this issue.

Several screening methods exist that may be used in personnel selection. Examples include the use of minimum or desired qualifications, resume/application review, scored biodata instruments, oral interviews, work performance measures (e.g., writing samples), and tests (cognitive ability, personality, job knowledge). Development and implementation of such screening methods is sometimes done by human resources departments; larger organizations hire consultants or firms that specialize in developing personnel selection systems.

Personnel Assessment Tools: Tests and Procedures

Any test or procedure used to measure an individual's employment or career-related qualifications and interests can be considered a personnel assessment tool. There are many types of personnel assessment tools. These include *traditional knowledge and ability tests, inventories, subjective procedures*, and *projective instruments*. In this guide, the term *test* will be used as a generic term to refer to any instrument or procedure that samples behaviour or performance. Personnel assessment tools differ in;

- Purpose, e.g., selection, placement, promotion, career counselling, or training
- What they are designed to measure, e.g., abilities, skills, work styles, work values, or vocational interests
- What they are designed to predict, e.g., job performance, managerial potential, career success, job satisfaction, or tenure
- Format, e.g., paper-and-pencil, work-sample, or computer simulation
- Level of standardization, objectivity, and quantifiability-Assessment tools and procedures vary greatly on these factors. For example, there are subjective evaluations of resumes, highly structured achievement tests, interviews having varying degrees of structure, and personality inventories with no specific right or wrong answers.

All assessment tools used to make employment decisions, regardless of their format, level of standardization, or objectivity, are subject to professional and legal standards. For example, both the evaluation of a resume and the use of a highly standardized achievement test must comply with applicable laws. Assessment tools used solely for career exploration or counselling are usually not held to the same legal standards.

Relationship between the Personnel Assessment Process and Tests and Procedures

A personnel test or a procedure provides only part of the picture about a person. On the other hand, the personnel assessment process combines and evaluates all the information gathered about a person to make career or employment-related decisions.

What do Tests Measure?

People differ on many psychological and physical characteristics. These characteristics are called *constructs*. For example, people skilful in verbal and mathematical reasoning are considered high on *mental ability*. Those who have little physical stamina and strength are labeled low on *endurance* and *physical strength*. The terms *mental ability, endurance* and *physical strength* are constructs. *Constructs* are used to identify personal characteristics and to sort people in terms of how much they possess of such characteristics.

Constructs cannot be seen or heard, but we can observe their effects on other variables. For example, we don't observe physical strength but we can observe people with great strength lifting heavy objects and people with limited strength attempting, but failing, to lift these

Tests, inventories, and procedures are assessment tools that may be used to measure an individual's abilities, values, and personality traits. They are components of the assessment process.

- observations
- resume evaluations
- application blanks/questionnaires
- biodata inventories
- interviews
- work samples/performance tests
- achievement tests
- general ability tests
- specific ability tests
- physical ability tests
- personality inventories
- honesty/integrity inventories
- interest inventories
- work values inventories
- assessment centers

- drug tests
- medical tests.

Assessment process Systematic approach to combining and evaluating all the information gained from testing and using it to make career or employment-related decisions.

Why do Organizations Conduct Assessment?

Organizations use assessment tools and procedures to help them perform the following human resource functions:

- Selection. Organizations want to be able to identify and hire the best people for the job and the organization in a fair and efficient manner. A properly developed assessment tool may provide a way to select successful sales people, concerned customer service representatives, and effective workers in many other occupations.
- Placement. Organizations also want to be able to assign people to the appropriate job level. For example, an organization may have several managerial positions, each having a different level of responsibility. Assessment may provide information that helps organizations achieve the best fit between employees and jobs.
- Training and development. Tests are used to find out whether employees have mastered training materials. They can help identify those applicants and employees who might benefit from either remedial or advanced training. Information gained from testing can be used to design or modify training programs. Test results also help individuals identify areas in which self-development activities would be useful.
- Promotion. Organizations may use tests to identify employees who possess managerial potential or higher level capabilities, so that these employees can be promoted to assume greater duties and responsibilities.
- Career exploration and guidance. Tests are sometimes used to help people make educational and vocational

choices. Tests may provide information that helps individuals choose occupations in which they are likely to be successful and satisfied.

- Program evaluation. Tests may provide information that the organization can use to determine whether employees are benefiting from training and development programs.

Some Situations in which an Organization may Benefit from Testing

Some situations include the following:

- Current selection or placement procedures result in poor hiring decisions.
- Employee productivity is low.
- Employee errors have serious financial, health, or safety consequences.
- There is high employee turnover or absenteeism.
- Present assessment procedures do not meet current legal and professional standards.

Importance of using Tests in a Purposeful Manner

Assessment instruments, like other tools, can be extremely helpful when used properly, but counter-productive when used inappropriately. Often inappropriate use stems from not having a clear understanding of what you want to measure and why you want to measure it. Having a clear understanding of the purpose of your assessment system is important in selecting the appropriate assessment tools to meet that purpose. This brings us to an important principle of assessment.

Principle of Assessment

Use assessment tools in a *purposeful manner*. It is critical to have a clear understanding of what needs to be measured and for what purpose.

Assessment strategies should be developed with a clear understanding of the knowledge, skills, abilities, characteristics, or personal traits you want to measure. It is also essential to have a clear idea of what each assessment tool you are considering using is designed to measure.

Limitations of Personnel Tests and Procedures-fallibility of Test Scores

Professionally developed tests and procedures that are used as part of a planned assessment program may help you select and hire more qualified and productive employees. However, it is essential to understand that *all assessment tools are subject to errors,* both in measuring a characteristic, such as verbal ability, and in predicting performance criteria, such as success on the job. This is true for all tests and procedures, regardless of how objective or standardized they might be.

- Do not expect any test or procedure to measure a personal trait or ability with perfect accuracy for every single person.
- Do not expect any test or procedure to be completely accurate in predicting performance.

There will be cases where a test score or procedure will predict someone to be a good worker, who, in fact, is not. There will also be cases where an individual receiving a low score will be rejected, who, in fact, would actually be capable and a good worker. Such errors in the assessment context are called selection errors. Selection errors cannot be completely avoided in any assessment program.

Why do organizations conduct testing despite these errors? The answer is that appropriate use of professionally developed assessment tools on average enables organizations to make more effective employment-related decisions than use of simple observations or random decision making.

Using a single test or procedure will provide you with a limited view of a person's employment or career-related qualifications. Moreover, you may reach a mistaken conclusion by giving too much weight to a single test result. On the other hand, using a variety of assessment tools enables you to get a more complete picture of the individual. The practice of using a variety of tests and procedures to more fully assess people is referred to as the *whole-person approach* to personnel assessment. This will help reduce the number of selection errors made and will boost the effectiveness of your decision making. This leads to an important principle of assessment.

Principle of Assessment

Do not rely too much on any one test to make decisions. Use the *whole-person approach* to assessment.

Vocational Guidance

A vocation is a career or calling and the word is derived from the Latin *vocare*, which means "to call." Vocational guidance means helping someone find his or her calling or at least a suitable career choice. Vocations or careers can be loosely categorized into areas such as service, technical, mechanical, creative, health and business.

Vocational training rather than vocational guidance is available at career colleges and this is usually for entry-level careers. For example, a career college with a health vocational curriculum may offer education and training programs for nurse's aide and medical assistant careers, while business-oriented vocational schools may have marketing assistant and bookkeeping program offerings.

A career college or vocational school differs from regular colleges and universities as the focus isn't on academics, but rather on training students for a specific career. Vocational or career colleges are also sometimes referred to as community colleges or trade schools.

Vocational guidance is often started in high school although some high schools also have vocational training programs. Vocational exploration courses offer students the opportunity to research different career possibilities as well as learn which vocational areas they have aptitude or talent in. For instance, many vocational guidance classes give tests to the students that test their ability with numbers, words, mechanical concepts and many more subjects. Tests designed to measure an individual's personality traits, intelligence quotient (IQ) as well as his or her main values and interests are administered and analysed by career counsellors.

Once career counsellors and the students have looked over the test results, career options can be chosen that fit best with each individual. Vocational guidance doesn't stop there as many other considerations must be made when deciding on a career direction. The type and number of years of education must be considered. Salary and working conditions are other important considerations in career selection. The likely demand for the occupation in the next decade or more is a crucial element when choosing a vocation since this affects the likelihood of finding jobs in a certain career field.

Vocational guidance isn't just for high school students. Rather it's for anyone either starting a career or changing careers. Some people may have several different careers in their life, while others may stay in the same field during all their working years.

Personnel Selection : Job Analysis and Workers Analysis

What is Job Analysis? Job Analysis is a process to identify and determine in detail the particular job duties and requirements and the relative importance of these duties for a given job. Job Analysis is a process where judgements are made about data collected on a job.

Why is Job Analysis performed? What is the purpose of Job Analysis? Job Analysis is used to show the *relatedness* of employment procedures used by the employer. The procedures supported by job analysis include:

- Training
- Personnel Selection
- Job Evaluation, and
- Performance Appraisal.

Who conducts Job Analysis? Job Analysis may be conducted by the employer's Human Resources department or by a trained Job Analyst/Consultant.

How do I conduct a Job Analysis? The steps to conduct a Job Analysis are outlined below:

- Identify the Job(s) to be analysed.
- Determine the procedures to be used (methods) in collecting job data.
- Implement the job analysis methods.
- Review the data collected through Job Analysis.
- Summarize and document the data collected.

How are Jobs Analysed?

Who is involved in a Job Analysis? The Job Analysis may be conducted by a member of the employer's Human Resources department. This analysis may be in conjunction with the job incumbent (if the position is not vacant), the incumbent's supervisor, and possibly subject matter experts (SMEs).

Do I need a consultant for Job Analysis? When is a consultant needed for Job Analysis? A consultant is not necessary for Job Analysis. However, consultants may provide a more independent (unbiased) analysis of the job. Their analysis may not be affected by the internal politics of the organization. Also, a consultant may be needed for situations in which a large number of jobs will be analysed in a relatively short period of time. A consultant in this situation may be better able to concentrate on the job analysis task as their main function whereas internal employees probably still have their regular jobs to perform.

What are the products of a Job Analysis? A job description is the main product of a job analysis.

Can an employer be sued over inadequate or missing Job Analysis?

Are there Federal guidelines for Job Analysis? The Uniform Guidelines on Employee Selection Procedures states that a thorough job analysis is needed for supporting a selection procedure.

The Americans with Disabilities Act specifically states:

No covered entity shall discriminate against a qualified individual with a disability because of the disability of such individual in regard to job application procedures, the hiring, advancement, or discharge of employees, employee compensation, job training, and other terms, conditions, and privileges of employment.

The Act defines "*qualified individual with a disability*" as someone with a disability who: "with or without reasonable accommodation, can perform the essential functions of the employment position that such individual holds or desires." Essential functions may be determined through a Job Analysis.

Is there software to perform Job Analysis? HR-Guide offers an on-line form for creating Position Description Questionnaires. You may use this application to create the form that will be useful in collecting the job information. Is there software to help me manage Job Analysis? Yes. HR.Superb. Net allows you to access, store, create, and update job descriptions on-line.

What are sources of information for conducting a Job Analysis? Before a Job Analysis is conducted, the job analyst should review external sources if job information including:

- Dictionary of Occupational Titles
- U.S. Standard Occupational Classification System
- Other on-line job descriptions.

What methods are used for Job Analysis? The main methods of job analysis are:

- Interviews
- Questionnaires
- Observation.

What is Functional Job Analysis? Functional Job Analysis (FJA) was used by U.S. Employment Service job analysts to classify jobs for the DOT. The most recent version of FJA uses seven scales to describe what workers do in jobs: (1) Things, (2) Data, (3) People, (4) Worker Instructions, (5) Reasoning, (6) Math, and (7) Language.

What is the Position Analysis Questionnaire? This questionnaire, developed by McCormick, Jeanneret, and Mecham (1972), is a standardized job analysis instrument. It consists of 187 job elements that describe generic human work behaviours. This questionnaire was designed to be used for a wide variety of jobs.

What is the Critical Incident Technique? This method of Job Analysis focuses on identifying the *critical incidents* that distinguish satisfactory workers from unsatisfactory workers. This is based on the theory that certain tasks are crucial to satisfactory job performance, while others are not. In this method, the job analyst interviews incumbents and/or supervisors to identify a list of critical incidents. The identification of required Knowledges, Skills, and Abilities (KSAs) is made by examining the incidents—their causes and solutions. This technique is useful for developing work sample tests.

What is the Job Element Method? This method of Job Analysis, developed by Ernest Primoff, is a worker oriented method and is used primarily with lesser skilled workers and industrial occupations. This method, like the Critical Incident Technique, focuses on satisfactory workers. This method attempts to identify the characteristics of satisfactory workers (*job elements*). Once identified, these elements are used to develop appropriate selection tests. The steps to perform a Job Element job analysis are:

- Select a group of experts (may include incumbents and supervisors)
- Conduct brainstorming sessions to identify job elements (the KSA's of satisfactory workers).
- Assign weights to each of the elements based on the following criteria:
    a. proportion of barely acceptable workers who have the job element;
    b. effectiveness of the element in picking a superior worker;
    c. the trouble likely to occur if the element is not considered; and
    d. practicality—the effect of including the job element on the organization's ability to fill job openings.
- Analyse the Job Element data.

4

Industrial Working Environment

A work environment can be identified as the place that one works. i.e.-in an office building in a cube, at home at the kitchen table, from a car or truck, at a construction site. All are work environments. We tend, however, to hear about "healthy work environments." This can point to other factors in the work environment, such as co-workers, air quality, ergonomic seating, management (the boss!), child care, parking, noise, and even the size of one's cube. A work environment doesn't require a job. It requires that work has to be done in some place. Say you need to do homework. Where do you do it? At school in study hall? At your kitchen table? On the floor at a friend's house? These can also be considered work environments.

An effective work environment is vital to the success of small businesses and large corporations alike. When problems remain unsolved and rules never get implemented, the result can be an unproductive staff and a stale work environment.

People working together with a common denominator will accomplish tasks with greater ease and have higher expectations of themselves and their work. (success and passion)A positive work environment is critical no matter how many employees you have. It is management that fosters the work atmosphere so they are responsible for conducting things in a way that helps raise people's spirits. There are four basic beliefs:

- Hope
- Trust
- Pleasure
- Opportunity.

All this will help to create a positive work environment.

Trust

Chaos is created with petty rules. A productive and professional & successful employee is moulded by the boundaries set before them. Strict and unyielding rules that leave little to no room for personal judgment and ownership of one's work can only destroy motivation and ultimately decrease productivity.

"Fussy" rules only add chaos to work environment.

It is my personal experience that boundaries mold a self-motivated staff member into a productive professional. Strict, unreasonable demands are the result of a dominant strong managed system. They leave no room for individual judgment and "no ownership" of one's work. This drastically reduces the motivation to complete tasks efficiently.

In an establishment that trusts its employees, people will make the ultimate sacrifice to assist their company in succeeding. Praise goes along way in our personal and professional life.

Optimism will help a group thrive by fuelling the aspirations of employees for achievement. The best employees seem to thrive off of the praise they receive when they tackle a tough problem and see it through to resolution.

When a company trusts its employees, those workers are far more likely to make sacrifices to help the company through difficult times. A kind word here and there goes a long way in both the professional and person spheres of influence.

Enjoyment in a Successful Work Place

Enjoyment... Yes, even the business owner and manager want to wake up the next morning with that "desire" to want to be at work! Real enjoyment at work comes when you and your team are deeply committed to a problem, and you persevere together to tackle it. It isn't the laughs and giggles that waste company time.

Opportunity in the Work Environment

Without a chance to grow, workers will not live up to their successful potential. We all need some kind of motivation that helps us on the road to attaining our goals. Those that punch a clock and do the same thing day in and day out are most likely looking for a better opportunity.

You have to be able to relate with your workers when you are a business owner so that you understand what is important to them. Asking them where they envision themselves in the future is a great way to find out what motivates them. If you offer employees the opportunity for advancement, then they are more likely to say that they will still be working for you. Make every day a success

Promoting from within is always a good idea as it motivates people to want to do their best so that they can make it to the next level.

It is important for companies to take a careful look at the work atmosphere on a regular basis. This helps reduce the possibility of lawsuits and lost assets. Understand that your employees should be valued and then make certain the work atmosphere reflects that.

Opportunity

People generally need some sort of challenge to motivate themselves. Effective leadership means offering people the chance to grow. Recognize their contribution with positive feedback, raises, and advancement to more challenging positions. People who are willing to expand into new things while working with a diverse set of co-workers will learn new roles and expand their view of the world.

These people may be few and far between, but they enrich the work environment and contribute to a stronger organization. As leader, you are empowered with the ability to inspire people and increase their productivity. By generating an atmosphere that is conducive to trust, hope, pleasure, and the potential for personal growth, you are creating a more powerful team and cultivating future leaders at the same time.

Hostile Work Environment

A hostile work environment exists when an employee experiences workplace harassment and fears going to work because of the offensive, intimidating, or oppressive atmosphere generated by the harasser.

A hostile work environment may also be defined as when a boss or manager begins to engage in a manner designed to make you quit in retaliation for your actions. Suppose you report safety violations at work, get injured at work, attempt to join a union, complain to upper level management about a problem at work, or act as a whistleblower in any respect.

Then, the company's response is to do all manner of things to make you quit, like writing you up for work rules you didn't break, reducing your hours, scheduling you for hours that are in total conflict with what you can do, or reducing your salary. The company's reaction can be viewed as creating a hostile work environment, one that makes it impossible to work and is an attempt to make you quit so that the employer does not have to pay unemployment benefits.

The anti-discrimination statutes governing hostile work environment are not a general civility code. Thus, federal law does not prohibit simple teasing, offhand comments, or isolated incidents that are not extremely serious. Rather, the conduct must be so objectively offensive as to alter the conditions of the individual's employment. The conditions of employment are altered only if the harassment culminates in a tangible employment action or is sufficiently severe or pervasive to create a hostile work environment.

Efficiency, Time-motion Study and Therbligs

The idea of a Time and Motion Study is often still associated with production lines and manufacturing industry. It gained a bad reputation as a source of disagreement between "management" and "workers". However if used properly it can be of benefit to modern companies and their workforce. This is a massive field-what follows is a brief overview.

History of Scientific Management

Time and Motion studes have their roots in the work of Frederick Winslow Taylor who in 1911 published his famous article "The Principles of Scientific Management". Essentially this involved getting the best person for each job and training them to do it the best way possible. Although Taylor believed in cooperation between management and workers, "Taylorism" can be seen as formalising the management/worker divide. Management would be responsible for deciding how things were done with workers simply doing what they were told. It was seen as dehumanising, reducing skilled workers to the status of mechanical parts and resources.

Gilbreths

Time and Motion study was refined in the early twentieth century by Frank and Lillian Gilbreth. The Gilbreths' preferred "motion study" to Taylor's "time study", however the term "Time and Motion" has tended to stick in popular terminology.

The Gilbreths studied the actions taken by workers at certain task with the aim of streamlining the processes involved. One of their most famous experiments involved analysing the work of bricklayers and significantly reducing the number of "operations" involved. This change benefited both employer (increased productivity) and employee (decreased fatigue).

Therbligs

The Gilbreths developed a categorisation system for the different basic activities which went to make up a task. These were called *Therbligs* (an anagram of "Gilbreths"). The basic Therbligs numbered around 15 (the system developed over time) and included such actions as "find", "select" and "rest". Each of these was represented by an icon, for example an eye for "find". The activity of a worker could then be plotted on a *Simo Chart* ("Simultaneous Motion Chart") for optimisation.

Hawthorne Effect

One problem for Time and Motion studies is what is known as the Hawthorne Effect (named after a factory not a person). This in essence says that employees change their behaviour when they know that they are being measured-the mere act of performing a study can improve performance. It's a form of "observer effect" akin to a productivity placebo.

The Hawthorne Effect also showed that productivity tends to improve *whatever* changes are made, then return to normal over time. This recognises that workers are human beings and that knowing they are valued can in itself inspire better performance.

The Hawthorne Effect doesn't undermine the value of Time and Motion studies but does emphasise that people are the most significant element of any workplace.

MTM

The original Time and Motion Study concepts led during the twentieth century to the development of Predetermined Motion Time Systems (PMTS) such as Methods-Time-Measurement (MTM). This was released in 1948 by Maynard, Stegemerten, & Schwab and is today found in three versions: MTM-1, MTM-2 and MTM-3

Mutual Benefits

In the"bad old days" of industrial relations, Time and Motion studies were often seen as a tool for the management to exploit the workers. The Time and Motion study-sometimes carried out in secret-could be used to pressurise people to work harder or lose their jobs. It's not surprising that many workers came to resent the whole concept of time & motion.

It needn't be that way. Modern analysis methodologies and software packages have little in common with the old image of a "Motion Man" timing workers with a stopwatch. A Time and Motion study carried out openly with full buy-in from all concerned can be of mutual benefit. Improvements can be made to working conditions and methods that both improve productivity and make working less stressful or reduce fatigue.

Perhaps the best way to ensure full cooperation is to ensure that any benefits of the study are *shared* between company and workforce. If efficiency improvements are identified then the gains can be shared between shareholders and workers, with the latter benefiting from greater wages or shorter hours.

Unfortunately too many companies today still see a Time and Motion study as simply a way to increase profits with no benefit returning to the workforce who are ultimately responsible for those profits.

Motivation, Incentives and Methods of Payment

Although some theorists like Herzberg believe that money is not a positive motivator (although lack of it can de-motivate), pay systems are designed to motivate employees. The scientific/Theory X approach, in particular, argues that workers respond to financial rewards. Getting employee pay right (often referred to as the "remuneration package") is a crucial task for a business.

Why is pay important?

- It is an important cost for a business (in some "labour-intensive" businesses, payroll costs are over 50% of total costs)
- People feel strongly about it. Pay helps to satisfy many needs (e.g. security, esteem needs, resources to pursue self-actualisation)
- Pay is the subject of much important business legislation (e.g. national minimum wage; equal opportunities legislation)
- It helps attract reliable employees with the skills the business needs for success
- Pay also helps retain employees – rather than them leave and perhaps join a competitor
- For most employees, the remuneration package is the most important part of a job – and certainly the most visible part of any job offer.

There are many methods of financial reward (these are covered in separate revision notes);

- Time-rate pay
- Piece-rate pay
- Commission
- Performance-related pay
- Bonuses
- Shares and options
- Benefits in kind ("fringe benefits")
- Pensions.

Because pay is a complex issue, there are several ways in which businesses determine how much to pay, and which methods to use:

- Job evaluation/content; this is usually the most important factor. What is involved in the job being paid? How does it compare with similar jobs?
- Fairness – pay needs to be perceived and be seen to match the level of work
- Negotiated pay rates – the rate of pay may have been determined elsewhere and the business needs to ensure that it complies with these rates.
- Market rates – another important influence – particularly where there is a standard pattern of supply and demand in the relevant labour market. If a business tries to pay below the "market rate" then it will probably have difficulty in recruiting and retaining suitable staff
- Individual performance – increasingly, businesses include an element of "performance-related" reward in their pay structures.

However, it is important to remember that pay is only one element of motivation and will work best where management also give attention to:

- Developing good management and supervision;
- Designing jobs and organising work groups to make them as satisfying as possible;
- Providing feedback to staff about their performance and training and development;

- Making effective arrangements for communications and consultation.

Employee Motivation and Productivity

The success of any business depends largely on the motivation of the employees. Human resources are essential to the prosperity, productivity and performance of any company. Motivation is the key to creating an environment where optimal performance is possible. So how do you ensure that individual motivation is at its peak within your workplace?

Every person has their own set of motivations and personal incentives to work hard or not as the case may be. Some are motivated by recognition whilst others are motivated by cash incentives. Whatever the employees motivation, the key to promoting that motivation as an employer is understanding and incentive.

Employee incentive programs go a long way towards ensuring employees feel appreciated and worthwhile. This alone can help with employee motivation across the board. The great thing about these programs is they are very individualized. That is you tailor your programs to suit the needs and wants of your employees. Incentive programs increase motivation because they are not only encouraging productive performance but also show employees the company cares.

Perhaps the most significant impact of increased employee motivation is that of increased productivity. This is a central aim when adopting an incentive program. If you can increase employee motivation, productivity will follow and with that the inevitable increased bottom line.

Employee incentive programs promote work place harmony, employee performance and most of all employee motivation. This is the key to long term benefits for your company. Motivated employees means staff retention and company loyalty, these are two things that will have a significant impact on the growth and development of your business.

Employee incentive programs work by offering rewards for outstanding performance, hard work or results. Employees who meet targets, go beyond the call of duty or simply do a good job are rewarded for their efforts. The rewards and incentives vary and can be as individual as the employees themselves. Employee incentive programs work because they offer diverse rewards that meet the needs of the company as a whole.

In order to maximize employee motivation via employee incentives it is useful to discuss the program with employees. Spend some time figuring out what your employees actually want out of an incentive program. Find out what motivates them and how they want to be rewarded for productive performance. If you take the time to do this then you will be able to implement a program based on the individualized needs of your employees. A distinctive tailor made program will increase employee motivation and in turn your profits.

Employee motivation is essential to the success of any company big or small. In the modern workplace human resources are valued above all others. Motivated employees are productive, happy and committed. The spin off of this includes reduced employee turnover, results driven employees, company loyalty and work place harmony.

Factors Affecting Labour Productivity

In a survey of manufacturing growth and performance in Britain, it was found that:

"The factors affecting labour productivity or the performance of individual work roles are of broadly the same type as those that affect the performance of manufacturing firms as a whole. They include: (1) physical-organic, location, and technological factors; (2) cultural belief-value and individual attitudinal, motivational and behavioural factors; (3) international influences – e.g. levels of innovativeness and efficiency on the part of the owners and managers of inward investing foreign companies; (4) managerial-organizational and wider economic and political-legal environments; (5) levels of flexibility in internal labour markets and the organization of work activities – e.g. the presence or absence of traditional craft demarcation lines and barriers to occupational entry; and (6) individual rewards and payment systems, and the effectiveness of personnel managers and others in recruiting, training, communicating with, and performance-motivating employees on the basis of pay and other incentives. The emergence of computers has been noted as a significant factor in increasing labour productivity in the late 1990's, by some, and as an insignificant factor by others, such as R.J. Gordon. Although computers have existed for most of the 20th century, some economic researchers have noted a lag in productivity growth caused by computers that didn't come until the late 1990's."

Industrial Incentives

In each section of Personal Tax (income tax), Indirect taxes (sales, excise & customs duty) and the corporate taxes there are certain rebates given to the tax payer if he fits in the prescribed criteria. These concessions or Tax Holidays as they call are meant to attract more and more people to pay tax. These rebates also mean less 'pinch' on the pockets and a good fast growth of economy.

Rebate is a deduction from tax payable. Since these are the best tax-slashing devices, it is absolutely essential to have a clear, concise and complete insight into these.

In computing the amount of income-tax on the total income of an assessee with which he is chargeable for any assessment year, there shall be allowed from the amount of income-tax, in accordance with and subject to the provisions of certain sections, the deductions specified in those sections.

The aggregate amount of the deductions under such sections shall not, in any case, exceed the amount of income tax on the total income of the assessee with which he is chargeable for any assessment year.

General Tax Incentives

The Government offers many incentives to investors in India with a view to stimulating industrial growth and development. The incentives offered are normally in line with the government's economic philosophy, and are revised regularly to accommodate new areas of emphasis. The following are some of the important incentives offered, which significantly reduce the effective tax rates for the beneficiary companies:

- Five year tax holiday for:
  - o Power projects.
  - o Firms engaged in exports.
  - o New industries in notified states and for new industrial units established, in electronic hardware/ software parks.
  - o Export Oriented Units and units in Free Trade Zones.
  - o As of 1994-95 budget firms engaged in providing infrastructure facilities, can also avail of this benefit.
- Tax deductions of 100 per cent of export profits.
- Deduction of 30 per cent of net (total) income for 10 years for new industrial undertakings.
- Deduction of 50 per cent on foreign exchange earnings by construction companies, hotels and on royalty, commission etc. earned in foreign exchange.
- Deduction in respect of certain inter-corporate dividends to the extent of dividend declared.

5

Job Satisfaction and Industrial Psychology

Job satisfaction describes how content an individual is with his or her job. The happier people are within their job, the more satisfied they are said to be. Job satisfaction is not the same as motivation, although it is clearly linked. Job design aims to enhance job satisfaction and performance, methods include job rotation, job enlargement and job enrichment. Other influences on satisfaction include the management style and culture, employee involvement, empowerment and autonomous work position. Job satisfaction is a very important attribute which is frequently measured by organizations. The most common way of measurement is the use of rating scales where employees report their reactions to their jobs. Questions relate to rate of pay, work responsibilities, variety of tasks, promotional opportunities the work itself and co-workers. Some questioners ask yes or no questions while others ask to rate satisfaction on 1-5 scale (where 1 represents "not at all satisfied" and 5 represents "extremely satisfied").

Definitions

Job satisfaction has been defined as a pleasurable emotional state resulting from the appraisal of one's job; an affective reaction to one's job; and an attitude towards one's job. Weiss (2002) has argued that job satisfaction is an attitude but points out that researchers should clearly distinguish the objects of cognitive evaluation which are affect (emotion), beliefs and behaviours. This definition suggests that we form attitudes towards our jobs by taking into account our feelings, our beliefs, and our behaviours

History

One of the biggest preludes to the study of job satisfaction was the Hawthorne studies. These studies (1924-1933), primarily credited to Elton Mayo of the Harvard Business School, sought to find the effects of various conditions (most notably illumination) on workers' productivity. These studies ultimately showed that novel changes in work conditions temporarily increase productivity (called the Hawthorne Effect). It was later found that this increase resulted, not from the new conditions, but from the knowledge of being observed. This finding provided strong evidence that people work for purposes other than pay, which paved the way for researchers to investigate other factors in job satisfaction.

Scientific management (aka Taylorism) also had a significant impact on the study of job satisfaction. Frederick Winslow Taylor's 1911 book, Principles of Scientific Management, argued that there was a single best way to perform any given work task. This book contributed to a change in industrial production philosophies, causing a shift from skilled labour and piecework towards the more modern ==

Headline text of assembly lines and hourly wages. The initial use of scientific management by industries greatly increased productivity because workers were forced to work at a faster pace. However, workers became exhausted and dissatisfied, thus leaving researchers with new questions to answer regarding job satisfaction. It should also be noted that the work of W.L. Bryan, Walter Dill Scott, and Hugo Munsterberg set the tone for Taylor's work.

Some argue that Maslow's hierarchy of needs theory, a motivation theory, laid the foundation for job satisfaction theory. This theory explains that people seek to satisfy five specific needs in life – physiological needs, safety needs, social needs, self-esteem needs, and self-actualization. This model served as a good basis from which early researchers could develop job satisfaction theories. Job satisfaction can also be seen within the broader context of the range of issues which affect an individual's experience of work, or their quality of working life. Job satisfaction can be understood in terms of its relationships with other key factors, such as general well-being, stress at work, control at work, home-work interface, and working conditions.

Models of Job Satisfaction

Affect Theory

Edwin A. Locke's Range of Affect Theory (1976) is arguably the most famous job satisfaction model. The main premise of this theory is that satisfaction is determined by a discrepancy between what one wants in a job and what one has in a job. Further, the theory states that how much one values a given facet of work (e.g. the degree of autonomy in a position) moderates how satisfied/dissatisfied one becomes when expectations are/aren't met. When a person values a particular facet of a job, his satisfaction is more greatly impacted both positively (when expectations are met) and negatively (when expectations are not met), compared to one who doesn't value that facet. To illustrate, if Employee A values autonomy in the workplace and Employee B is indifferent about autonomy, then Employee A would be more satisfied in a position that offers a high degree of autonomy and less satisfied in a position with little or no autonomy compared to Employee B. This theory also states that too much of a particular facet will produce stronger feelings of dissatisfaction the more a worker values that facet.

Dispositional Theory

Another well-known job satisfaction theory is the Dispositional Theory Template:JacksonApril 2007. It is a very general theory that suggests that people have innate dispositions that cause them to have tendencies toward a certain level of satisfaction, regardless of one's job. This approach became a notable explanation of job satisfaction in light of evidence that job satisfaction tends to be stable over time and across careers and jobs. Research also indicates that identical twins have similar levels of job satisfaction. A significant model that narrowed the scope of the Dispositional Theory was the Core Self-evaluations Model, proposed by Timothy A. Judge in 1998. Judge argued that there are four Core Self-evaluations that determine one's disposition towards job satisfaction: self-esteem, general self-efficacy, locus of control, and neuroticism. This model states that higher levels of self-esteem (the value one places on his/her self) and general self-efficacy (the belief in one's own competence) lead to higher work satisfaction. Having an internal locus of control (believing one has control over her\his own life, as opposed to outside forces having control) leads to higher job satisfaction. Finally, lower levels of neuroticism lead to higher job satisfaction.

Two-Factor Theory (Motivator-Hygiene Theory)

Frederick Herzberg's Two factor theory (also known as Motivator Hygiene Theory) attempts to explain satisfaction and motivation in the workplace This theory states that satisfaction and dissatisfaction are driven by different factors – motivation and hygiene factors, respectively. An employee's motivation to work is continually related to job satisfaction of a subordinate. Motivation can be seen as an inner force that drives individuals to attain personal and organizational goals. Motivating factors are those aspects of the job that make people want to perform, and provide people with satisfaction, for example achievement in work, recognition, promotion opportunities. These motivating factors are considered to be intrinsic to the job, or the work carried out. Hygiene factors include aspects of the working environment such as pay, company policies, supervisory practices, and other working conditions.

While Hertzberg's model has stimulated much research, researchers have been unable to reliably empirically prove the model, with Hackman & Oldham suggesting that Hertzberg's original formulation of the model may have been a methodological artifact. Furthermore, the theory does not consider individual differences, conversely predicting all employees will react in an identical manner to changes in motivating/hygiene factors. Finally, the model has been criticised in that it does not specify how motivating/hygiene factors are to be measured.

Job Characteristics Model

Hackman & Oldham proposed the Job Characteristics Model, which is widely used as a framework to study how particular job characteristics impact on job outcomes, including job satisfaction. The model states that there are five core job characteristics which impact three critical psychological states (experienced meaningfulness, experienced responsibility for outcomes, and knowledge of the actual results), in turn influencing work outcomes (job satisfaction, absenteeism, work motivation, etc.). The five core job characteristics can be combined to form a motivating potential score (MPS) for a job, which can be used as an index of how likely a job is to affect an employee's attitudes and behaviours——. A meta-analysis of studies that assess the framework of the model provides some support for the validity of the JCM.

Communication Overload and Communication Underload

One of the most important aspects of an individual's work in a modern organization concerns the management of communication demands that he or she encounters on the job. Demands can be characterized as a communication load, which refers to "the rate and complexity of communication inputs an individual must process in a particular time frame." Individuals in an organization can experience communication over-load and communication under-load which can affect their level of job satisfaction. Communication overload can occur when "an individual receives too many messages in a short period of time which can result in unprocessed information or when an individual faces more complex messages that are more difficult to process." Due to this process, "given an individual's style of work and motivation to complete a task, when more inputs exist than outputs, the individual perceives a condition of overload which can be positively or negatively related to job satisfaction. In comparison, communication under load can occur when messages or inputs are sent below the individual's ability to process them." According to the ideas of communication over-load and under-load, if an individual does not receive enough input on the job or is unsuccessful in processing these inputs, the individual is more likely to become dissatisfied, aggravated, and unhappy with their work which leads to a low level of job satisfaction.

Measuring Job Satisfaction

There are many methods for measuring job satisfaction. By far, the most common method for collecting data regarding job satisfaction is the Likert scale (named after Rensis Likert). Other less common methods of for gauging job satisfaction include: Yes/No questions, True/False questions, point systems, checklists, and forced choice answers. This data is typically collected using an Enterprise Feedback Management (EFM) system.

The Job Descriptive Index (JDI), created by Smith, Kendall, & Hulin (1969), is a specific questionnaire of job satisfaction that has been widely used. It measures one's satisfaction in five facets: pay, promotions and promotion opportunities, coworkers, supervision, and the work itself. The scale is simple, participants answer either yes, no, or can't decide (indicated by '?') in response to whether given statements accurately describe one's job.

The Job in General Index is an overall measurement of job satisfaction. It is an improvement to the Job Descriptive Index because the JDI focuses too much on individual facets and not enough on work satisfaction in general.

Other job satisfaction questionnaires include: the Minnesota Satisfaction Questionnaire (MSQ), the Job Satisfaction Survey (JSS), and the Faces Scale. The MSQ measures job satisfaction in 20 facets and has a long form with 100 questions (five items from each facet) and a short form with 20 questions (one item from each facet).

The JSS is a 36 item questionnaire that measures nine facets of job satisfaction. Finally, the Faces Scale of job satisfaction, one of the first scales used widely, measured overall job satisfaction with just one item which participants respond to by choosing a face.

Superior-Subordinate Communication

Superior-subordinate communication is an important influence on job satisfaction in the workplace. The way in which subordinate's perceive a supervisor's behaviour can positively or negatively influence job satisfaction. Communication behaviour such as facial expression, eye contact, vocal expression, and body movement is crucial to the superior-subordinate relationship. Nonverbal messages play a central role in interpersonal interactions with respect to impression formation, deception, attraction, social influence, and emotional expression. Nonverbal immediacy from the supervisor helps to increase interpersonal involvement with their subordinates impacting job satisfaction. The manner in which supervisors communicate their subordinates may be more important than the verbal content. Individuals who dislike and think negatively about their supervisor are less willing to communicate or have motivation to work where as individuals who like and think positively of their supervisor are more likely to communicate and are satisfied with their job and work environment. The relationship of a subordinate with their supervisor is a very important aspect in the workplace. Therefore, a supervisor who uses nonverbal immediacy, friendliness, and open communication lines is more willing to receive positive feedback and high job satisfaction from a subordinate where as a supervisor who is antisocial, unfriendly, and unwilling to communicate will naturally receive negative feedback and very low job satisfaction from their subordinate's in the workplace.. motions == Mood and emotions while working are the raw materials which cumulate to form the affective element of job satisfaction. Moods tend to be longer lasting but often weaker states of uncertain origin, while emotions are often more intense, short-lived and have a clear object or cause.

There is some evidence in the literature that state moods are related to overall job satisfaction. Positive and negative emotions were also found to be significantly related to overall job satisfaction.

Frequency of experiencing net positive emotion will be a better predictor of overall job satisfaction than will intensity of positive emotion when it is experienced. Emotion regulation and emotion labour are also related to job satisfaction. Emotion work (or emotion management) refers to various efforts to manage emotional states and displays. Emotion regulation includes all of the conscious and unconscious efforts to increase, maintain, or decrease one or more components of an emotion. Although early studies of the consequences of emotional labour emphasized its harmful effects on workers, studies of workers in a variety of occupations suggest that the consequences of emotional labour are not uniformly negative.

It was found that suppression of unpleasant emotions decreases job satisfaction and the amplification of pleasant emotions increases job satisfaction. The understanding of how emotion regulation relates to job satisfaction concerns two models:

1. emotional dissonance. Emotional dissonance is a state of discrepancy between public displays of emotions and internal experiences of emotions, that often follows the process of emotion regulation.Emotional dissonance is associated with high emotional exhaustion, low organizational commitment, and low job satisfaction.
2. Social interaction model. Taking the social interaction perspective, workers' emotion regulation might beget responses from others during interpersonal encounters that subsequently impact their own job satisfaction. For example: The accumulation of favorable responses to displays of pleasant emotions might positively affect job satisfaction.

performance of emotional labour that produces desired outcomes could increase job satisfaction.

Relationships and Practical Implications

Job Satisfaction can be an important indicator of how employees feel about their jobs and a predictor of work behaviours such as organizational citizenship, absenteeism, and turnover. Further, job satisfaction can partially mediate the relationship of personality variables and deviant work behaviours.

One common research finding is that job satisfaction is correlated with life satisfaction. This correlation is reciprocal, meaning people who are satisfied with life tend to be satisfied with their job and people who are satisfied with their job tend to be satisfied with life. However, some research has found that job satisfaction is not significantly related to life satisfaction when other variables such as nonwork satisfaction and core self-evaluations are taken into account.

An important finding for organizations to note is that job satisfaction has a rather tenuous correlation to productivity on the job. This is a vital piece of information to researchers and businesses, as the idea that satisfaction and job performance are directly related to one another is often cited in the media and in some non-academic management literature. A recent meta-analysis found an average uncorrected correlation between job satisfaction and productivity to be r=.18; the average true correlation, corrected for research artifacts and unreliability, was r=.30. Further, the meta-analysis found that the relationship between satisfaction and performance can be moderated by job complexity, such that for high-complexity jobs the correlation between satisfaction and performance is higher (ñ=.52) than for jobs of low to moderate complexity (ñ=.29). Job Satisfaction also high relationship with intention to quit. It is found in many research that Job Satisfaction can lead to Intention to Stay/Quit in an organization. Recent research has also shown that Intention to Quit can have effect like poor performance orientation, organizational deviance, and poor organizational citizenship behaviours. In short, the relationship of satisfaction to productivity is not necessarily straightforward and can be influenced by a number of other work-related constructs, and the notion that "a happy worker is a productive worker" should not be the foundation of organizational decision-making.

With regard to job performance, employee personality may be more important than job satisfaction. The link between job satisfaction and performance is thought to be a spurious relationship; instead, both satisfaction and performance are the result of personality.

The Work Curve

In economics, labour is a measure of the work done by human beings. It is conventionally contrasted with such other factors of production as land and capital. There are theories which have developed a concept called human capital (referring to the skills that workers possess, not necessarily their actual work), although there are also counter posing macro-economic system theories that think human capital is a contradiction in terms.

Compensation and Measurement

Wage is a basic compensation for paid labour, and the compensation for labour per period of time is referred to as the wage rate. Other frequently used terms include:

- wage = payment per unit of time (typically an hour)
- earnings = payment accrued over a period (typically a week, a month, or a year)
- total compensation = earnings + other benefits for labour
- income = total compensation + unearned income
- economic rent = total compensation-opportunity cost

Economists measure labour in terms of hours worked, total wages, or efficiency.

- total cost = fixed cost + variable cost.

Demand for Labour and Wage Determination

Labour demand is a derived demand, in other words the employer's cost of production is the wage, in which the business or firm benefits from an increased output or revenue. The determinants of employing the addition to labour depend on the Marginal Revenue Product (MRP) of the worker. The MRP is calculated by multiplying the price of the end product or service by the Marginal Physical Product of the worker. If the MRP is greater than a firm's Marginal Cost, then the firm will employ the worker. The firm only employs however up to the point where MRP=MC, not lower, in economic theory.

Wage differences exist, particularly in mixed and fully/ partly flexible labour markets. For example, the wages of a doctor and a port cleaner, both employed by the NHS, differ greatly. But why? There are many factors concerning this issue.

This includes the MRP of the worker. A doctor's MRP is far greater than that of the port cleaner. In addition, the barriers to becoming a doctor are far greater than that of becoming a port cleaner. For example to become a doctor takes a lot of education and training which is costly, and only those who are socially and intellectually advantaged can succeed in such a demanding profession. The port cleaner however requires minimal training. The supply of doctors therefore would be much more inelastic than the supply of port cleaners. The demand would also be inelastic as there is a high demand for doctors, so the NHS will pay higher wage rates to attract the profession.

The MRP of the worker is affected by other inputs to production with which the worker can work (e.g. machinery), often aggregated under the term "capital". It is typical in economic models for greater availability of capital for a firm to increase the MRP of the worker, all else equal. The education and training noted in the last paragraph are counted as "human capital". Since the amount of physical capital affects MRP, and since financial capital flows can affect the amount of physical capital available, MRP and thus wages can be affected by financial capital flows within and between countries, and the degree of capital mobility within and between countries.

Two Ways of Analysing Labour Markets

There are two sides to labour economics. Labour economics can generally be seen as the application of microeconomic or macroeconomic techniques to the labour market. Microeconomic techniques study the role of individuals and individual firms in the labour market. Macroeconomic techniques look at the interrelations between the labour market, the goods market, the money market, and the foreign trade market. It looks at how these interactions influence macro variables such as employment levels, participation rates, aggregate income and Gross Domestic Product. (Morendy Octora)

The Macroeconomics of Labour Markets

The labour force is defined as the number of individuals age 16 and over, excluding those in the military, who are either employed or actively looking for work. The participation rate is the number of people in the labour force divided by the size of the adult civilian noninstitutional population (or by the population of working age that is not institutionalised). The nonlabour force includes those who are not looking for work, those who are institutionalised such as in prisons or psychiatric wards, stay-at home spouses, children, and those serving in the military. The unemployment level is defined as the labour force minus the number of people currently employed. The unemployment rate is defined as the level of unemployment divided by the labour force. The employment rate is defined as the number of people currently employed divided by the adult population (or by the population of working age). In these statistics, self-employed people are counted as employed.

Variables like employment level, unemployment level, labour force, and unfilled vacancies are called stock variables because they measure a quantity at a point in time. They can be contrasted with flow variables which measure a quantity over a duration of time. Changes in the labour force are due to flow variables such as natural population growth, net immigration, new entrants, and retirements from the labour force. Changes in unemployment depend on: inflows made up of non-employed people starting to look for jobs and of employed people who lose their jobs and look for new ones; and outflows of people who find new employment and of people who stop looking for employment. When looking at the overall macroeconomy, several types of unemployment have been identified, including:

- Frictional unemployment — This reflects the fact that it takes time for people to find and settle into new jobs. If 12 individuals each take one month before they start a new job, the aggregate unemployment statistics will record this as a single unemployed worker. Technological advancement often reduces frictional unemployment, for example: internet search engines have reduced the cost and time associated with locating employment.

- Structural unemployment — This reflects a mismatch between the skills and other attributes of the labour force and those demanded by employers. If 4 workers each take six months off to re-train before they start a new job, the aggregate unemployment statistics will record this as two unemployed workers. Technological change often increases structural unemployment, for example: technological implementation might require workers to re-train to adapt to the new technology. The effects of globalisation have ensured that some domestic industries have expanded whilst others contract which contributes to this factor of unemployment.
- Natural rate of unemployment — This is the summation of frictional and structural unemployment, that excludes cyclical contributions of unemployment e.g. recession's. It is the lowest rate of unemployment that a stable economy can expect to achieve, seeing as some frictional and structural unemployment is inevitable. Economists do not agree on the natural rate, with estimates ranging from 1% to 5%, or on its meaning — some associate it with "non-accelerating inflation". The estimated rate varies from country to country and from time to time.
- Demand deficient unemployment — In Keynesian economics, any level of unemployment beyond the natural rate is most likely due to insufficient demand in the overall economy. During a recession, aggregate expenditure is deficient causing the underutilisation of inputs (including labour). Aggregate expenditure (AE) can be increased, according to Keynes, by increasing consumption spending (C), increasing investment spending (I), increasing government spending (G), or increasing the net of exports minus imports (X"M).

{AE = C + I + G + (X"M)}

Neoclassical Microeconomics of Labour Markets

Neo-classical economists view the labour market as similar to other markets in that the forces of supply and demand jointly determine price (in this case the wage rate) and quantity (in this case the number of people employed). However, the labour market differs from other markets (like the markets for goods or the money market) in several ways. Perhaps the most important of these differences is the function of supply and demand in setting price and quantity.

In markets for goods, if the price is high there is a tendency in the long run for more goods to be produced until the demand is satisfied. With labour, overall supply cannot effectively be manufactured because people have a limited amount of time in the day, and people are not manufactured. The income effect suggests a rise in overall wages will, in many situations, not result in more supply of labour: it may result in less supply of labour as workers take more time off to spend their increased wages. The substitution effect of a higher wage might cause people to work more, as the opportunity cost to work less is greater than it was prior to the increase. While available empirical evidence is mixed, some analysts suggest the income and substitution effects cancel each other out, resulting in no supply increase. Within the overall labour market, particular segments are thought to be subject to more normal rules of supply and demand as workers are likely to change job types in response to differing wage rates.

The labour market also acts as a non-clearing market. Whereas most markets have a point of equilibrium without excess surplus or demand, the labour market is expected to have a persistent level of unemployment. Contrasting the labour market to other markets also reveals persistent compensating differentials among similar workers.

The competitive assumption leads to clear conclusions — workers earn their marginal product of labour.

Neoclassical Microeconomic Model — Supply

Households are suppliers of labour. In microeconomics theory, people are assumed to be rational and seeking to maximize their utility function. In this labour market model, their utility function is determined by the choice between income and leisure. However, they are constrained by the waking hours available to them.

Let w denote hourly wage. Let k denote total waking hours. Let L denote working hours. Let ð denote other incomes or benefits. Let A denote leisure hours.

The utility function and budget constraint can be expressed as following: max U(w L + ð, A) such that L + A d" k.

This can be shown in a graph that illustrates the trade-off between allocating your time between leisure activities and income generating activities. The linear constraint line indicates that there are only 24 hours in a day, and individuals must choose how much of this time to allocate to leisure activities and how much to working. (If multiple days are being considered the maximum number of hours that could be allocated towards leisure or work is about 16 due to the necessity of sleep) This allocation decision is informed by the curved indifference curve labelled IC. The curve indicates the combinations of leisure and work that will give the individual a specific level of utility. The point where the highest indifference curve is just tangent to the constraint line (point A), illustrates the short-run equilibrium for this supplier of labour services.

The Income/Leisure Trade-off in the Short Run

If the preference for consumption is measured by the value of income obtained, rather than work hours, this diagram can be used to show a variety of interesting effects. This is because the slope of the budget constraint becomes the wage rate. The point of optimization (point A) reflects the equivalency between the wage rate and the marginal rate of substitution, leisure for income (the slope of the indifference curve). Because the marginal rate of substitution, leisure for income, is also the ratio of the marginal utility of leisure (MU^L) to the marginal utility of income (MU^Y), one can conclude:

Effects of a Wage Increase

If wages increase, this individual's constraint line pivots up from X,Y_1 to X,Y_2. He/she can now purchase more goods and services. His/her utility will increase from point A on IC_1 to point B on IC_2. To understand what effect this might have on the decision of how many hours to work, you must look at the income effect and substitution effect. The wage increase shown in the previous diagram can be decompiled into two separate effects. The pure income effect is shown as the movement from point A to point C in the next diagram. Consumption increases from Y_A to Y_C and — assuming leisure is a normal good — leisure time increases from X_A to X_C (employment time decreases by the same amount; X_A to X_C).

The Income and Substitution effects of a Wage Increase

But that is only part of the picture. As the wage rate rises, the worker will substitute work hours for leisure hours, that is, will work more hours to take advantage of the higher wage rate, or in other words substitute away from leisure because of its higher opportunity cost. This substitution effect is represented by the shift from point C to point B. The net impact of these two effects is shown by the shift from point A to point B. The relative magnitude of the two effects depends on the circumstances. In some cases the substitution effect is greater than the income effect (in which case more time will be allocated to working), but in other cases the income effect will be greater than the substitution effect (in which case less time is allocated to working). The intuition behind this latter case is that the worker has reached the point where his marginal utility of leisure outweighs his marginal utility of income. To put it in less formal (and less accurate) terms: there is no point in earning more money if you don't have the time to spend it.

The Labour Supply Curve

If the substitution effect is greater than the income effect, the labour supply curve (diagram to the left) will slope upwards to the right, as it does at point E for example. This individual will continue to increase his supply of labour services as the wage rate increases up to point F where he is working H_F hours (each period of time). Beyond this point he will start to reduce the amount of labour hours he supplies (for example at point G he has reduced his work hours to H_G). Where the supply curve is sloping upwards to the right (positive wage elasticity of labour supply), the substitution effect is greater than the income effect. Where it slopes upwards to the left (negative elasticity), the income effect is greater than the substitution effect. The direction of slope may change more than once for some individuals, and the labour supply curve is likely to be different for different individuals.

Other variables that affect this decision include taxation, welfare, and work environment.

Neoclassical Microeconomic Model — Demand

This article has examined the labour supply curve which illustrates at every wage rate the maximum quantity of hours a worker will be willing to supply to the economy per period of time. Economists also need to know the maximum quantity of hours an employer will demand at every wage rate. To understand the quantity of hours demanded per period of time it is necessary to look at product production. That is, labour demand is a derived demand: it is derived from the output levels in the goods market.

A firm's labour demand is based on its marginal physical product of labour (MPL). This is defined as the additional output (or physical product) that results from an increase of one unit of labour (or from an infinitesimally small increase in labour). If you are not familiar with these concepts, you might want to look at production theory basics before continuing with this article.

The Marginal Physical Product of Labour

In most industries, and over the relevant range of outputs, the marginal physical product of labour is declining. That is, as more and more units of labour are employed, their additional output begins to decline. This is reflected by the slope of the MPP_L curve in the diagram to the right. If the marginal physical product of labour is multiplied by the value of the output that it produces, we obtain the Value of marginal physical product of labour:

$$MPP_L * P_Q = VMPP_L$$

The value of marginal physical product of labour ($VMPP_L$) is the value of the additional output produced by an additional unit of labour. This is illustrated in the diagram by the $VMPP_L$ curve that is above the MPP_L.

In competitive industries, the $VMPP_L$ is in identity with the marginal revenue product of labour (MRP_L). This is because in competitive markets price is equal to marginal revenue, and marginal revenue product is defined as the marginal physical product times the marginal revenue from the output (MRP = MPP * MR).

A Firm's Labour Demand in the Short Run

The marginal revenue product of labour can be used as the demand for labour curve for this firm in the short run. In competitive markets, a firm faces a perfectly elastic supply of labour which corresponds with the wage rate and the marginal resource cost of labour ($W = S_L = MFC_L$). In imperfect markets, the diagram would have to be adjusted because MFC_L would then be equal to the wage rate divided by marginal costs. Because optimum resource allocation requires that marginal factor costs equal marginal revenue product, this firm would demand L units of labour as shown in the diagram.

Neoclassical Microeconomic Model — Equilibrium

The demand for labour of this firm can be summed with the demand for labour of all other firms in the economy to obtain the aggregate demand for labour. Likewise, the supply curves of all the individual workers (mentioned above) can be summed to obtain the aggregate supply of labour. These supply and demand curves can be analysed in the same way as any other industry demand and supply curves to determine equilibrium wage and employment levels. (Morendy Octora)

Information Approaches

In the classical model it is assumed that both sides know how much work effort and marginal product the employee contributes.

In many real-life situations this is far from the case. The firm does not necessarily know how hard a worker is working or how productive they are. This provides an incentive for workers to shirk from providing their full effort — since it is difficult for the employer to identify the hard-working and the shirking employees, there is no incentive to work hard and productivity falls overall.

One solution used recently (stock options) grants employees the chance to benefit directly from the firm's success. However, this solution has attracted criticism as executives with large stock option packages have been suspected of acting to over-inflate share values to the detriment of the long-run welfare of the firm.

Another aspect of uncertainty results from the firm's imperfect knowledge about worker ability. If a firm is unsure about a worker's ability, it pays a wage assuming that the worker's ability is the average of similar workers. This wage undercompensates high ability workers and may drive them away from the labour market. Such phenomenon is called adverse selection and can sometimes lead to market collapse.

There are many ways to overcome adverse selection in labour market. One important mechanism is called signalling, pioneered by Michael Spence. In his classical paper on job signalling, Spence showed that even if education does not increase productivity, high ability workers may still acquire it just to signal their abilities. Employers can then use education as a signal to infer worker ability and pay higher wages to better educated workers.

Work Done by a Variable Force

The basic work relationship W=Fx is a special case which applies only to constant force along a straight line. That relationship gives the area of the rectangle shown, where the force F is ploted as a function of distance. In the more general case of a force which changes with distance, the work may still be calculated as the area under the curve. For example, for the work done to stretch a spring, the area under the curve can be readily determined as the area of the triangle. The power of calculus can also be applied since the integral of the force over the distance range is equal to the area under the force curve:

Performance Appraisal

A performance appraisal, employee appraisal, performance review, or (career) development discussion is a method by which the job performance of an employee is evaluated (generally in terms of quality, quantity, cost, and time) typically by the corresponding manager or supervisor. A performance appraisal is a part of guiding and managing career development. It is the process of obtaining, analysing, and recording information about the relative worth of an employee to the organization. Performance appraisal is an analysis of an employee's recent successes and failures, personal strengths and weaknesses, and suitability for promotion or further training. It is also the judgement of an employee's performance in a job based on considerations other than productivity alone.

Aims

Generally, the aims of a performance appraisal are to:

- Give employees feedback on performance
- Identify employee training needs
- Document criteria used to allocate organizational rewards
- Form a basis for personnel decisions: salary increases, promotions, disciplinary actions, bonuses, etc.
- Provide the opportunity for organizational diagnosis and development
- Facilitate communication between employee and administration
- Validate selection techniques and human resource policies to meet federal Equal Employment Opportunity requirements.
- To improve performance through counselling, coaching and development.

Methods

A common approach to assessing performance is to use a numerical or scalar rating system whereby managers are asked to score an individual against a number of objectives/attributes.

In some companies, employees receive assessments from their manager, peers, subordinates, and customers, while also performing a self assessment. This is known as a *360-degree appraisal* and forms good communication patterns. The most popular methods used in the performance appraisal process include the following:

- Management by objectives
- 360-degree appraisal
- Behavioural observation scale
- Behaviourally anchored rating scales.

Trait-based systems, which rely on factors such as integrity and conscientiousness, are also commonly used by businesses. The scientific literature on the subject provides evidence that assessing employees on factors such as these should be avoided. The reasons for this are twofold:

1) Because trait-based systems are by definition based on personality traits, they make it difficult for a manager to provide feedback that can cause positive change in employee performance. This is caused by the fact that personality dimensions are for the most part static, and while an employee can change a specific behaviour they cannot change their personality. For example, a person who lacks integrity may stop lying to a manager because they have been caught, but they still have low integrity and are likely to lie again when the threat of being caught is gone.

2) Trait-based systems, because they are vague, are more easily influenced by office politics, causing them to be less reliable as a source of information on an employee's true performance. The vagueness of these instruments allows managers to fill them out based on who they want to/feel should get a raise, rather than basing scores on specific behaviours employees should/should not be engaging in. These systems are also more likely to leave a company open to discrimination claims because a manager can make biased decisions without having to back them up with specific behavioural information.

Employment Integrity Testing

Integrity as defined by Webster's Dictionary is a firm adherence to a code of especially moral or artistic values. Some synonyms are uprightness, honesty, probity, rectitude, truthfulness, veracity, trustworthiness, fairness, honor, moral fiber, principle, soundness, wholeness, and oneness. All of these words describe the type of employee one would like to hire.

Integrity testing, pre employment screening, pre-employment screening tests, employee assessments, credibility testing and employment testing are all synonyms for the analyses used in detecting employee concealment. These tests are supplemental to background checks and can also be administered after candidates have started to work. With today's technology a well trained organization can objectively evaluate a candidate's potential both positive and negative. Industrial espionage is one of the most important security issues in the business world today and regular integrity testing can assist in the reduction of negligent hiring liability.

These supplemental tests can augment the requirement by all US states that require employers to complete criminal background checks for certain jobs, which may include teaching, childcare and healthcare professions that involve contact with vulnerable segments of our society. The advantage of the integrity test is that it does not require the access to a candidate's criminal records, it gives pertinent information about how that person measures up to the company's code of conduct. According to ADP and the United States Department of Justice (DOJ) pre employment screening has become commonplace and has gained popularity of the last 25 years.

US Laws

The US laws can be interpreted differently and privacy advocates are quick to point out what can and cannot be accessed by companies. However, by using a test that evaluates the candidate on the spot and does not require outside involvement eliminates those issues. Integrity tests evaluate the integrity of the candidate not whether the information on the resume is correct. For that reason this type of test is invaluable.

Pre Employment Screening Tests

Pre-employment screening tests are an invaluable tool to Human Resource Professionals. They enable the company to verify the veracity of the information provided to them by the potential employee. However, these background tests and credit checks require authorizations and may not create a correct profile of the candidate. Supplemental tests that can verify the characteristics. These tests are called Integrity Tests.

Periodic Employment Testing

This type of reusable testing enables employers to verify that the employees that are currently working are performing to the company's code of conduct. In addition it enables companies to obtain an accurate assessment of its' workforce.

Fatigue and Boredom

Temporary loss of strength and energy resulting from hard physical or mental work is termed as fatigue. It's a feeling of tiredness and drop in energy levels that doesn't go away when you rest.

The concept of fatigue is pretty hard to define as every individual has his own idea of what being tired means. In case of physical fatigue your muscles cannot do things as easily as they usually do. You might notice this when you carry grocery bags or climb stairs. On other hand psychological fatigue makes it difficult for you to concentrate for as long as you used to. Sometimes it can be a combination of illness, work stress and unhealthy lifestyle. In severe cases it can reduce your overall physical and mental performance to quite an extent.

Most of the times fatigue can be caused by one or more of your habits or routines. it can be a normal and important response to physical exertion, poor eating habits, emotional stress, boredom and on top of all, lack of sleep, the most common cause, of course. In some cases, however, fatigue is a symptom of an underlying medical problem that requires immediate medical attention.

Fatigue can also be caused by a number of illnesses and diseases. In such cases, a person usually finds that he or she needs more rest and sleep. There are a numbers of reasons that cause fatigue:

- Anaemia (lack of Iron)
- Infections (for example, flu)
- Depression
- Cancers
- Low Metabolism (when the body is too slow to convert food into energy).
- Diabetes
- Chronic Fatigue Syndrome (a condition that causes fatigue and exhaustion without explanation).

Chances are that you know what's causing your fatigue, so just by making a few lifestyle changes you can get the energy, zeal and enthusiasm back in your life. Consider these different ways to help you regain your energy levels.

Dietary Recommendations:

- Start your day with a healthy breakfast to boost your metabolism. Choose a carbohydrate rich breakfast such as cereals or whole grain bead.
- Never restrict the intake of your carbohydrates. Crash diets can sometimes lead to unbalanced levels of vitamins and minerals in body which lead to fatigue and exhaustion.
- Eat a balanced food. Reduce amount of high sugar, high salt and high fat meals. Use low fat dairy products and lean meat.
- Don't overeat. Try to have small frequent meals rather than overeating. Eating small quantities more frequently makes them easier to digest and results in constant sugar as well as insulin levels in blood.
- Eat iron rich food, for example, red meat, spinach and apples.
- Keep an eye on your caffeine intake. It has been observed that people with 5 or more caffeinated drinks (coffee, tea and cola) per day are prone to anxiety, irritability and reduced performance.

- Drink at least 8 glasses of water. A well hydrated body functions very efficiently.

Sleep Recommendations

- Sleep at least 8 hours a day. Make the necessary changes to ensure a better night's sleep.
- Learn to relax. Learn the technique such as meditation or yoga and find the one that suits you the most.
- Avoid caffeinated drinks after dinner. Don't go to bed immediately after your dinner. A full stomach can cause poor quality sleep.
- Don't use sleeping pills. They are not a long term cure for insomnia.

Lifestyle Related Recommendations

- Don't smoke. Our body uses glucose as fuel. Fuel requires oxygen to burn. Smoking reduces the oxygen levels in the body thus keeping fuel from burning efficiently and hence the energy levels stay low.
- Stay away from alcohol. Alcohol is a depressant and can lead to insomnia.
- Exercise regularly. Physical activity is known to improve fitness, health and well being. It also boosts the energy levels and minimizes stress.
- Try to eliminate all the factors that can cause disturbed sleep, like uncomfortable sleeping surface, noise leeks etc.
- Try having a balanced diet with all the essential nutrients like vitamins and minerals. They best way to a balanced diet is to eat everything once in a while. Quick fix foods, such as caffeinated drinks or chocolate bars offer a temporary energy boost that quickly wears off and worsens fatigue.
- Stop thinking too much about your problems.

Workplace Related Recommendations

- Prefer the job in which you have to work during the day. Night shift workers usually disturb their sleeping pattern by working when their body is programmed to sleep.

- Practices like irregular working hours, stressful environment (too much noise or heat), hard physical labour, long work hours and even working alone can lead to extreme fatigue.
- Workplace stress like conflict with colleagues, dissatisfaction, non compensation, heavy workloads and boredom can also lead to fatigue.
- Workaholic. Don't reserve all the energy for career alone. Spend quality time with family and loved ones to reduce stress.
- Financial targets are most crucial in life, but they are not everything. Have a balanced life for time to be spent on entertainment and hanging out. Laughter is the best medicine and an energy booster one can have.

Some studies also suggest that psychological factors are present in at least 50 percent of fatigue cases. Individuals going through long periods of sadness and hopelessness commonly experience chronic tiredness.

So if you are getting 7 to 8 hours of sleep and you are still tiered, its time for a checkup to uncover the causes for fatigue. Diagnosis of fatigue causing factor is very hard, as there is a vast range of symptoms to be held responsible. Try to incorporate as many recommendations as you can into your lifestyle. Despite all that, if you feel stressed out and exhausted, please contact your doctor on the earliest to find out the underlying reason for the fatigue.

Boredom

Boredom has been defined by C. D. Fisher in terms of its central psychological processes: "an unpleasant, transient affective state in which the individual feels a pervasive lack of interest in and difficulty concentrating on the current activity." M. R. Leary and others describe boredom as "an affective experience associated with cognitive attentional processes." In positive psychology, boredom is described as a response to a moderate challenge for which the subject has more than enough skill.

There are three types of boredom, all of which involve problems of engagement of attention. These include times when we are prevented from engaging in some wanted activity, when we are forced to engage in some unwanted activity, or when we are simply unable, for no apparent reason, to maintain engagement in any activity or spectacle. Boredom proneness is a tendency to experience boredom of all types. This is typically assessed by the Boredom Proneness Scale. Consistent with the definition provided above, recent research has found that boredom proneness is clearly and consistently associated with failures of attention. Boredom and boredom proneness are both theoretically and empirically linked to depression and depressive symptoms. Nonetheless, boredom proneness has been found to be as strongly correlated with attentional lapses as with depression. Although boredom is often viewed as a trivial and mild irritant, proneness to boredom has been linked to a very diverse range of possible psychological, physical, educational, and social problems.

Philosophy

Boredom is a condition characterized by perception of one's environment as dull, tedious, and lacking in stimulation. This can result from leisure and a lack of aesthetic interests. Labour, however, and even art may be alienated and passive, or immersed in tedium. There is an inherent anxiety in boredom; people will expend considerable effort to prevent or remedy it, yet in many circumstances, it is accepted as suffering to be endured. Common passive ways to escape boredom are to sleep or to think creative thoughts (daydream). Typical active solutions consist in an intentional activity of some sort, often something new, as familiarity and repetition lead to the tedious.

Boredom also plays a role in existentialist thought. In contexts where one is confined, spatially or otherwise, boredom may be met with various religious activities, not because religion would want to associate itself with tedium, but rather, partly because boredom may be taken as the essential human condition, to which God, wisdom, or morality are the ultimate answers.

Boredom is in fact taken in this sense by virtually all existentialist philosophers as well as by Schopenhauer. Heidegger wrote about boredom in two texts available in English, in the 1929/30 semester lecture course *The Fundamental Concepts of Metaphysics*, and again in the essay *What is Metaphysics?* published in the same year. In the lecture, Heidegger included about 100 pages on boredom, probably the most extensive philosophical treatment ever of the subject. He focused on waiting at train stations in particular as a major context of boredom. In Kierkegaard's remark in *Either/Or*, that "patience cannot be depicted" visually, there is a sense that any immediate moment of life may be fundamentally tedious. Blaise Pascal in the Pensées discusses the human condition in saying "we seek rest in a struggle against some obstacles. And when we have overcome these, rest proves unbearable because of the boredom it produces", and later states that "only an infinite and immutable object – that is, God himself – can fill this infinite abyss."

Without stimulus or focus, the individual is confronted with nothingness, the meaninglessness of existence, and experiences existential anxiety. Heidegger states this idea nicely: "Profound boredom, drifting here and there in the abysses of our existence like a muffling fog, removes all things and men and oneself along with it into a remarkable indifference. This boredom reveals being as a whole." Arthur Schopenhauer used the existence of boredom in an attempt to prove the vanity of human existence, stating, "...for if life, in the desire for which our essence and existence consists, possessed in itself a positive value and real content, there would be no such thing as boredom: mere existence would fulfil and satisfy us."

Erich Fromm and other thinkers of critical theory speak of boredom as a common psychological response to industrial society, where people are required to engage in alienated labour. According to Fromm, boredom is "perhaps the most important source of aggression and destructiveness today." For Fromm, the search for thrills and novelty that characterizes consumer culture are not solutions to boredom, but mere distractions from boredom which, he argues, continues unconsciously. Above and beyond taste and character, the universal case of boredom consists in any instance of *waiting*, as Heidegger noted, such as in line, for someone else to arrive or finish a task, or while one is travelling somewhere. The automobile requires fast reflexes, making its operator busy and hence, perhaps for other reasons as well, making the ride more tedious despite being over sooner.

Causes and Effects

Although it has not been widely studied, research on boredom suggests that boredom is a major factor impacting diverse areas of a person's life. People ranked low on a boredom-proneness scale were found to have better performance in a wide variety of aspects of their lives, including career, education, and autonomy. Boredom can be a symptom of clinical depression. Boredom can be a form of learned helplessness, a phenomenon closely related to depression. Some philosophies of parenting propose that if children are raised in an environment devoid of stimuli, and are not allowed or encouraged to interact with thei- environment, they will fail to develop the mental capacities to do so.

In a learning environment, a common cause of boredom is lack of understanding; for instance, if one is not following or connecting to the material in a class or lecture, it will usually seem boring. However, the opposite can also be true; something that is too easily understood, simple or transparent, can also be boring. Boredom is often inversely related to learning, and in school it may be a sign that a student is not challenged enough, or too challenged. An activity that is predictable to the students is likely to bore them.

A study of 1989 indicated that an individual's impression of boredom may be influenced by the individuals degree of attention, as a higher acoustic level of distraction from the environment correlated with higher reportings of boredom.

Boredom has been studied as being related to drug abuse among teens. Boredom has been proposed as a cause of pathological gambling behaviour. A study found results consistent with the hypothesis that pathological gamblers seek stimulation to avoid states of boredom and depression. Since the advent of the internet and other communicative means, access to curing boredom has new mediums. Video games and web pages have all provide the end user a different experience in their attempt to cure boredom.

Industrial Accidents

An accident at work is defined as an external, sudden, unexpected, unintended, during the execution of work or arising out of it, which may lead to an industrial injury and/or fatality and/or material and/or environmental damages.The accident is a preceding "event" while the resulting damage,be it injury, fatality, material or environmental damages are all consequences of this event.

Where the accidents involve multiple fatalities they are often referred to as industrial disasters.

Occupational Injury

An industrial injury is bodily damage resulting from working.

In the United States in 2007, 5,488 workers died from job injuries, and 49,000 died from work-related injuries. NIOSH estimates that 4 million workers in the U.S. in 2007 suffered from non-fatal work related injuries or illnesses.

The most usual organs involved are the spine, hands, the head, lungs, eyes, skeleton, and skin. According to data from the National Institute for Occupational Safety and Health and the Bureau of Labour Statistics, an average of 15 workers die from traumatic injuries each day in the United States, and an additional 200 workers are hospitalized.

Common causes of industrial injury are poor ergonomics, manual handling of heavy loads, misuse or failure of equipment, exposure to general hazards, inadequate safety training and clothing, jewellery or long hair that becomes tangled in machinery.

General hazards in a work environment include electricity, explosive materials, fire, flammable gases, heat, height, high pressure gases and liquids, hot gases and liquids, powerful or sharp moving machinery, oxygen-free gases or spaces, poisonous gases, radiation, toxic materials, work on, near or under water, work on, near or under weak or heavy structures.

There are many methods of preventing or reducing industrial injuries, including anticipation of problems by risk assessment, safety training, control banding, personal protective equipment safety guards, mechanisms on machinery, and safety barriers. In addition, past problems can be analysed to find their root causes by using a technique called root cause analysis.

Workplace Safety

Workplace safety & health is a category of management responsibility in places of employment.

To ensure the safety and health of workers, managers establish a focus on safety that can include elements such as:

- management leadership and commitment
- employee engagement
- accountability
- ensuring all task are carried out safely and efficiently and effectivily
- safety programs, policies, and plans
- safety processes, procedures, and practices
- safety goals and objectives
- safety inspections for workplace hazards
- safety program audits
- safety tracking & metrics
- hazard identification and control
- safety committees to promote employee involvement
- safety education and training
- safety communications to maintain a high level of awareness on safety.

Occupational Disease

An occupational disease is any chronic ailment that occurs as a result of work or occupational activity. It is an aspect of occupational safety and health. An occupational disease is typically identified when it is shown that it is more prevalent in a given body of workers than in the general population, or in other worker populations. Occupational hazards that are of a traumatic nature (such as falls by roofers) are not considered to be occupational diseases.

Under the law of workers' compensation in many jurisdictions, there is a presumption that specific disease are caused by the worker being in the work environment and the burden is on the employer or insurer to show that the disease came about from another cause.

Examples

Some well-known occupational diseases include:

Lung Diseases

Occupational lung diseases include asbestosis among asbestos miners and those who work with friable asbestos insulation, as well as black lung (coalworker's pneumoconiosis) among coal miners, and byssinosis among workers in parts of the cotton textile industry.

Occupational asthma has a vast number of occupations at risk.

Bad indoor air quality may predispose for diseases in the lungs as well as in other parts of the body.

Skin Diseases

Occupational skin diseases and conditions are generally caused by chemicals and having wet hands for long periods while at work. Eczema is by far the most common, but urticaria, sunburn and skin cancer are also of concern.

High-risk occupations include:

- Hairdressing
- Catering
- Healthcare
- Printing
- Metal machining

- Motor vehicle repair
- Construction.

Other Diseases of Concern

- Carpal tunnel syndrome among persons who work in the poultry industry and information technology.
- Lead poisoning affecting workers in many industries that processed or employed lead or lead compounds.

Maladjusted Industrial Worker

The industrial case work has been defined as an art in which knowledge of the science of human relations are used to mobilize capacities in the individual and resources in the industry and community appropriate for better adjustment between the industrial client and all or any part of his total environment. The industrial client in this article is the employees and managers who face socio-emotional and organisational problems, in their work or social environment in an in the industrial setting. The purpose of industrial casework according to this definition is to help the client to make a better adjustment. Industrial casework helps a person meet a problem, fill needs and receive services. The means to this purpose are the mobilization of appropriate industrial and community resources depending upon the needs of each industrial client.

Science of Human Relation

Knowledge of science of human relations is necessary because the case industrial worker deals intimately with employees and managers in the organisation. The knowledge of how human personality grows, changes, reacts to stressors normally or abnormally serves as a framework in which the individual client is better understood. To understand individual it is very helpful to know as much as possible about the common characteristics of human nature.

The relationship between the industrial caseworker and the client is the medium through which the knowledge of human nature and of the individual is used. Knowledge alone, without skill in relationship is inadequate. The relationship is the channel of the entire case work process, though it flow the mobilization of the capacities of the individual and the mobilization of the industrial and community resources, through the skill in interviewing, study, diagnosis and treatment.

Casework Relationship

The casework relation ship is has been compared to an atmosphere, to flesh & blood, to a bridge and to an atmosphere. The essence of the relationship has been call an interplay, a mutual emotional exchange, an attitude, a dynamic interaction, a medium a connection, between two parties, (the industrial worker and the industrial case worker) a professional mediating and a mutual process. The materials of this dynamic interaction is described as personalities, thoughts, feelings, actions ingredients from both parties and the sum total of all that happens between the participants.

The purpose of the relationship is described as creating an atmosphere, the development of the personality, better solutions to the clients problems, the means of carrying out functions, starting and focusing reality of emotional problems. The relationship has general and specific purposes. More over in some cases the relationship is the principal for of treatment. While in others it is an aid to treatment.

The Purpose of Casework Relationship

In general the purpose of the relationship is a part of the over all-purpose of entire casework process. To help the client which is psychosocial need and problems. In addition the relationship has more proximate purpose. All of which can be categorized as creating an atmosphere in which the industrial client free to engage effectively in the study diagnosis and treatment. Since, each casework situation is individual occurring in agencies with different functions and with clients who differ in personality, needs and problems. The relationship may serve one or more proximate purposes in each case.

Industrial Casework

The case work relationship is a dynamic interaction of attitudes and emotions between the industrial case worker and the individual employee in an industrial setting, with the purpose of helping the individual employee to achieve a better adjustment between himself and his environment.

Casework Process

Study: The initial phase of the casework relationship is to study the problem faced by the industrial client. This understanding required the information of the social, psychological, economical, health, organisational and related facts on the industrial client. Detailed data gathering and understanding is the purpose of casework relationship in the first phase of interaction.

Diagnosis: Based on the data gathered it is the effort of the caseworker to identify the symptoms of the problem faced whether is emotional, psychosocial or others. A proper diagnosis required the effective understanding and analysis of facts and figures.

Treatment: In the treatment phase, the caseworker helps the client to understand the problem by himself by detailing and referring all the related facts and figures. In majority cases, the client finds the solution to the problem by himself with the support of the caseworker. While in some cases if the problem is beyond the capacities and abilities to resolve it, there the caseworker refer the case to some treatment agencies and help him to solve the problem.

Scope of Casework in Labour Setting

In the factory setting one meets the working men with different economic, political and socio cultural back ground and tradition, with different physical capacities, mental abilities, emotional qualities and institutional moves they have came together to make their living through work. When they come with a social mind set, which is inadequate to become an industrial man, he find himself maladjusted and his behaviour turn to become abnormal to work and work organisation. An organisation more concentrate to business surplus and in the acute state of competition and business changes there is little time to spend some time with the worker to resolve the personal crisis. Remove the maladjusted personnel from the payroll and appoint another who is competent enough to perform the functions may be the organisational solution. They don't have the knowledge or skill to intervene into personal problems of the employees.

Mistreated by the management and neglected by labour unions he is always anxious to know about his job and how he fits in the total scheme of things, what his status in the organisation is and where he stands in the hierarchy of relationship, how he is respected by his fellow workers and what role he plays in promoting prosperity of the entire enterprise from where he seeks his own satisfaction. Thus he works under condition, which is more open than not, results in indiscipline and low morale. He thinks that the existing pattern of labour management relations hardly provides proper machinery for amicable settlement of differences and creates conditions of industrial peace. Above all the worker is under the greatest handicap of the paucity proper referral agencies.

In many organisations service conditions are often intolerable. There is high task orientation and less relationship orientation managerial approach in addition to capital incentive approaches. Here the management neglects the greatest asset, human resources, and it affect the morale and motivation of employees at work. A worker may be good in his skill and knowledge to contribute best to the organisation. But because of lack of experience in handling human problems at work, the managers in the organisation have to leave those worker problems aside. His service conditions are often intolerable the climate of human relations at the work places is hopelessly impaired and the personnel organisation where he works to rarely knit. The organisational climate, prevalent practices and the managerial approaches thus affect the worker adjustment of the members in their work situation.

Lack of integration of the personal and organisational goal is the main factor that leads to maladjustment of the workers in the organisation. Organisational stress is one of the major intervention areas of the industrial casework process. Many stress inducing factors like lack of supervisory support, lack of acceptance of the innovative suggestions, feeling of inequality, inadequate authority, lack of group cohesiveness, job requirement capability mismatch, role conflict role ambiguity etc. are all directly affecting the individual worker at the personal level and develop maladjustments. In the day-to-day work relationships he often comes in clash with the supervisor, strains his relation with him and he is charge sheeted for insubordination. A feeling enter his mind that he is misunderstood by the management that they are prejudiced against him. Due to the lack of adequate proper training accounts keeping he commits a clerical error and is unfortunately charged for the misappropriation of companies fund. He may be exposed to many disciplinary actions. The disciplinary actions affect the reputation of the worker in the industry. The single way to cope up with this problem is to quit the employment to protect his self-esteem. Organisation may not take effort to correct the individual worker and help him to identify his mistake. A proper guidance and better support itself can lead employees to better performance and high integrity. Absenteeism and the labour turnover are the best examples of the individual workers maladjustment in the organisational setting. Indian organisations are facing these problems in its acute level. The problems at the organisational level and the psychosocial level of employees in the labour setting have better opportunity to resolve those crisis thorough Industrial case work process.

Conclusion

Many problems situations, which the industrial man meets in his working life, are largely indicative of the nature and scope of social casework in the industrial setting in India. The worker wants to solve his situations but since by himself he is unable to find the situation he needs some guidance and some confidence and encouragement and the case worker must extend helping hand to him who deserves empathy, support, advices and solutions to his problems.

Executive Development

Executive development is the whole of activities aimed at developing the skills and competencies of those that (will) have executive positions in organisations. While "executive" and "manager" and "leader" are often used interchangeably, "executive" is commonly used to signify the top 5% to 10% of the organization. Similarly, "development" and "training" and "education" are often used as synonyms, however "development" is generally seen as the more encompassing of the three in terms of activities that build skills and competencies.

While it is typical to find organizations that have dedicated corporate training & development people and processes, it is not always the case that an organization will have a dedicated executive development set of activities. In some organizations (typically large multi-nationals), there is a separate executive development team, in other organizations executive development is handled as one of many activities by the larger corporate training group, and in yet other scenarios there is no executive development activity to speak of.

In contrast to other corporate training & development activities, which have as their core purpose to build tactical skills for employees, executive development plays a different role for the organization. Indeed some executive development is conducted for the purpose of building tactical skills (sometimes referred to as "hard skills" such as business fundamentals-finance, marketing, operations and also "soft skills" such as communication and team building), yet executive development is also used to evaluate future potential future executives as well as a mechanism for the CEO and the executive team to cascade their strategies, goals, and even elements of the culture to the rest of the management team and ultimately the organization. In the best of cases, executive development not only helps an organization execute its key strategies, it can also help provide input to the strategy creation process. In this way, executive development is much more strategic than typical corporate training & development which is used for most employees of an organization.

Philosophies and Practices There is a wide range of practices in the field of executive development today. On one hand, there are organizations that have for many years, if not decades, had very thorough executive development functions that conduct a wide variety of high profile and highly regarded set of activities (GE's Crotonville is the classic example). On the other end of the spectrum, there are some organizations that have curtailed many of the executive development activities and spending in the wake of the economic crisis of 2008/2009. As one looks across different companies, and against the backdrop of different periods, there exists a wide variety of executive development activity.

As well, the main philosophy of executive development is quite different depending on the organization. For some, the development process has and continues to play a very strategic role in the organization-is it with and through executive development activities that organizational strategies are formed, communicated, and reinforced with senior management. In other organizations, development of executives is seen as an inherently positive activity, which akin to insurance, is probably better to have than not. In organizations where development has not had an opportunity to prove its value, it may be seen as a waste of time and rarely something that the organization commits its leaders' precious time toward.

Reporting & Structure Most often the executive development function reports into the head of Talent Management, the head of HR, or into the Chief Learning Officer (CLO). In rare cases, it reports into an operating executive (i.e. COO). Executive development can be very effective under any reporting structure– what is key is executive level sponsorship and access to senior line leaders who can help ensure development is aligned with and supports the company's strategy.

Most often, the head of executive development will have additional resources working along side him/her. These may be in the form of direct reports, and/or HR business partners and shared resources in the Talent Management function. While the majority of executive development professionals are the more senior talent management professionals in the organization (based on expertise, education such as graduate degree, and tenure), in some cases and perhaps more frequently organizations are putting "outsiders" in charge of executive development who have not spent the bulk of their career in

Talent Management or Human Resources (some examples include CBS Corporation and the U.S. Navy). Among the reasons for this are to bring a fresh perspective into the role and to bring strategy and operational expertise into the function. On the supplier side, there exists a rich ecosystem of development professionals; essentially any part of the executive development process can be procured from an outside firm or set of individual consultants and coaches.

Primary Activities Executive Development activities generally fall into two broad categories: Assessment and Development as outlined below.

Assessment:

- Capability Requirements – Provide input into the organization's strategy formulation process by identifying what is required of executives from a capability perspective
- Capability Assessment – Measure existing capabilities against required capabilities
- Gap Analysis – Identify gap between requirements and current assessment, with an eye toward what capabilities cab be "built" (development) vs. "bought" external hiring.

Development:

- Segment executive population– Create groupings of executives, by level, geography, business unit, or other affiliation (C-suite track, high potential's, critical roles etc.)
- Architect – Create development activities and experiences for the different segmentations
- Deliver – Coordinate across the ecosystem of internal and external partners to deliver development experiences and manage execution of executive development initiatives, etc.
- Measure & Refine – Conduct post activity ROI (typically Kirkpatrick Level I-IV), make course corrections, summarize and report results.

Some of the adjacent Talent Management activities that executive development may have involvement with include the succession planning process (typically not CEO or CEO-1, but below), executive onboarding (ideally both external hiring and internal changes), structuring on the job developmental assignments, and working with alumni of development programs, and alumni of the organization.

Developmental Options Executive development professionals have a wide variety of activities they can choose to deploy including in order of most commonly found:

- OTJ (On the job) stretch assignments, line and staff roles, rotational assignments
- Executive coaching
- Mentoring
- Custom workshops and activities
- Action learning
- Business school open enrollment courses
- Online courses and resources.

Best Practices The following are a set of best practices most often found in organizations that have long standing development activities which are highly regarded in and outside of the organization.

- Articulate a clear and compelling vision – Leaders have many competing priorities, and need a compelling set of reasons to support development activities. The development team needs to build a compelling case and consistent themes across its development strategy.
- Build support across key sponsors-Executive development professionals need to have a deep set of contacts both inside of the organization and across many functions and outside with thought leaders and experts. Many organizations have found that Advisory Boards, which seek to create a formal process of soliciting the input from stakeholders as highly effective. Relationships with internal executives, who are increasingly used as "faculty" to delivery development,

are important to nurture. A strong professional network is the "currency" of the development professional.

- Ground development in business challenges – When in doubt, development that is rooted in solving current and significant business challenges will always prevail over development that is designed to round out a leader or a group of professionals.
- Shorten the timeline – Especially in light of budget cutbacks that are all too common in organizations today, it is important that development is focused on solving current operating cycle issues and challenges. Development plans that span many quarters risk never being fully implemented.
- Market successes – Successful development professionals, like any other professionals in the organization, are quite good at highlighting their impact for the organization and making sure to create "buzz" for their work and activities. Whether through formal ROI studies or informal anecdotal reviews that are circulated to strategic individuals, it is key to promote success.

Executive Development 2.0 Below are key factors that are impacting the field of executive development:

- Time frame – The speed with hich organizations need to revise strategies, launch new products and services, expand their global footprint, etc. continues to accelerate; more rapid means of enabling the organization and its leaders to make these changes are required from the development function.
- Share of mind – Executives are incredibly taxed with an increasing set of responsibilities; mid-level management has been reduced and the number of stakeholders (community, environment, government, etc.) has increased, all putting incredible pressure on leaders. Development that is not of immediate value risks elimination.
- Budget – The current economic situation has put great pressure on all expenses across the organization,

executive development is no exception. Centralized development budgets are all targets, while certain activities such as executive coaching that may be paid out of a business unit budget may be more insulated from cutbacks.

- HR – As many organizations have become more results oriented and quantitative for all support functions, there is increased pressure for HR and all of its components to "raise its game" and prove in business terms its impact.

These factors are creating a new operating context for executive development professionals. In response to this new environment, The Institute of Executive Development has articulated a vision of what Executive Development 2.0 will look like:

- The purpose of the function is to drive the organizational strategy (not solely build skills)
- The content will be based on current business imperatives
- The timeline is focused on the immediate 12 months, not longer
- The format will include more on the job and action learning (vs. formal workshops and programs)
- The audience will include stakeholders such as customers and partners
- The budget will be measured more in terms of investment of executive's time (vs. funds).

While executive development continues to become enriched by many approaches, one approach, adult development and its subfield Positive Adult Development is beginning to create opportunities for what has been essentially reserved for academic research to become an increasing part of executive practices.

6

Job Evaluation in Industrial Environment

Job evaluation is the process of systematically determining a relative internal value of a job in an organization. In all cases the idea is to evaluate the job, not the person doing it.

Job evaluation is the process of determining the worth of one job in relation to that of the other jobs in a company so that a fair and equitable wage and salary system can be established.

Evaluation Types

- *Job Ranking* is the most simple form. Basically one just orders the jobs according to perceived seniority. This is easy to do in a small organization, but gets more and more difficult as different jobs exist within the company.
- Pair Comparison introduces more rigor by comparing jobs in pairs, but really it's a more structured way of building a basic rank order.
- Benchmarking or slotting sets up certain jobs that are analysed in detail. These are then used for comparison to slot jobs against these benchmarks.
- Job Matching allocates benchmarks too, but when a position is matched the elements of the job that differ are re-evaluated. Usually this evaluation will be done with a Point Factor Analysis (PFA) or classification system, okay.

Point Factor Analysis

Point Factor Analysis (PFA) is the old-school (but fair) bureaucratic method for determining a score for each job. Jobs are broken down into factors such as "knowledge required". A set of closed questions in each factor break down to detail such as "level of education". The responses to these questions are given a score, and totaled for each factor. Each factor is given a weight, and this effects the contribution made to the overall total score by that factor.

Factors can be weighted according to their significance to the organization, and this allows the pay scheme to be linked to the organization's strategy.

Job Classification

Job classification can be at the whole job or factor level. Each factor (or the whole job) is a single question that has very clearly defined levels. Compared to an equivalent PFA scheme classification, it has fewer but more complex questions requiring more job analysis from whoever is answering the questionnaire.

The modern trend appears to be away from complex PFA schemes towards factor classification methods. This puts more responsibility in the hands of whoever is doing the analysis. this is also known as the understanding the job rate in order to get the place of the position

A United Kingdom Perspective

The late 1990s saw a move towards widespread introduction of job evaluation across government with the introduction of the Single Status Agreement for Local Authorities, Agenda for Change in the NHS, Framework Agreement in Higher Education and similar moves in the Armed Forces and Civil Service.

In an organization, different employees perform different jobs and their salary is also not the same. But how does companies decide the importance and hierarchy of jobs. The answer is job evaluation. Job evaluation means determining the relative worth of a job by comparing it with other jobs. Job evaluation is done on the basis of the value of the particular job and how important it is to the organization. After evaluation, they are placed in order of their importance and a job hierarchy is formed. Wages are decided based on job evaluation and job hierarchy. Systematic job evaluation is the responsibility of every employer.

Definitions

- According to the British Institute Of Management, "Job evaluation is the process of analysis and assessment of jobs to ascertain reliably their relative worth, using the assessment as a basis for a balanced wage structure.
- According to Edwin B. Flippo, "Job evaluation is a systematic and orderly process of determining the worth of a job in relation to other jobs."

Principles of Job Evaluation

- Rate The Job And Not The Man: Job evaluation should be done only to rate the job and not the employees performing them. The evaluator should understand that the job requirement is fixed and definite.
- Easily Explainable Elements Of Rating: The elements selected for rating purpose should be easily explainable. The elements selected should be few and should cover the essential requisite of every job.
- Exposure Of Plan To Employees: The process of job evaluation should be told to employees. Employees should be given clear-cut explanation and maximum co-operation should be garnered from them.
- Employee Participation In Rating: Employee should participate in the rating of jobs of their own departments.

Objectives of Job Evaluation

- To establish impartial judgement
- To establish satisfactory wage and salary
- To select employees more accurately
- To promote employee goodwill
- To provide management with a basis for proper control
- To determine the rate of pay for each job.

Process of Job Evaluation

The process of job evaluation is lengthy and has to be taken in a systematic manner. The process of job evaluation involves the following steps:

- Securing Acceptance From Employees: Before starting the process of job evaluation, the management must explain the purpose and uses of the job evaluation programme to the employees. The acceptance of the job evaluation programme by the employees will also avoid possible opposition from them in the future.
- Forming Job Evaluation Committee: A single person should not be entrusted with the responsibility to evaluate all the key jobs in an organization. A committee of experienced employees and HR experts should be created for this purpose.
- Deciding The Jobs To Be Evaluated: Evaluating every job in the organization is time consuming and costly. So, only important jobs are evaluated. For this, certain key jobs in each department are identified and evaluated.
- Analysing And Preparing Job Description: In this step, the job selected for evaluation is analysed in great detail. This is necessary for the preparation of job description and it's successful performance.
- Selecting The Method Of Evaluation: In this step, the method of job evaluation is selected. The method is selected keeping the job factors and organizational demands in mind. The benefits of job evaluation is available only when the method selected is appropriate.
- Classifying Jobs: In this step, the relative worth of various jobs is found out and arranged in order of importance. This classification of jobs on the basis of weightage is a major step in the process of job evaluation.
- Executing The Programme: Once the job evaluation process is over, the management must explain it to the employees and solve their doubts. After this, the action plan is put into execution.

- Periodical Review: Job evaluation is a ever changing process and it requires periodical review. In the absence of periodical review all the relevant job factors will not be evaluated properly.

Advantages of Job Evaluation

- Indicates the relative worth of different jobs
- Establishes a hierarchy of jobs
- Useful for introducing a satisfactory, rational and balanced wage structure
- Provides scientific base for promotions and transfers
- Avoids injustice to employees
- Removes grievances and disputes among employees.

Quality of Work Life and Quality Circles

Quality of Working Life is a term that had been used to describe the broader job-related experience an individual has.

Whilst there has, for many years, been much research into job satisfaction (1), and, more recently, an interest has arisen into the broader concepts of stress and subjective well-being (2), the precise nature of the relationship between these concepts has still been little explored. Stress at work is often considered in isolation, wherein it is assessed on the basis that attention to an individual's stress management skills or the sources of stress will prove to provide a good enough basis for effective intervention. Alternatively, job satisfaction may be assessed, so that action can be taken which will enhance an individual's performance. Somewhere in all this, there is often an awareness of the greater context, whereupon the home-work context is considered, for example, and other factors, such as an individual's personal characteristics, and the broader economic or cultural climate, might be seen as relevant. In this context, subjective well-being is seen as drawing upon both work and non-work aspects of life.

However, more complex models of an individuals experience in the workplace often appear to be set aside in an endeavour to simplify the process of trying to measuring "stress" or some similarly apparently discrete entity. It may be, however, that the consideration of the bigger, more complex picture is essential, if targeted, effective action is to be taken to address quality of working life or any of it's sub-components in such a way as to produce real benefits, be they for the individual or the organisation.

Quality of working life has been differentiated from the broader concept of Quality of Life. To some degree, this may be overly simplistic, as Elizur and Shye,(1990)(3) concluded that quality of work performance is affected by Quality of Life as well as Quality of working life. However, it will be argued here that the specific attention to work-related aspects of quality of life is valid.

Whilst Quality of Life has been more widely studied (4), Quality of working life, remains relatively unexplored and unexplained. A review of the literature reveals relatively little on quality of working life. Where quality of working life has been explored, writers differ in their views on its' core constituents.

It is argued that the whole is greater than the sum of the parts as regards Quality of working Life, and, therefore, the failure to attend to the bigger picture may lead to the failure of interventions which tackle only one aspect. A clearer understanding of the inter-relationship of the various facets of quality of working life offers the opportunity for improved analysis of cause and effect in the workplace.

This consideration of Quality of working Life as the greater context for various factors in the workplace, such as job satisfaction and stress, may offer opportunity for more cost-effective interventions in the workplace. The effective targeting of stress reduction, for example, may otherwise prove a hopeless task for employers pressured to take action to meet governmental requirements. Various authors and researchers have proposed models of Quality of working life which include a wide range of factors. Selected models are reviewed below.

Hackman and Oldham (1976)(5) drew attention to what they described as psychological growth needs as relevant to the consideration of Quality of working life. Several such needs were identified; Skill variety, Task Identity, Task significance, Autonomy and Feedback. They suggested that such needs have to be addressed if employees are to experience high quality of working life.

In contrast to such theory based models, Taylor (1979)(6) more pragmatically identified the essential components of Quality of working life as; basic extrinsic job factors of wages, hours and working conditions, and the intrinsic job notions of the nature of the work itself. He suggested that a number of other aspects could be added, including; individual power, employee participation in the management, fairness and equity, social support, use of one's present skills, self development, a meaningful future at work, social relevance of the work or product, effect on extra work activities. Taylor suggested that relevant Quality of working life concepts may vary according to organisation and employee group.

Warr and colleagues (1979)(7), in an investigation of Quality of working life, considered a range of apparently relevant factors, including work involvement, intrinsic job motivation, higher order need strength, perceived intrinsic job characteristics, job satisfaction, life satisfaction, happiness, and self-rated anxiety. They discussed a range of correlations derived from their work, such as those between work involvement and job satisfaction, intrinsic job motivation and job satisfaction, and perceived intrinsic job characteristics and job satisfaction. In particular, Warr et al. found evidence for a moderate association between total job satisfaction and total life satisfaction and happiness, with a less strong, but significant association with self-rated anxiety.

Thus, whilst some authors have emphasised the workplace aspects in Quality of working life, others have identified the relevance of personality factors, psychological well being, and broader concepts of happiness and life satisfaction.

Factors more obviously and directly affecting work have, however, served as the main focus of attention, as researchers have tried to tease out the important influences on Quality of working life in the workplace. Mirvis and Lawler (1984)(8) suggested that Quality of working life was associated with satisfaction with wages, hours and working conditions, describing the "basic elements of a good quality of work life" as; safe work environment, equitable wages, equal employment opportunities and opportunities for advancement.

Baba and Jamal (1991)(9) listed what they described as typical indicators of quality of working life, including: job satisfaction, job involvement, work role ambiguity, work role conflict, work role overload, job stress, organisational commitment and turn-over intentions. Baba and Jamal also explored routinisation of job content, suggesting that this facet should be investigated as part of the concept of quality of working life.

Some have argued that quality of working life might vary between groups of workers. For example, Ellis and Pompli (2002)(10) identified a number of factors contributing to job dissatisfaction and quality of working life in nurses, including: Poor working environments, Resident aggression, Workload, Unable to deliver quality of care preferred, Balance of work and family, Shiftwork, Lack of involvement in decision making, Professional isolation, Lack of recognition, Poor relationships with supervisor/peers, Role conflict, Lack of opportunity to learn new skills.

Sirgy et al.; (2001)(11) suggested that the key factors in quality of working life are: Need satisfaction based on job requirements, Need satisfaction based on Work environment, Need satisfaction based on Supervisory behaviour, Need satisfaction based on Ancillary programmes, Organizational commitment. They defined quality of working life as satisfaction of these key needs through resources, activities, and outcomes stemming from participation in the workplace. Maslow's needs were seen as relevant in underpinning this model, covering Health & safety, Economic and family, Social, Esteem, Actualisation, Knowledge and Aesthetics, although the relevance of non-work aspects is play down as attention is focussed on quality of work life rather than the broader concept of quality of life.

These attempts at defining quality of working life have included theoretical approaches, lists of identified factors, correlational analyses, with opinions varying as to whether such definitions and explanations can be both global, or need to be specific to each work setting.

Bearfield, (2003)(12) used 16 questions to examine quality of working life, and distinguished between causes of dissatisfaction in professionals, intermediate clerical, sales and service workers, indicating that different concerns might have to be addressed for different groups.

The distinction made between job satisfaction and dissatisfaction in quality of working life reflects the influence of job satisfaction theories. Herzberg at al., (1959)(13) used "Hygiene factors" and "Motivator factors" to distinguish between the separate causes of job satisfaction and job dissatisfaction. It has been suggested that Motivator factors are intrinsic to the job, that is; job content, the work itself, responsibility and advancement. The Hygiene factors or dissatisfaction-avoidance factors include aspects of the job environment such as interpersonal relationships, salary, working conditions and security. Of these latter, the most common cause of job dissatisfaction can be company policy and administration, whilst achievement can be the greatest source of extreme satisfaction.

An individual's experience of satisfaction or dissatisfaction can be substantially rooted in their perception, rather than simply reflecting their "real world". Further, an individual's perception can be affected by relative comparison – am I paid as much as that person-and comparisons of internalised ideals, aspirations, and expectations, for example, with the individual's current state.

In summary, where it has been considered, authors differ in their views on the core constituents of Quality of Working Life.

It has generally been agreed however that Quality of Working Life is conceptually similar to well-being of employees but differs from job satisfaction which solely represents the workplace domain.

Quality of Working Life is not a unitary concept, but has been seen as incorporating a hierarchy of perspectives that not only include work-based factors such as job satisfaction, satisfaction with pay and relationships with work colleagues, but also factors that broadly reflect life satisfaction and general feelings of well-being. More recently, work-related stress and the relationship between work and non-work life domains have also been identified as factors that should conceptually be included in Quality of Working Life.

Measurement

Whilst there has, for many years, been much research into job satisfaction, and, more recently, an interest has arisen into the broader concepts of stress and subjective well-being, the precise nature of the relationship between these concepts has still been little explored. Stress at work is often considered in isolation, wherein it is assessed on the basis that attention to an individual's stress management skills or the sources of stress will prove to provide a good enough basis for effective intervention. Alternatively, job satisfaction may be assessed, so that action can be taken which will enhance an individual's performance. Somewhere in all this, there is often an awareness of the greater context, whereupon the home-work context is considered, for example, and other factors, such as an individual's personal characteristics, and the broader economic or cultural climate, might be seen as relevant. In this context, subjective well-being is seen as drawing upon both work and non-work aspects of life.

However, more complex models of an individuals experience in the workplace often appear to be set aside in an endeavo

The Job & Career Satisfaction Job and Career satisfaction (JCS) scale of the Work-Related Quality of Life scale (WRQoL) is said to reflect an employee's feelings about, or evaluation of, their satisfaction or contentment with their job and career and the training they receive to do it. Within the WRQoL measure, JCS is reflected by questions asking how satisfied people feel about their work. It has been proposed that this Positive Job Satisfaction factor is influenced by various issues including clarity of goals and role ambiguity, appraisal, recognition and reward, personal development career benefits and enhancement and training needs.

The General well-being (GWB) scale of the Work-Related Quality of Life scale, aims to assess the extent to which an individual feels good or content in themselves, in a way which may be independent of their work situation. It is suggested that general well-being both influences, and is influenced by work. Mental health problems, predominantly depression and anxiety disorders, are common, and may have a major impact on the general well-being of the population. The WRQoL GWB factor assesses issues of mood, depression and anxiety, life satisfaction, general quality of life, optimism and happiness.

The WRQoL Stress at Work sub-scale (SAW) reflects the extent to which an individual perceives they have excessive pressures, and feel stressed at work. The WRQoL SAW factor is assessed through items dealing with demand and perception of stress and actual demand overload. Whilst it is possible to be pressured at work and not be stressed at work, in general, high stress is associated with high pressure.

The Control at Work (CAW) subsacle of the WRQoL scale addresses how much employees feel they can control their work through the freedom to express their opinions and being involved in decisions at work. Perceived control at work as measureed by the Work-Related Quality of Life scale is recognized as a central concept in the understanding of relationships between stressful experiences, behaviour and health. Control at work, within the theoretical model underpinning the WRQoL, is influenced by issues of communication at work, decision making and decision control.

The WRQoL Home-Work Interface scale (HWI) measures the extent to which an employer is perceived to support the family and home life of employees. This factor explores the interrelationship between home and work life domains. Issues that appear to influence employee HWI include adequate facilities at work, flexibile working hours and the understanding of managers.

The Working Conditions scale of the WRQoL assesses the extent to which the employee is satisfied with the fundamental resources, working conditions and security necessary to do their job effectively. Physical working conditions influence employee health and safety and thus employee Quality of working life. This scale also taps into satisfaction with the resources provided to help people do their jobs.

Applications

Regular assessment of Quality of Working Life can potentially provide organisations with important information about the welfare of their employees, such as job satisfaction, general well-being, work-related stress and the home-work interface. Studies in the UK University sector have shown a valid measure of Quality of Working Life exists and can be used as a basis for effective interventions.

Worrall and Cooper recently reported that a low level of well-being at work is estimated to cost about 5-10% of Gross National Product per annum, yet Quality of Working Life as a theoretical construct remains relatively unexplored and unexplained within the organisational psychology research literature.

A large chunk of most peoples' lives will be spent at work. Most people recognise the importance of sleeping well, and actively try to enjoy the leisure time that they can snatch. But all too often, people tend to see work as something they just have to put up with, or even something they don't even expect to enjoy.

Some of the factors used to measure quality of working life pick up on things that don't actually make people feel good, but which seem to make people feel bad about work if those things are absent. For example, noise – if the place where someone works is too noisy, they might get frequent headaches, or find they can not concentrate, and so feel dissatisfied. But when it is quiet enough they don't feel pleased or happy-they just don't feel bad. This can apply to a range of factors that affect someone's working conditions.

Other things seem to be more likely to make people feel good about work and themselves once the basics are OK at work. Challenging work (not too little, not too much) can make them feel good. Similarly, opportunities for career progression and using their abilities can contribute to someone's quality of working life. The recent publication of National Institute of Clinical Excellence (NICE) public health guidance 22; Promoting mental wellbeing through productive and healthy working conditions emphasises the core role of assessment and understanding of the way working environments pose risks for psychological wellbeing through lack of control and excessive demand. The emphasis placed by NICE on assessment and monitoring wellbeing springs from the fact that these processes are the key first step in identifying areas for improveming quality of working life and addressing risks at work.

Employee Stress

There have been so many reports of worldwide workplace stress recently that it would be perfectly reasonable to conclude that everyone everywhere is stressed out, burned out and depressed.

Every employee feels work-related stress. That's normal. Complaining about it is normal too. Many employers take it in stride that they complain about their jobs, their bosses, their co-workers. So is that occasional outburst that just releases enough pressure to allow you to calm down and get back to work.

What is not normal is sustained and prolonged stress. Kronos, Inc. a human resources consulting firm, recently conducted a Harris poll of American workers. Half of these American workers say work leaves them "overtired and overwhelmed." That alone is not alarming until you dig a little deeper and realize these workers develop chronic, often serious, stress-induced health problems.

Workplace stress has been on human resource professional's radar for years. But management considered the solution as soft stuff. A few execs threw HR a bone and agreed to offer "warm and fuzzy feel-good" training as long as it didn't interfere with business or cost too much. Others expected employees just to tough it out.

That is until recently. What always seems to get attention in the boardrooms however is money, especially the type that eats away at the bottom lines. With skyrocketing insurance and health care costs now getting the full attention of nearly every executive and small business owner, many solutions are focused on what many HR and organizational professionals knew for years-workplace stress is not only a major obstacle to continuous improvements in productivity, but the root cause of much of the increase in workplace health care costs.

To confirm the connection, all you have to do is watch and listen to workers and the link between the bottom line and chronic stress is obvious. Donna is a forty-something mother of two children. Described by everyone who knows her as loyal, hard-working, and generous, Donna doesn't believe it does any good to complain. "Everyone has their own problems", she says. "I'm just grateful that mine aren't worse."

But lately, Donna hasn't been feeling so good. She blames much of her aches, pains and "minor depression" on getting old. A former athlete, Donna now finds herself being a juggler of work and family commitments. She's beginning to feel like the better she gets at juggling, the more she is asked to juggle.

Donna just doesn't have much time for herself anymore, and that includes exercise. She joined the gym and tries to walk at lunch but there always seems to be one more obligation that interferes with what she considers her "free" time – another project meeting at work, getting the kids to doctor appointments, volunteering at the Chamber, working on her postgraduate degree, covering for co-workers on vacations – you get the picture.

Like millions of other people, Donna eats when she's stressed. Stress + Eating + No Exercise equals extra pounds. Donna by her own admission is at least 30 pounds overweight. The once trim and fit Donna has now officially joined the obese American's club. Being overweight and out of shape stresses her out even more-but she swears by the first of the year she'll change her ways. Of course, this is what she said last year and the year before that, too.

Donna has been staying later and arriving earlier in addition to taking work home on the weekends. Her company put a freeze on hiring last year and a few people who left weren't replaced. Just recently, they agreed to bring on a few tempsto-hire but their dependability was terrible and few of them had the skills or experience to help Donna. She decided it was easier to do the work herself.

And to add one more thing to her daily routine, Donna's mother-in-law moved in. An independent woman, her mother-in-law refused to go to a retirement home but was just too forgetful to live alone anymore. Donna adored this woman but now had one more person to take care for. What made this transition so difficult was that her husband's job now required him to travel overnight at least 3 or 4 days each week.

As a result of more work, more family responsibilities and less balance in her life, Donna's blood pressure went up, her cholesterol skyrocketed, her joints were hurting and she was just diagnosed with adult onset diabetes. Research now confirms that stress induces the onset of every one of these conditions–obesity, hypertension, arthritis, diabetes. Fortunately today's wonder drugs brought her blood pressure down, controlled her cholesterol, relieved the pain, and reduced her blood sugar count. On the surface this was great news. Donna never missed work and just like John Cameron Swayze used to say in the Timex watch commercials, she "took a licking, but just keeps on ticking."

But the problem with chronic stress is its damage is insidious. You can cover up the symptoms, but the stress just keeps eating away at you. Chronic stress eventually dampens our ability to keep track of information resulting in mistakes and lost productivity. Our immune system is compromised, making us even more susceptible to infections, as simple as the common cold, and even more serious autoimmune diseases. People under chronic stress eventually pay the price with their bodies. Employers who tolerate and even encourage workplace stress are beginning to pay the price with their wallets.

What has finally grabbed senior management's attention is the effect workplace stress has on the bottom line. The American Institute on Stress reports chronic stress adds over $300 billion each year to cover associated health care costs and absentee rates, according to. That is like writing an extra paycheck exceeding over $600 to every "stressed" worker without getting anything in return. Even worse the cost for health insurance of a single employee jumped from $1.80 to $3.80 per hour over the last few years. How much of this was caused by workplace stress is anyone's guess but considering this research, its substantial.

Research, published in the February 2004 British Medical Journal, found that the risk for a worker having a heart attack and hospitalization doubled after downsizings, along with a number of other conditions. The risk occurred at a higher incidence following rapid expansion too. A Massachusetts-based study dating back to 1972 showed the surest predictor of heart disease was job dissatisfaction.. A recent study conducted by LLuminari® found that 54 percent of workers leave work fatigued. Ten percent of workers are too tired to enjoy their leisure time.

The result? Nearly one out of five workers is at risk for stress-related health problems. In addition to a threefold risk for heart and cardiovascular problems, stressed employees are two to three times more likely to suffer from anxiety, back pain, substance abuse, injuries, infections, cancers, and obesity. The cost of insuring and taking care of these stressed and frazzled workers is beginning to exceed the gains made from increased productivity per worker enjoyed over the last two years.

One solution being kicked around to control employer-paid health costs is cost sharing with employees. While I am the first to agree that employees must begin to share responsibility in taking care of themselves, my advice to all executives and human resources professionals is to be very, very careful in taking this strategy. It is not without its potentially catastrophic consequences.

First of all, cost sharing reduces the take-home pay, which for many employees, will just add more stress to their stretched checkbooks. While cost-sharing might be a financially sound strategy on the surface, its impact on morale might just result in higher turnover and lower productivity. With a critical shortage of skilled workers already handicapping many industries, senior management must look at all the effects cost-sharing carefully.

Second, employees with higher deductibles and co-pays postpone early intervention and wait until situations turn acute. This is like stealing from Peter to pay Paul. Office visits are replaced with emergency room visits and longer hospital stays. Short term treatment is replaced with long term therapy and costly prescription drugs.

Third, hard-working and trusted employees will push themselves to the edge for their boss. They never miss a day, even when sick. More often than not, they prolong their recovery and infect their co-workers as well. Ironically, many organizations reward ("what we need is more employees like you") these employees for this selfless abuse to the point that a long term disability resulting from overwork is almost the ultimate display of loyalty. Unfortunately for the employer, disability comes with an unrecoverable price tag – the loss of a productive worker and higher health care utilization rates.

While reducing workplace stress is not the magic bullet for health care cost containment, all employers need to remember is this: Chronic disease is expensive to treat and workplace stress is now linked to chronic conditions.

Facts about Workplace Stress

Workplace stress costs the nation more than $300 billion each year in health care, missed work and stress reduction efforts.

Only 45 percent (Source: BLS) of private-sector employees are covered by or participate in employer-sponsored programs, employers who provide health insurance benefits experienced on average cost of $3,80 per hour for participating employees in 2003. That cost has more than doubled in four years. (Source: Employment Policy Foundation, Employment Trends)

1 out of 5 workers are at risk for stress related health problems. (Source: LLuminari® Landmark Study)

1 in 10 are so tired at the end of the work day that they do not enjoy their non-work time. (Source: LLuminari® Landmark Study)

1 in 5 stated that their work regularly interfered with their responsibilities at home and kept them from spending time with their family. (Source: LLuminari® Landmark Study)

Workers who report they are stressed incur health care costs that are 46 percent higher, or $600 more per person, than other employees. The risk of a heart attack doubled among permanent after a major round of downsizing, with the risk growing to five times normal after four years. (British Medical Journal, Feb 2004).

The indirect costs of diabetes are e stimated to be $40 billion in 2002. In 2002, diabetes accounted for a loss of nearly 88 million disability days and 176,000 cases of permanent disability were caused by diabetes, at a cost of $7.5 billion. The cost of lost productivity related to obesity (BMI > 30) among Americans ages 17–64 is $3.9 billion. This value considers the following annual numbers (for 1994):

- Workdays lost related to obesity: 39.3 million
- Physician office visits related to obesity: 62.7 million
- Restricted activity days related to obesity: 239.0 million
- Bed-days related to obesity: 89.5 million.

Alcoholism causes 500 million lost work days annually. Absenteeism among alcoholics or problem drinkers is 3.8 to 8.3 times greater than normal and up to 16 times greater among all employees with alcohol and other drug-related problems. (US Department of Labour)

Family members of alcoholics and substance users use ten times as much sick leave and have higher than average health care claims than family members of non alcoholic and substance using families. (HSS and NCADD Fact Sheet)

Up to 40 percent of industrial fatalities can be linked to alcohol use. Forty-seven percent of all industrial injuries are attributed to alcohol use.

Consumer Psychology

The study of consumers helps firms and organizations improve their marketing strategies by understanding issues such as how:

- The psychology of how consumers think, feel, reason, and select between different alternatives (e.g., brands, products, and retailers);
- The psychology of how the consumer is influenced by his or her environment (e.g., culture, family, signs, media);
- The behaviour of consumers while shopping or making other marketing decisions;
- Limitations in consumer knowledge or information processing abilities influence decisions and marketing outcome;
- How consumer motivation and decision strategies differ between products that differ in their level of importance or interest that they entail for the consumer; and
- How marketers can adapt and improve their marketing campaigns and marketing strategies to more effectively reach the consumer.

One "official" definition of consumer behaviour is "The study of individuals, groups, or organizations and the processes they use to select, secure, use, and dispose of products, services, experiences, or ideas to satisfy needs and the impacts that these processes have on the consumer and society." Although it is not necessary to memorize this definition, it brings up some useful points:

- Behaviour occurs either for the individual, or in the context of a group (e.g., friends influence what kinds of clothes a person wears) or an organization (people on the job make decisions as to which products the firm should use).
- Consumer behaviour involves the use and disposal of products as well as the study of how they are purchased. Product use is often of great interest to the marketer, because this may influence how a product is best positioned or how we can encourage increased consumption. Since many environmental problems result from product disposal (e.g., motor oil being sent into sewage systems to save the recycling fee, or garbage piling up at landfills) this is also an area of interest.

- Consumer behaviour involves services and ideas as well as tangible products.
- The impact of consumer behaviour on society is also of relevance. For example, aggressive marketing of high fat foods, or aggressive marketing of easy credit, may have serious repercussions for the national health and economy.

There are four main applications of consumer behaviour:

- The most obvious is for *marketing strategy*—i.e., for making better marketing campaigns. For example, by understanding that consumers are more receptive to food advertising when they are hungry, we learn to schedule snack advertisements late in the afternoon. By understanding that new products are usually initially adopted by a few consumers and only spread later, and then only gradually, to the rest of the population, we learn that (1) companies that introduce new products must be well financed so that they can stay afloat until their products become a commercial success and (2) it is important to please initial customers, since they will in turn influence many subsequent customers' brand choices.
- A second application is *public policy*. In the 1980s, Accutane, a near miracle cure for acne, was introduced. Unfortunately, Accutane resulted in severe birth defects if taken by pregnant women. Although physicians were instructed to warn their female patients of this, a number still became pregnant while taking the drug. To get consumers' attention, the Federal Drug Administration (FDA) took the step of requiring that very graphic pictures of deformed babies be shown on the medicine containers.
- *Social marketing* involves getting ideas across to consumers rather than selling something. Marty Fishbein, a marketing professor, went on sabbatical to work for the Centers for Disease Control trying to reduce the incidence of transmission of diseases through illegal drug use. The best solution, obviously, would be

if we could get illegal drug users to stop. This, however, was deemed to be infeasible. It was also determined that the practice of sharing needles was too ingrained in the drug culture to be stopped. As a result, using knowledge of consumer attitudes, Dr. Fishbein created a campaign that encouraged the cleaning of needles in bleach before sharing them, a goal that was believed to be more realistic.

- As a final benefit, studying consumer behaviour should make us better consumers. Common sense suggests, for example, that if you buy a 64 liquid ounce bottle of laundry detergent, you should pay less per ounce than if you bought two 32 ounce bottles. In practice, however, you often pay a size *premium* by buying the larger quantity. In other words, in this case, knowing this fact will sensitize you to the need to check the unit cost labels to determine if you are *really* getting a bargain.

There are several units in the market that can be analysed.

Modern selling uses psychology not manipulation. Understanding what triggers people to buy makes the difference between a sale and a failure.

A desire to buy something often involves a subconscious decision. In fact, I claim that 95% of buying decisions are indeed subconscious.

Knowing the subconscious reasons why people buy, and using this information in a fair and constructive way, will trigger greater sales response — often far beyond what you could imagine.

There are 30 triggers in all — many of them are very subtle, and many of them are the exact opposite of what you would expect. I will reveal a few of them to you in a moment. Each trigger, when deployed, has the power to increase sales and response beyond what you would normally expect.

There are triggers, for example, that will cause your prospect to feel guilty if they don't purchase your product. Let me give you an example. Whenever you receive in the mail a sales solicitation with free personalized address stickers, you often feel guilty if you use the stickers and don't send something back— often far in excess of the value of the stickers. Fundraising companies use this method a great deal. You receive 50 cents worth of stickers and send back a $20 bill.

Another example are those surveys that are sent out asking for you to spend about 20 minutes of your time filling them out. Enclosed in the mailing you, might find a dollar bill included to encourage you to feel guilty, and entice you to fill out the survey. And you often spend a lot more than one dollar of your time to do that.

Guilt is a strong motivator. I have to admit that I've used guilt in many selling situations, in mail order ads and on TV— with great success, I might add.

I call one of the most powerful triggers a "satisfaction conviction," which is a guarantee of satisfaction. But don't confuse this with the typical trial period you find in mail order, i.e., "If you're not happy within 30 days, you can return your purchase for a full refund." A satisfaction conviction is different. Basically it takes the trial period and adds something that makes it go well beyond the trial period.

For example, if I were offering a subscription, instead of saying, "If at anytime you're not happy with your subscription, we'll refund your unused portion," and instead said, "If at any time you're not happy with your subscription, let us know and we'll refund your entire subscription price — even if you decide to cancel just before the last issue."

Basically you're saying to your prospect that you are absolutely certain that they'll like the subscription, that you are willing to go beyond what is traditionally offered with other subscriptions. This in fact gives the reader the sense that the company really knows it has a winning product and solidly stands behind the product and your satisfaction.

Consumer behaviour is the study of when, why, how, and where people do or do not buy product. It blends elements from psychology, sociology, social anthropology and economics. It attempts to understand the buyer decision making process, both individually and in groups. It studies characteristics of individual consumers such as demographics and behavioural variables in an attempt to understand people's wants. It also tries to assess influences on the consumer from groups such as family, friends, reference groups, and society in general.

Customer behaviour study is based on consumer buying behaviour, with the customer playing the three distinct roles of user, payer and buyer.

Relationship marketing is an influential asset for customer behaviour analysis as it has a keen interest in the re-discovery of the true meaning of marketing through the re-affirmation of the importance of the customer or buyer. A greater importance is also placed on consumer retention, customer relationship management, personalisation, customisation and one-to-one marketing. Social functions can be categorized into social choice and welfare functions.

Each method for vote counting is assumed as social function but if Arrow's possibility theorem is used for a social function, social welfare function is achieved. Some specifications of the social functions are decisiveness, neutrality, anonymity, monotonicity, unanimity, homogeneity and weak and strong Pareto optimality. No social choice function meets these requirements in an ordinal scale simultaneously. The most important characteristic of a social function is identification of the interactive effect of alternatives and creating a logical relation with the ranks. Marketing provides services in order to satisfy customers. With that in mind, the productive system is considered from its beginning at the production level, to the end of the cycle, the consumer.

Black Box Model

The black box model shows the interaction of stimuli, consumer characteristics, decision process and consumer responses. It can be distinguished between interpersonal stimuli (between people) or intrapersonal stimuli (within people). The black box model is related to the black box theory of behaviourism, where the focus is not set on the processes *inside* a consumer, but the *relation* between the stimuli and the response of the consumer. The marketing stimuli are planned and processed by the companies, whereas the environmental stimulus are given by social factors, based on the economical, political and cultural circumstances of a society. The buyers black box contains the buyer characteristics and the decision process, which determines the buyers response.

The black box model considers the buyers response as a result of a conscious, rational decision process, in which it is assumed that the buyer has recognized the problem. However, in reality many decisions are not made in awareness of a determined problem by the consumer.

Information Search

Once the consumer has recognised a problem, they search for information on products and services that can solve that problem. Belch and Belch (2007) explain that consumers undertake both an internal (memory) and an external search.

Sources of information include:

- Personal sources
- Commercial sources
- Public sources
- Personal experience.

The relevant internal psychological process that is associated with information search is perception. Perception is defined as "the process by which an individual receives, selects, organises, and interprets information to create a meaningful picture of the world".

The Selective Perception Process

Stage Description;

- Selective exposure consumers select which promotional messages they will expose themselves to.
- Selective attention consumers select which promotional messages they will pay attention to.
- Selective comprehension consumer interpret messages in line with their beliefs, attitudes, motives and experiences.

- Selective retention consumers remember messages that are more meaningful or important to them.

The implications of this process help develop an effective promotional strategy, and select which sources of information are more effective for the brand.

Information Evaluation

At this time the consumer compares the brands and products that are in their evoked set. How can the marketing organization increase the likelihood that their brand is part of the consumer's evoked (consideration) set?

Consumers evaluate alternatives in terms of the functional and psychological benefits that they offer. The marketing organization needs to understand what benefits consumers are seeking and therefore which attributes are most important in terms of making a decision.

Purchase Decision

Once the alternatives have been evaluated, the consumer is ready to make a purchase decision. Sometimes purchase intention does not result in an actual purchase. The marketing organization must facilitate the consumer to act on their purchase intention.

The organisation can use variety of techniques to achieve this. The provision of credit or payment terms may encourage purchase, or a sales promotion such as the opportunity to receive a premium or enter a competition may provide an incentive to buy now. The relevant internal psychological process that is associated with purchase decision is integration. Once the integration is achieved, the organisation can influence the purchase decisions much more easily.

Postpurchase Evaluation

The EKB model was further developed by Rice (1993) which suggested there should be a feedback loop, Foxall (2005) further suggests the importance of the post purchase evaluation and that the post purchase evaluation is key due to its influences on future purchase patterns.

Internal Influences

Consumer behaviour is influenced by: demographics, psychographics (lifestyle), personality, motivation, knowledge, attitudes, beliefs, and feelings. Consumer behaviour concern with consumer need consumer actions in the direction of satisfying needs leads to his behaviour of every individuals depend on thinking

External Influences

Consumer behaviour is influenced by: culture, sub-culture, locality, royalty, ethnicity, family, social class, past experience reference groups, lifestyle, sex.

7

Psychology of Advertisement and Selling

Advertising is a form of communication intended to persuade an audience (viewers, readers or listeners) to purchase or take some action upon products, ideals, or services. It includes the name of a product or service and how that product or service could benefit the consumer, to persuade a target market to purchase or to consume that particular brand. These brands are usually paid for or identified through sponsors and viewed via various media. Advertising can also serve to communicate an idea to a large number of people in an attempt to convince them to take a certain action.

Commercial advertisers often seek to generate increased consumption of their products or services through branding, which involves the repetition of an image or product name in an effort to associate related qualities with the brand in the minds of consumers. Non-commercial advertisers that spend money to advertise items other than a consumer product or service include political parties, interest groups, religious organizations and governmental agencies. Nonprofit organizations may rely on free modes of persuasion, such as a public service announcement.

Modern advertising developed with the rise of mass production in the late 19th and early 20th centuries. Mass media can be defined as any media meant to reach a mass amount of people. Different types of media can be used to deliver these messages, including traditional media such as newspapers, magazines, television, radio, outdoor or direct mail; or new media such as websites and text messages. Advertising may be placed by an advertising agency on behalf of a company or other organization.

Industry

In 2010, spending on advertising was estimated at more than $300 billion in the United States and $500 billion worldwide.

Internationally, the largest ("big four") advertising conglomerates are Interpublic, Omnicom, Publicis, and WPP.

History

Egyptians used papyrus to make sales messages and wall posters. Commercial messages and political campaign displays have been found in the ruins of Pompeii and ancient Arabia. Lost and found advertising on papyrus was common in Ancient Greece and Ancient Rome. Wall or rock painting for commercial advertising is another manifestation of an ancient advertising form, which is present to this day in many parts of Asia, Africa, and South America. The tradition of wall painting can be traced back to Indian rock art paintings that date back to 4000 BC. History tells us that Out-of-home advertising and billboards are the oldest forms of advertising.

As the towns and cities of the Middle Ages began to grow, and the general populace was unable to read, signs that today would say cobbler, miller, tailor or blacksmith would use an image associated with their trade such as a boot, a suit, a hat, a clock, a diamond, a horse shoe, a candle or even a bag of flour. Fruits and vegetables were sold in the city square from the backs of carts and wagons and their proprietors used street callers (town criers) to announce their whereabouts for the convenience of the customers.

As education became an apparent need and reading, as well as printing, developed advertising expanded to include handbills. In the 17th century advertisements started to appear in weekly newspapers in England. These early print advertisements were used mainly to promote books and newspapers, which became increasingly affordable with advances in the printing press; and medicines, which were increasingly sought after as disease ravaged Europe. However, false advertising and so-called "quack" advertisements became a problem, which ushered in the regulation of advertising content.

As the economy expanded during the 19th century, advertising grew alongside. In the United States, the success of this advertising format eventually led to the growth of mail-order advertising.

In June 1836, French newspaper *La Presse* was the first to include paid advertising in its pages, allowing it to lower its price, extend its readership and increase its profitability and the formula was soon copied by all titles. Around 1840, Volney B. Palmer established a predecessor to advertising agencies in Boston. Around the same time, in France, Charles-Louis Havas extended the services of his news agency, Havas to include advertisement brokerage, making it the first French group to organize. At first, agencies were brokers for advertisement space in newspapers. N. W. Ayer & Son was the first full-service agency to assume responsibility for advertising content. N.W. Ayer opened in 1869, and was located in Philadelphia.

At the turn of the century, there were few career choices for women in business; however, advertising was one of the few. Since women were responsible for most of the purchasing done in their household, advertisers and agencies recognized the value of women's insight during the creative process. In fact, the first American advertising to use a sexual sell was created by a woman – for a soap product. Although tame by today's standards, the advertisement featured a couple with the message "The skin you love to touch".

In the early 1920s, the first radio stations were established by radio equipment manufacturers and retailers who offered programs in order to sell more radios to consumers. As time passed, many non-profit organizations followed suit in setting up their own radio stations, and included: schools, clubs and civic groups. When the practice of sponsoring programs was popularised, each individual radio program was usually sponsored by a single business in exchange for a brief mention of the business' name at the beginning and end of the sponsored shows. However, radio station owners soon realised they could earn more money by selling sponsorship rights in small time allocations to multiple businesses throughout their radio station's broadcasts, rather than selling the sponsorship rights to single businesses per show.

This practice was carried over to television in the late 1940s and early 1950s. A fierce battle was fought between those seeking to commercialise the radio and people who argued that the radio spectrum should be considered a part of the commons – to be used only non-commercially and for the public good. The United Kingdom pursued a public funding model for the BBC, originally a private company, the British Broadcasting Company, but incorporated as a public body by Royal Charter in 1927. In Canada, advocates like Graham Spry were likewise able to persuade the federal government to adopt a public funding model, creating the Canadian Broadcasting Corporation. However, in the United States, the capitalist model prevailed with the passage of the Communications Act of 1934 which created the Federal Communications Commission. To placate the socialists, the U.S. Congress did require commercial broadcasters to operate in the "public interest, convenience, and necessity". Public broadcasting now exists in the United States due to the 1967 Public Broadcasting Act which led to the Public Broadcasting Service and National Public Radio.

In the early 1950s, the DuMont Television Network began the modern practice of selling advertisement time to multiple sponsors. Previously, DuMont had trouble finding sponsors for many of their programs and compensated by selling smaller blocks of advertising time to several businesses. This eventually became the standard for the commercial television industry in the United States. However, it was still a common practice to have single sponsor shows, such as The United States Steel Hour. In some instances the sponsors exercised great control over the content of the show—up to and including having one's advertising agency actually writing the show. The single sponsor model is much less prevalent now, a notable exception being the Hallmark Hall of Fame.

The 1960s saw advertising transform into a modern approach in which creativity was allowed to shine, producing unexpected messages that made advertisements more tempting to consumers' eyes. The Volkswagen ad campaign—featuring such headlines as "Think Small" and "Lemon" (which were used to describe the appearance of the car)—ushered in the era of modern advertising by promoting a "position" or "unique selling proposition" designed to associate each brand with a specific idea in the reader or viewer's mind. This period of American advertising is called the Creative Revolution and its archetype was William Bernbach who helped create the revolutionary Volkswagen ads among others. Some of the most creative and long-standing American advertising dates to this period.

The late 1980s and early 1990s saw the introduction of cable television and particularly MTV. Pioneering the concept of the music video, MTV ushered in a new type of advertising: the consumer tunes in *for* the advertising message, rather than it being a by-product or afterthought. As cable and satellite television became increasingly prevalent, specialty channels emerged, including channels entirely devoted to advertising, such as QVC, Home Shopping Network, and ShopTV Canada.

Marketing through the Internet opened new frontiers for advertisers and contributed to the "dot-com" boom of the 1990s. Entire corporations operated solely on advertising revenue, offering everything from coupons to free Internet access. At the turn of the 21st century, a number of websites including the search engine Google, started a change in online advertising by emphasizing contextually relevant, unobtrusive ads intended to help, rather than inundate, users. This has led to a plethora of similar efforts and an increasing trend of interactive advertising.

The share of advertising spending relative to GDP has changed little across large changes in media. For example, in the US in 1925, the main advertising media were newspapers, magazines, signs on streetcars, and outdoor posters. Advertising spending as a share of GDP was about 2.9 percent. By 1998, television and radio had become major advertising media. Nonetheless, advertising spending as a share of GDP was slightly lower—about 2.4 percent.

A recent advertising innovation is "guerrilla marketing", which involve unusual approaches such as staged encounters in public places, giveaways of products such as cars that are covered with brand messages, and interactive advertising where the viewer can respond to become part of the advertising message. Guerrilla advertising is becoming increasing more popular with a lot of companies. This type of advertising is unpredictable and innovative, which causes consumers to buy the product or idea. This reflects an increasing trend of interactive and "embedded" ads, such as via product placement, having consumers vote through text messages, and various innovations utilizing social network services such as Facebook.

Public Service Advertising

The same advertising techniques used to promote commercial goods and services can be used to inform, educate and motivate the public about non-commercial issues, such as HIV/AIDS, political ideology, energy conservation and deforestation.

Advertising, in its non-commercial guise, is a powerful educational tool capable of reaching and motivating large audiences. "Advertising justifies its existence when used in the public interest—it is much too powerful a tool to use solely for commercial purposes." Attributed to Howard Gossage by David Ogilvy.

Public service advertising, non-commercial advertising, public interest advertising, cause marketing, and social marketing are different terms for (or aspects of) the use of sophisticated advertising and marketing communications techniques (generally associated with commercial enterprise) on behalf of non-commercial, public interest issues and initiatives.

In the United States, the granting of television and radio licenses by the FCC is contingent upon the station broadcasting a certain amount of public service advertising. To meet these requirements, many broadcast stations in America air the bulk of their required public service announcements during the late night or early morning when the smallest percentage of viewers are watching, leaving more day and prime time commercial slots available for high-paying advertisers.

Public service advertising reached its height during World Wars I and II under the direction of more than one government.

Marketing Mix

The marketing mix has been the key concept to advertising. The marketing mix was suggested by Jeremy McCarthy, professor at Harvard Business School, in the 1960s. The marketing mix consists of four basic elements called the four P's Product is the first P representing the actual product. Price represents the process of determining the value of a product. Place represents the variables of getting the product to the consumer like distribution channels, market coverage and movement organization. The last P stands for Promotion which is the process of reaching the target market and convincing them to go out and buy the product. Geana, Mugur Valentin.

Types of Advertising

Virtually any medium can be used for advertising. Commercial advertising media can include wall paintings, billboards, street furniture components, printed flyers and rack cards, radio, cinema and television adverts, web banners, mobile telephone screens, shopping carts, web popups, skywriting, bus stop benches, human billboards, magazines, newspapers, town criers, sides of buses, banners attached to or sides of airplanes ("logojets"), in-flight advertisements on seatback tray tables or overhead storage bins, taxicab doors, roof mounts and passenger screens, musical stage shows, subway platforms and trains, elastic bands on disposable diapers, doors of bathroom stalls, stickers on apples in supermarkets, shopping cart handles (grabertising), the opening section of streaming audio and video, posters, and the backs of event tickets and supermarket receipts. Any place an "identified" sponsor pays to deliver their message through a medium is advertising.

Digital Advertising

The TV commercial is generally considered the most effective mass-market advertising format, as is reflected by the high prices TV networks charge for commercial airtime during popular TV events. The annual Super Bowl football game in the United States is known as the most prominent advertising event on television. The average cost of a single thirty-second TV spot during this game has reached US$3 million (as of 2009). The majority of television commercials feature a song or jingle that listeners soon relate to the product. Virtual advertisements may be inserted into regular television programming through computer graphics. It is typically inserted into otherwise blank backdrops or used to replace local billboards that are not relevant to the remote broadcast audience. More controversially, virtual billboards may be inserted into the background where none exist in real-life. This technique is especially used in televised sporting events Virtual product placement is also possible.; Infomercials: An infomercial is a long-format television commercial, typically five minutes or longer. The word "infomercial" combining the words "information" & "commercial". The main objective in an infomercial is to create an impulse purchase, so that the consumer sees the presentation and then immediately buys the product through the advertised toll-free telephone number or website. Infomercials describe, display, and often demonstrate products and their features, and commonly have testimonials from consumers and industry professionals.

Radio Advertising

Radio advertising is a form of advertising via the medium of radio. Radio advertisements are broadcast as radio waves to the air from a transmitter to an antenna and a thus to a receiving device. Airtime is purchased from a station or network in exchange for airing the commercials. While radio has the obvious limitation of being restricted to sound, proponents of radio advertising often cite this as an advantage.

Online Advertising

Online advertising is a form of promotion that uses the

Internet and World Wide Web for the expressed purpose of delivering marketing messages to attract customers. Examples of online advertising include contextual ads that appear on search engine results pages, banner ads, in text ads, Rich Media Ads, Social network advertising, online classified advertising, advertising networks and e-mail marketing, including e-mail spam.

Product Placements

Covert advertising, also known as guerrilla advertising, is when a product or brand is embedded in entertainment and media. For example, in a film, the main character can use an item or other of a definite brand, as in the movie *Minority Report*, where Tom Cruise's character John Anderton owns a phone with the *Nokia* logo clearly written in the top corner, or his watch engraved with the *Bulgari* logo.

Another example of advertising in film is in *I, Robot*, where main character played by Will Smith mentions his *Converse* shoes several times, calling them "classics," because the film is set far in the future. *I, Robot* and *Spaceballs* also showcase futuristic cars with the *Audi* and *Mercedes-Benz* logos clearly displayed on the front of the vehicles. Cadillac chose to advertise in the movie *The Matrix Reloaded*, which as a result contained many scenes in which Cadillac cars were used. Similarly, product placement for Omega Watches, Ford, VAIO, BMW and Aston Martin cars are featured in recent James Bond films, most notably *Casino Royale*. In "Fantastic Four: Rise of the Silver Surfer", the main transport vehicle shows a large Dodge logo on the front. *Blade Runner* includes some of the most obvious product placement; the whole film stops to show a Coca-Cola billboard.

Physical Advertising

Press Advertising

Press advertising describes advertising in a printed medium such as a newspaper, magazine, or trade journal. This encompasses everything from media with a very broad readership base, such as a major national newspaper or magazine, to more narrowly targeted media such as local newspapers and trade journals on very specialized topics. A form of press advertising is classified advertising, which allows private individuals or companies to purchase a small, narrowly targeted ad for a low fee advertising a product or service. Another form of press advertising is the Display Ad, which is a larger ad (can include art) that typically run in an article section of a newspaper.

Billboard advertising: Billboards are large structures located in public places which display advertisements to passing pedestrians and motorists. Most often, they are located on main roads with a large amount of passing motor and pedestrian traffic; however, they can be placed in any location with large amounts of viewers, such as on mass transit vehicles and in stations, in shopping malls or office buildings, and in stadiums.

Mobile Billboard Advertising

Mobile billboards are generally vehicle mounted billboards or digital screens. These can be on dedicated vehicles built solely for carrying advertisements along routes preselected by clients, they can also be specially equipped cargo trucks or, in some cases, large banners strewn from planes. The billboards are often lighted; some being backlit, and others employing spotlights. Some billboard displays are static, while others change; for example, continuously or periodically rotating among a set of advertisements. Mobile displays are used for various situations in metropolitan areas throughout the world, including: Target advertising, One-day, and long-term campaigns, Conventions, Sporting events, Store openings and similar promotional events, and Big advertisements from smaller companies.

In-store Advertising

In-store advertising is any advertisement placed in a retail store. It includes placement of a product in visible locations in a store, such as at eye level, at the ends of aisles and near checkout counters, eye-catching displays promoting a specific product, and advertisements in such places as shopping carts and in-store video displays.

Celebrity Branding

This type of advertising focuses upon using celebrity power, fame, money, popularity to gain recognition for their products and promote specific stores or products. Advertisers often advertise their products, for example, when celebrities share their favorite products or wear clothes by specific brands or designers. Celebrities are often involved in advertising campaigns such as television or print adverts to advertise specific or general products. The use of celebrities to endorse a brand can have its downsides, however. One mistake by a celebrity can be detrimental to the public relations of a brand. For example, following his performance of eight gold medals at the 2008 Olympic Games in Beijing, China, swimmer Michael Phelps' contract with Kellogg's was terminated, as Kellogg's did not want to associate with him after he was photographed smoking marijuana.

Sales Promotions

Sales promotions are another way to advertise. Sales promotions are double purposed because they are used to gather information about what type of customers you draw in and where they are, and to jumpstart sales. Sales promotions include things like contests and games, sweepstakes, product giveaways, samples coupons, loyalty programs, and discounts. The ultimate goal of sales promotions is to stimulate potential customers to action.

Media and Advertising Approaches

Increasingly, other media are overtaking many of the "traditional" media such as television, radio and newspaper because of a shift toward consumer's usage of the Internet for news and music as well as devices like digital video recorders (DVRs) such as TiVo. Advertising on the World Wide Web is a recent phenomenon. Prices of Web-based advertising space are dependent on the "relevance" of the surrounding web content and the traffic that the website receives.

Digital signage is poised to become a major mass media because of its ability to reach larger audiences for less money. Digital signage also offer the unique ability to see the target audience where they are reached by the medium. Technology advances has also made it possible to control the message on digital signage with much precision, enabling the messages to be relevant to the target audience at any given time and location which in turn, gets more response from the advertising. Digital signage is being successfully employed in supermarkets. Another successful use of digital signage is in hospitality locations such as restaurants and malls.

E-mail advertising is another recent phenomenon. Unsolicited bulk E-mail advertising is known as "e-mail spam". Spam has been a problem for email users for many years.

Some companies have proposed placing messages or corporate logos on the side of booster rockets and the International Space Station. Controversy exists on the effectiveness of subliminal advertising and the pervasiveness of mass messages.

Unpaid advertising (also called "publicity advertising"), can provide good exposure at minimal cost. Personal recommendations ("bring a friend", "sell it"), spreading buzz, or achieving the feat of equating a brand with a common noun (in the United States, "Xerox" = "photocopier", "Kleenex" = tissue, "Vaseline" = petroleum jelly, "Hoover" = vacuum cleaner, "Nintendo" (often used by those exposed to many video games)= video games, and "Band-Aid" = adhesive bandage) — these can be seen as the pinnacle of any advertising campaign. However, some companies oppose the use of their brand name to label an object. Equating a brand with a common noun also risks turning that brand into a genericized trademark-turning it into a generic term which means that its legal protection as a trademark is lost.

As the mobile phone became a new mass media in 1998 when the first paid downloadable content appeared on mobile phones in Finland, it was only a matter of time until mobile advertising followed, also first launched in Finland in 2000. By 2007 the value of mobile advertising had reached $2.2 billion and providers such as Admob delivered billions of mobile ads.

More advanced mobile ads include banner ads, coupons, Multimedia Messaging Service picture and video messages, advergames and various engagement marketing campaigns. A particular feature driving mobile ads is the 2D Barcode, which replaces the need to do any typing of web addresses, and uses the camera feature of modern phones to gain immediate access to web content. 83 percent of Japanese mobile phone users already are active users of 2D barcodes.

A new form of advertising that is growing rapidly is social network advertising. It is online advertising with a focus on social networking sites. This is a relatively immature market, but it has shown a lot of promise as advertisers are able to take advantage of the demographic information the user has provided to the social networking site. Friendertising is a more precise advertising term in which people are able to direct advertisements toward others directly using social network service.

From time to time, The CW Television Network airs short programming breaks called "Content Wraps," to advertise one company's product during an entire commercial break. The CW pioneered "content wraps" and some products featured were Herbal Essences, Crest, Guitar Hero II, CoverGirl, and recently Toyota.

Recently, there appeared a new promotion concept, "ARvertising", advertising on Augmented Reality technology.

Current Trends

Rise in New Media

With the dawn of the Internet came many new advertising opportunities. Popup, Flash, banner, Popunder, advergaming, and email advertisements (the last often being a form of spam) are now commonplace. Particularly since the rise of "entertaining" advertising, some people may like an advertisement enough to wish to watch it later or show a friend. In general, the advertising community has not yet made this easy, although some have used the Internet to widely distribute their ads to anyone willing to see or hear them. In the last three quarters of 2009 mobile and internet advertising grew by 18.1% and 9.2% respectively. Older media advertising saw declines: "10.1% (TV), "11.7% (radio), "14.8% (magazines) and "18.7% (newspapers).

Niche Marketing

Another significant trend regarding future of advertising is the growing importance of the niche market using niche or targeted ads. Also brought about by the Internet and the theory of The Long Tail, advertisers will have an increasing ability to reach specific audiences. In the past, the most efficient way to deliver a message was to blanket the largest mass market audience possible. However, usage tracking, customer profiles and the growing popularity of niche content brought about by everything from blogs to social networking sites, provide advertisers with audiences that are smaller but much better defined, leading to ads that are more relevant to viewers and more effective for companies' marketing products. Among others, Comcast Spotlight is one such advertiser employing this method in their video on demand menus. These advertisements are targeted to a specific group and can be viewed by anyone wishing to find out more about a particular business or practice at any time, right from their home. This causes the viewer to become proactive and actually choose what advertisements they want to view.

Crowdsourcing

The concept of crowdsourcing has given way to the trend of user-generated advertisements. User-generated ads are created by consumers as opposed to an advertising agency or the company themselves, most often they are a result of brand sponsored advertising competitions. For the 2007 Super Bowl, the Frito-Lays division of PepsiCo held the Crash the Super Bowl contest, allowing consumers to create their own Doritos commercial. Chevrolet held a similar competition for their Tahoe line of SUVs. Due to the success of the Doritos user-generated ads in the 2007 Super Bowl, Frito-Lays relaunched the competition for the 2009 and 2010 Super Bowl. The resulting ads were among the most-watched and most-liked Super Bowl ads. In fact, the winning ad that aired in the 2009 Super Bowl was ranked by the USA Today Super Bowl Ad Meter as the top ad for the year while the winning ads that aired in the 2010 Super Bowl were found by Nielsen's BuzzMetrics to be the "most buzzed-about".

This trend has given rise to several online platforms that host user-generated advertising competitions on behalf of a company. Founded in 2007, Zooppa has launched ad competitions for brands such as Google, Nike, Hershey's, General Mills, Microsoft, NBC Universal, Zinio, and Mini Cooper. Crowdsourced advertisements have gained popularity in part to its cost effective nature, high consumer engagement, and ability to generate word-of-mouth. However, it remains controversial, as the long-term impact on the advertising industry is still unclear.

Global Advertising

Advertising has gone through five major stages of development: domestic, export, international, multi-national, and global.

For global advertisers, there are four, potentially competing, business objectives that must be balanced when developing worldwide advertising: building a brand while speaking with one voice, developing economies of scale in the creative process, maximising local effectiveness of ads, and increasing the company's speed of implementation. Born from the evolutionary stages of global marketing are the three primary and fundamentally different approaches to the development of global advertising executions: exporting executions, producing local executions, and importing ideas that travel.

Advertising research is key to determining the success of an ad in any country or region. The ability to identify which elements and/or moments of an ad that contributes to its success is how economies of scale are maximised. Once one knows what works in an ad, that idea or ideas can be imported by any other market. Market research measures, such as Flow of Attention, Flow of Emotion and branding moments provide insight into what is working in an ad in any country or region because the measures are based on the visual, not verbal, elements of the ad.

Diversification

In the realm of advertising agencies, continued industry diversification has seen observers note that "big global clients don't need big global agencies any more". This is reflected by the growth of non-traditional agencies in various global markets, such as Canadian business TAXI and SMART in Australia and has been referred to as "a revolution in the ad world".

New Technology

The ability to record shows on digital video recorders (such as TiVo) allow users to record the programs for later viewing, enabling them to fast forward through commercials. Additionally, as more seasons of pre-recorded box sets are offered for sale of television programs; fewer people watch the shows on TV. However, the fact that these sets are sold, means the company will receive additional profits from the sales of these sets. To counter this effect, many advertisers have opted for product placement on TV shows like Survivor.

Advertising Education

Advertising education has become widely popular with bachelor, master and doctorate degrees becoming available in the emphasis. A surge in advertising interest is typically attributed to the strong relationship advertising plays in cultural and technological changes, such as the advance of online social networking. A unique model for teaching advertising is the student-run advertising agency, where advertising students create campaigns for real companies. Organizations such as American Advertising Federation and AdU Network partner established companies with students to create these campaigns.

Criticisms

While advertising can be seen as necessary for economic growth, it is not without social costs. Unsolicited Commercial Email and other forms of spam have become so prevalent as to have become a major nuisance to users of these services, as well as being a financial burden on internet service providers. Advertising is increasingly invading public spaces, such as schools, which some critics argue is a form of child exploitation.

In addition, advertising frequently uses psychological pressure on the intended consumer, which may be harmful.

Regulation

In the US many communities believe that many forms of outdoor advertising blight the public realm. As long ago as the 1960s in the US there were attempts to ban billboard advertising in the open countryside. Cities such as São Paulo have introduced an outright ban with London also having specific legislation to control unlawful displays.

There have been increasing efforts to protect the public interest by regulating the content and the influence of advertising. Some examples are: the ban on television tobacco advertising imposed in many countries, and the total ban of advertising to children under 12 imposed by the Swedish government in 1991. Though that regulation continues in effect for broadcasts originating within the country, it has been weakened by the European Court of Justice, which had found that Sweden was obliged to accept foreign programming, including those from neighboring countries or via satellite. Greece's regulations are of a similar nature, "banning advertisements for children's toys between 7 am and 10 pm and a total ban on advertisement for war toys".

In Europe and elsewhere, there is a vigorous debate on whether (or how much) advertising to children should be regulated. This debate was exacerbated by a report released by the Kaiser Family Foundation in February 2004 which suggested fast food advertising that targets children was an important factor in the epidemic of childhood obesity in the United States.

In New Zealand, South Africa, Canada, and many European countries, the advertising industry operates a system of self-regulation. Advertisers, advertising agencies and the media agree on a code of advertising standards that they attempt to uphold. The general aim of such codes is to ensure that any advertising is 'legal, decent, honest and truthful'. Some self-regulatory organizations are funded by the industry, but remain independent, with the intent of upholding the standards or codes like the Advertising Standards Authority in the UK. In the UK most forms of outdoor advertising such as the display of billboards is regulated by the UK Town and County Planning system. Currently the display of an advertisement without consent from the Planning Authority is a criminal offense liable to a fine of £2,500 per offence. All of the major outdoor billboard companies in the UK have convictions of this nature.

Naturally, many advertisers view governmental regulation or even self-regulation as intrusion of their freedom of speech or a necessary evil. Therefore, they employ a wide-variety of linguistic devices to bypass regulatory laws (e.g. printing English words in bold and French translations in fine print to deal with the Article 120 of the 1994 Toubon Law limiting the use of English in French advertising). The advertisement of controversial products such as cigarettes and condoms are subject to government regulation in many countries. For instance, the tobacco industry is required by law in most countries to display warnings cautioning consumers about the health hazards of their products. Linguistic variation is often used by advertisers as a creative device to reduce the impact of such requirements.

Advertising Research

Advertising research is a specialized form of research that works to improve the effectiveness and efficiency of advertising. It entails numerous forms of research which employ different methodologies. Advertising research includes pre-testing (also known as copy testing) and post-testing of ads and/or campaigns—pre-testing is done before an ad airs to gauge how well it will perform and post-testing is done after an ad airs to determine the in-market impact of the ad or campaign on the consumer. Continuous ad tracking and the Communicus System are competing examples of post-testing advertising research types.

Evidence-based Advertising

Evidence-based advertising refers to advertising principles, which have been proven through experimental studies. They can be applied to an advertising campaign with high confidence of increasing persuasiveness regardless of time and place. Principles are usually accompanied with various conditions, which must be taken into consideration when applying them. According to Professor J. Scott Armstrong from The Wharton School, evidence-based principles "draw upon typical practice, expert opinion, factual evidence and empirical evidence."Innovation

Innovation is a change in the thought process for doing something, or the useful application of new inventions or discoveries. It may refer to an incremental emergent or radical and revolutionary changes in thinking, products, processes, or organizations.

Following Schumpeter (1934), contributors to the scholarly literature on innovation typically distinguish between invention, an idea made manifest, and innovation, ideas applied successfully in practice. In many fields, such as the arts, economics and government policy, something new must be substantially different to be innovative. In economics the change must increase value, customer value, or producer value. The goal of innovation is positive change, to make someone or something better. Innovation leading to increased productivity is the fundamental source of increasing wealth in an economy.

Innovation is an important topic in the study of economics, business, entrepreneurship, design, technology, sociology, and engineering. Colloquially, the word "innovation" is often synonymous with the output of the process. However, economists tend to focus on the process itself, from the origination of an idea to its transformation into something useful, to its implementation; and on the system within which the process of innovation unfolds. Since innovation is also considered a major driver of the economy, especially when it leads to new product categories or increasing productivity, the factors that lead to innovation are also considered to be critical to policy makers. In particular, followers of innovation economics stress using public policy to spur innovation and growth.

Those who are directly responsible for application of the innovation are often called pioneers in their field, whether they are individuals or organizations.

In the organizational context, innovation may be linked to performance and growth through improvements in efficiency, productivity, quality, competitive positioning, market share, etc. All organizations can innovate, including for example hospitals, universities, and local governments.

While innovation typically adds value, innovation may also have a negative or destructive effect as new developments clear away or change old organizational forms and practices. Organizations that do not innovate effectively may be destroyed by those that do. Hence innovation typically involves risk. A key challenge in innovation is maintaining a balance between process and product innovations where process innovations tend to involve a business model which may develop shareholder satisfaction through improved efficiencies while product innovations develop customer support however at the risk of costly R&D that can erode shareholder return. Innovation can be described as the result of some amount of time and effort into researching an idea, plus some larger amount of time and effort into developing this idea, plus some very large amount of time and effort into commercializing this idea into a market place with customers.

Innovation has been studied in a variety of contexts, including in relation to technology, commerce, social systems, economic development, and policy construction. There are, therefore, naturally a wide range of approaches to conceptualizing innovation in the scholarly literature.

Distinguishing from Invention

Invention is the embodiment of something new. While both invention and innovation have "uniqueness" implications, innovation also carries an undertone of profitability and market performance expectation.

An improvement on an existing form or embodiment, composition or processes might be an invention, an innovation, both or neither if it is not substantial enough. According to certain business literature, an idea, a change or an improvement is only an innovation when it is put to use and effectively causes a social or commercial reorganization.

In business, innovation can be easily distinguished from invention. Invention is the conversion of cash into ideas. Innovation is the conversion of ideas into cash. This is best described by comparing Thomas Edison with Nikola Tesla. Thomas Edison was an innovator because he made money from his ideas. Nikola Tesla was an inventor. Tesla spent money to create his inventions but was unable to monetize them. Innovators produce, market and profit from their innovations. Inventors may or may not profit from their work.

In Organizations

A convenient definition of innovation from an organizational perspective is given by Luecke and Katz (2003), who wrote:

"Innovation... is generally understood as the successful introduction of a new thing or method... Innovation is the embodiment, combination, or synthesis of knowledge in original, relevant, valued new products, processes, or services.

A content analysis on the term "innovation" carried out by Baregheh et al. (2009) within the organizational context, defines innovation as:

"Innovation is the multi-stage process whereby organizations transform ideas into new/improved products, service or processes, in order to advance, compete and differentiate themselves successfully in their marketplace."

Innovation typically involves creativity, but is not identical to it: innovation involves acting on the creative ideas to make some specific and tangible difference in the domain in which the innovation occurs. For example, Amabile et al. (1996) propose:

"All innovation begins with creative ideas... We define innovation as the successful implementation of creative ideas within an organization. In this view, creativity by individuals and teams is a starting point for innovation; the first is necessary but not sufficient condition for the second".

For innovation to occur, something more than the generation of a creative idea or insight is required: the insight must be put into action to make a genuine difference, resulting for example in new or altered business processes within the organization, or changes in the products and services provided.

"Innovation, like many business functions, is a management process that requires specific tools, rules, and discipline."

From this point of view emphasis is moved from the introduction of specific novel and useful ideas to the general organizational processes and procedures for generating, considering, and acting on such insights leading to significant organizational improvements in terms of improved or new business products, services, or internal processes.

Through these varieties of viewpoints, creativity is typically seen as the basis for innovation, and innovation as the successful implementation of creative ideas within an organization. It should be noted, however, that the term 'innovation' is used by many authors rather interchangeably with the term 'creativity' when discussing individual and organizational creative activity.

Economic Conceptions

Joseph Schumpeter defined economic innovation in "Theorie der Wirtschaftlichen Entwicklung" (1912). (The Theory of Economic Development, 1934, Harvard University Press, Boston.)

1. The introduction of a new good — that is one with which consumers are not yet familiar — or of a new quality of a good.
2. The introduction of a new method of production, which need by no means be founded upon a discovery scientifically new, and can also exist in a new way of handling a commodity commercially.
3. The opening of a new market, that is a market into which the particular branch of manufacture of the country in question has not previously entered, whether or not this market has existed before.
4. The conquest of a new source of supply of raw materials or half-manufactured goods, again irrespective of whether this source already exists or whether it has first to be created.

5. The carrying out of the new organization of any industry, like the creation of a monopoly position (for example through trustification) or the breaking up of a monopoly position.

Schumpeter's focus on innovation is reflected in Neo-Schumpeterian economics, developed by such scholars as Christopher Freeman and Giovanni Dosi.

Innovation is also studied by economists in a variety of other contexts, for example in theories of entrepreneurship or in Paul Romer's New Growth Theory. In network theory, innovation can be seen as "a new element introduced in the network which changes, even if momentarily, the costs of transactions between at least two actors, elements or nodes, in the network".

Market Outcome

Market outcome from innovation can be studied from different lenses. The industrial organizational approach of market characterization according to the degree of competitive pressure and the consequent modelling of firm behaviour often using sophisticated game theoretic tools, while permitting mathematical modelling, has shifted the ground away from the usual understanding of markets. The earlier visual framework in economics, of market demand and supply along price and quantity dimensions, has given way to powerful mathematical models which though intellectually satisfying has led policy makers and managers groping for more intuitive and less theoretical analyses to which they can relate to at a practical level.

In the management (strategy) From an academic point of view, there is often a divorce between industrial organisation theory and strategic management models. While many economists view management models as being too simplistic, strategic management consultants perceive academic economists as being too theoretical, and the analytical tools that they devise as too complex for managers to understand.

Innovation literature while rich in typologies and descriptions of innovation dynamics is mostly technology focused. Most research on innovation has been devoted to the process (technological) of innovation, or has otherwise taken a how to (innovate) approach.

Sources of Innovation

There are several sources of innovation. In the linear model of innovation the traditionally recognized source is *manufacturer innovation*. This is where an agent (person or business) innovates in order to sell the innovation. Another source of innovation, only now becoming widely recognized, is *end-user innovation*. This is where an agent (person or company) develops an innovation for their own (personal or in-house) use because existing products do not meet their needs. Eric von Hippel has identified end-user innovation as, by far, the most important and critical in his classic book on the subject, *Sources of Innovation*.

Joseph F. Engelberger, paraphrasing the conclusion of the 1967 US DoD program "Project Hindsight", says that innovations require only three things: 1. A recognized need, 2. Competent people with relevant technology, and 3. Financial support.

Innovation by businesses is achieved in many ways, with much attention now given to formal research and development for "breakthrough innovations." But innovations may be developed by less formal on-the-job modifications of practice, through exchange and combination of professional experience and by many other routes. The more radical and revolutionary innovations tend to emerge from R&D, while more incremental innovations may emerge from practice – but there are many exceptions to each of these trends. accelerated radical innovation is another buzzword topping radical innovation expressing the target to move things quicker than by relying on the ideas flowing in from inventors. User as customers buying products or using services are an important factor in innovation. Firms may incorporate users in focus groups (user centred approach), work closely with so called lead users (lead user approach)or users might adapt their products them selves. Regarding this user innovation, a great deal of innovation is done by those actually implementing and using technologies and products as part of their normal activities. In most of the times user innovators have some personal record motivating them. Sometimes user-innovators may become entrepreneurs, selling their product, they may choose to trade their innovation in exchange for other innovations, or they may be adopted by their suppliers. Nowadays, they may also choose to freely reveal their innovations, using methods like open source. In such networks of innovation the users or communities of users can further develop technologies and reinvent their social meaning.

Whether innovation is mainly supply-pushed (based on new technological possibilities) or demand-led (based on social needs and market requirements) has been a hotly debated topic. Similarly, what exactly drives innovation in organizations and economies remains an open question.

More recent theoretical work moves beyond this simple dualistic problem, and through empirical work shows that innovation does not just happen within the industrial supply-side, or as a result of the articulation of user demand, but through a complex set of processes that links many different players together – not only developers and users, but a wide variety of intermediary organisations such as consultancies, standards bodies etc. Work on social networks suggests that much of the most successful innovation occurs at the boundaries of organisations and industries where the problems and needs of users, and the potential of technologies can be linked together in a creative process that challenges both.

Value of Experimentation

When an innovative idea requires a new business model, or radically redesigns the delivery of value to focus on the customer, a real world experimentation approach increases the chances of market success. New business models and customer experiences can't be tested through traditional market research methods. Pilot programs for new innovations set the path in stone too early thus increasing the costs of failure. On the other hand, the good news is that recent years have seen considerable progress in identifying important key factors/principles or variables that affect the probability of success in innovation. Of course, building successful businesses is such a complicated process, involving subtle interdependencies among so many variables in dynamic systems, that it is unlikely to ever be made perfectly predictable. But the more business can master the variables and experiment, the more they will be able to create new companies, products, processes and services that achieve what they hope to achieve.

Diffusion

Once innovation occurs, innovations may be spread from the innovator to other individuals and groups. This process has been proposed that the life cycle of innovations can be described using the 's-curve' or diffusion curve.

The s-curve maps growth of revenue or productivity against time. In the early stage of a particular innovation, growth is relatively slow as the new product establishes itself. At some point customers begin to demand and the product growth increases more rapidly. New incremental innovations or changes to the product allow growth to continue. Towards the end of its life cycle growth slows and may even begin to decline. In the later stages, no amount of new investment in that product will yield a normal rate of return.

The s-curve derives from an assumption that new products are likely to have "product Life". i.e. a start-up phase, a rapid increase in revenue and eventual decline. In fact the great majority of innovations never get off the bottom of the curve, and never produce normal returns.

Innovative companies will typically be working on new innovations that will eventually replace older ones. Successive s-curves will come along to replace older ones and continue to drive growth upwards. In the figure above the first curve shows a current technology. The second shows an emerging technology that current yields lower growth but will eventually overtake current technology and lead to even greater levels of growth. The length of life will depend on many factors.

Goals

Programs of organizational innovation are typically tightly linked to organizational goals and objectives, to the business plan, and to market competitive positioning. One driver for innovation programs in corporations is to achieve growth objectives. As Davila et al. (2006) note;

> *"Companies cannot grow through cost reduction and reengineering alone... Innovation is the key element in providing aggressive top-line growth, and for increasing bottom-line results"*

In general, business organisations spend a significant amount of their turnover on innovation, such as making changes to their established products, processes and services. The amount of investment can vary from as low as a half a percent of turnover for organisations with a low rate of change to anything over twenty percent of turnover for organisations with a high rate of change.

The average investment across all types of organizations is four percent. For an organisation with a turnover of one billion currency units, this would represent an investment of forty million units. This budget will typically be spread across various functions including marketing, product design, information systems, manufacturing systems and quality assurance. The investment may vary by industry and by market positioning.

One survey across a large number of manufacturing and services organisations found, ranked in decreasing order of popularity, that systematic programs of organizational innovation are most frequently driven by:

1. Improved quality
2. Creation of new markets
3. Extension of the product range
4. Reduced labour costs
5. Improved production processes
6. Reduced materials
7. Reduced environmental damage
8. Replacement of products/services
9. Reduced energy consumption
10. Conformance to regulations.

These goals vary between improvements to products, processes and services and dispel a popular myth that innovation deals mainly with new product development. Most of the goals could apply to any organisation be it a manufacturing facility, marketing firm, hospital or local government. Whether innovation goals are successfully achieved or otherwise depends greatly on the environment prevailing in the firm.

Failure

Research findings vary, ranging from fifty to ninety percent of innovation projects judged to have made little or no contribution to organizational goals. One survey regarding product innovation quotes that out of three thousand ideas for new products, only one becomes a success in the marketplace. Failure is an inevitable part of the innovation process, and most successful organisations factor in an appropriate level of risk. Perhaps it is because all organisations experience failure that many choose not to monitor the level of failure very closely. The impact of failure goes beyond the simple loss of investment. Failure can also lead to loss of morale among employees, an increase in cynicism and even higher resistance to change in the future.

Innovations that fail are often potentially good ideas but have been rejected or postponed due to budgetary constraints, lack of skills or poor fit with current goals. Failures should be identified and screened out as early in the process as possible. Early screening avoids unsuitable ideas devouring scarce resources that are needed to progress more beneficial ones. Organizations can learn how to avoid failure when it is openly discussed and debated. The lessons learned from failure often reside longer in the organisational consciousness than lessons learned from success. While learning is important, high failure rates throughout the innovation process are wasteful and a threat to the organisation's future.

The causes of failure have been widely researched and can vary considerably. Some causes will be external to the organisation and outside its influence of control. Others will be internal and ultimately within the control of the organisation. Internal causes of failure can be divided into causes associated with the cultural infrastructure and causes associated with the innovation process itself. Failure in the cultural infrastructure varies between organizations but the following are common across all organisations at some stage in their life cycle (O'Sullivan, 2002):

1. Poor Leadership
2. Poor Organization
3. Poor Communication
4. Poor Empowerment
5. Poor Knowledge Management.

Common causes of failure within the innovation process in most organisations can be distilled into five types:

1. Poor goal definition
2. Poor alignment of actions to goals
3. Poor participation in teams
4. Poor monitoring of results
5. Poor communication and access to information.

Effective goal definition requires that organisations state explicitly what their goals are in terms understandable to everyone involved in the innovation process. This often involves stating goals in a number of ways. Effective alignment of actions to goals should link explicit actions such as ideas and projects to specific goals. It also implies effective management of action portfolios. Participation in teams refers to the behaviour of individuals in and of teams, and each individual should have an explicitly allocated responsibility regarding their role in goals and actions and the payment and rewards systems that link them to goal attainment. Finally, effective monitoring of results requires the monitoring of all goals, actions and teams involved in the innovation process.

Innovation can fail if seen as an organisational process whose success stems from a mechanistic approach i.e. 'pull lever obtain result'. While 'driving' change has an emphasis on control, enforcement and structure it is only a partial truth in achieving innovation. Organisational gatekeepers frame the organisational environment that "Enables" innovation; however innovation is "Enacted" – recognised, developed, applied and adopted – through individuals.

Individuals are the 'atom' of the organisation close to the minutiae of daily activities. Within individuals gritty appreciation of the small detail combines with a sense of desired organisational objectives to deliver (and innovate for) a product/ service offer.

From this perspective innovation succeeds from strategic structures that engage the individual to the organisation's benefit. Innovation pivots on intrinsically motivated individuals, within a supportive culture, informed by a broad sense of the future.

Innovation, implies change, and can be counter to an organisation's orthodoxy. Space for fair hearing of innovative ideas is required to balance the potential autoimmune exclusion that quells an infant innovative culture.

Measures

There are two fundamentally different types of measures for innovation: the organizational level and the political level. The measure of innovation at the organizational level relates to individuals, team-level assessments, private companies from the smallest to the largest. Measure of innovation for organizations can be conducted by surveys, workshops, consultants or internal benchmarking. There is today no established general way to measure organizational innovation. Corporate measurements are generally structured around balanced scorecards which cover several aspects of innovation such as business measures related to finances, innovation process efficiency, employees' contribution and motivation, as well benefits for customers. Measured values will vary widely between businesses, covering for example new product revenue, spending in R&D, time to market, customer and employee perception & satisfaction, number of patents, additional sales resulting from past innovations. For the political level, measures of innovation are more focussing on a country or region competitive advantage through innovation. In this context, organizational capabilities can be evaluated through various evaluation frameworks, such as those of the European Foundation for Quality Management. The OECD Oslo Manual (1995) suggests standard guidelines on measuring technological product and process innovation. Some people consider the Oslo Manual complementary to the Frascati Manual from 1963. The new Oslo manual from 2005 takes a wider perspective to innovation, and includes marketing and organizational innovation. These standards are used for example in the European Community Innovation Surveys.

Other ways of measuring innovation have traditionally been expenditure, for example, investment in R&D (Research and Development) as percentage of GNP (Gross National Product). Whether this is a good measurement of Innovation has been widely discussed and the Oslo Manual has incorporated some of the critique against earlier methods of measuring. The traditional methods of measuring still inform many policy decisions. The EU Lisbon Strategy has set as a goal that their average expenditure on R&D should be 3 % of GNP.

The Oslo Manual is focused on North America, Europe, and other rich economies. In 2001 for Latin America and the Caribbean countries it was created the Bogota Manual

Many scholars claim that there is a great bias towards the "science and technology mode" (S&T-mode or STI-mode), while the "learning by doing, using and interacting mode" (DUI-mode) is widely ignored. For an example, that means you can have the better high tech or software, but there are also crucial learning tasks important for innovation. But these measurements and research are rarely done.

A common industry view (unsupported by empirical evidence) is that comparative cost-effectiveness research (CER) is a form of price control which, by reducing returns to industry, limits R&D expenditure, stifles future innovation and compromises new products access to markets. Some academics claim the CER is a valuable value-based measure of innovation which accords truly significant advances in therapy (those that provide 'health gain') higher prices than free market mechanisms. Such value-based pricing has been viewed as a means of indicating to industry the type of innovation that should be rewarded from the public purse. The Australian academic Thomas Alured Faunce has developed the case that national comparative cost-effectiveness assessment systems should be viewed as measuring 'health innovation' as an evidence-based concept distinct from valuing innovation through the operation of competitive markets (a method which requires strong anti-trust laws to be effective) on the basis that both methods of assessing innovation in pharmaceuticals are mentioned in annex 2C.1 of the AUSFTA.

Political Level Studies

There are several international benchmarking studies of the innovation performance of countries (above called the political level), Global Innovation Index being one. Other examples are Richard Florida´s index for the Creative Class and the Innovation Capacity Index (ICI) published by a large number of international professors working in a collaborative fashion. The top scorers of ICI 2009-2010 being:1.Sweden 82.2, 2. Finland 77.8, 3. United States 3 77.5.

The Global Innovation Index is a global index measuring the level of innovation of a country, produced jointly by The Boston Consulting Group (BCG), the National Association of Manufacturers (NAM), and The Manufacturing Institute (MI), the NAM's nonpartisan research affiliate. NAM describes it as the "largest and most comprehensive global index of its kind".

The International Innovation Index is part of a large research study that looked at both the business outcomes of innovation and government's ability to encourage and support innovation through public policy. The study comprised a survey of more than 1,000 senior executives from NAM member companies across all industries; in-depth interviews with 30 of the executives; and a comparison of the "innovation friendliness" of 110 countries and all 50 U.S. states. The findings are published in the report, "The Innovation Imperative in Manufacturing: How the United States Can Restore Its Edge."

The report discusses not only country performance but also what companies are doing and should be doing to spur innovation. It looks at new policy indicators for innovation, including tax incentives and policies for immigration, education and intellectual property.

The latest index was published in March 2009. To rank the countries, the study measured both innovation inputs and outputs. Innovation inputs included government and fiscal policy, education policy and the innovation environment. Outputs included patents, technology transfer, and other R&D results; business performance, such as labour productivity and total shareholder returns; and the impact of innovation on business migration and economic growth.

8

Counterproductive Work Behaviour

Counterproductive work behaviour (CWB) is employee behaviour that goes against the goals of an organization. These behaviours can be intentional or unintentional and result from a wide range of underlying causes and motivations. It has been proposed that a person-by-environment interaction can be utilized to explain a variety of counter-productive behaviours. For instance, an employee who steals from the company may do so because of lax supervision (environment) and underlying psychopathology (person) that work in concert to result in the counterproductive behaviour.

Counterproductive work behaviour is a topic of research in industrial and organizational psychologyý.

Forms of Counterproductive Work Behaviour

The forms of counterproductive work behaviour with the most empirical examination are ineffective job performance, absenteeism, job turnover, theft, and accidents. Less common but potentially more detrimental forms of counterproductive behaviour have also been investigated including theft, violence, substance use, and sexual harassment.

Within organizations, ineffective job performance is often difficult to detect, diagnose the cause of, prevent, or resolve. This is because most performance measurement systems only assess the impact of various employee behaviours rather than the behaviours themselves. Performance data is the most common method of evaluating ineffective job performance and often includes personnel data, production data, subjective evaluations, and electronic performance monitoring.

The causes of ineffective job performance have been evaluated from different theoretical approaches including: attribution theory that links performance to employee characteristics, selection errors that evaluate mistakes of hiring the wrong employees, and inadequate socialization/training that evaluate the social environment and structured training employees receive.

Employers need to be careful to avoid the fundamental attribution error whereby performance is linked to characteristics of the employee rather than the environment.

Absenteeism is typically measured by time lost measures and frequency measures. It is weakly linked to affective predictors such as job satisfaction and commitment. Research has found that women are more likely to be absent than men, and that the absence control policies and culture of an organization will predict absenteeism.

Research on employee job turnover has attempted to understand the causes of individual decisions to leave an organization. It has been found that lower performance, lack of reward contingencies for performance, and better external job opportunities.

Accidents are a serious and costly form of counterproductive behaviour. Most research on this topic has attempted to evaluate characteristics of the work-place environment that lead to accidents and determination of ways to avoid accidents. There has also been some research on the characteristics of accident-prone employees has found they are typically younger, more distractible, and less socially adjusted than other employees.

Strike

Strike action, often simply called a strike, is a work stoppage caused by the mass refusal of employees to work. A strike usually takes place in response to employee grievances. Strikes became important during the industrial revolution, when mass labour became important in factories and mines. In most countries, they were quickly made illegal, as factory owners had far more political power than workers. Most western countries partially legalized striking in the late 19th or early 20th centuries.

Strikes are sometimes used to put pressure on governments to change policies. Occasionally, strikes destabilise the rule of a particular political party. A notable example is the Gdañsk Shipyard strike led by Lech Wa³êsa. This strike was significant in the struggle for political change in Poland, and was an important mobilised effort that contributed to the fall of the Iron Curtain.

History

The strike tactic has a very long history. Towards the end of the 20th dynasty, under Pharaoh Ramses III in ancient Egypt on 14 November 1152 BC, the artisans of the Royal Necropolis at Deir el-Medina organized the first known strike or workers' uprising in recorded history.

The event was reported in detail on a papyrus at the time, which has been preserved, and is currently located in Turin. The strike is narrated by John Romer in *Ancient Lives: The story of the Pharaohs' Tombmakers* The strike so terrified the Egyptian authorities, as such rebellion was virtually unheard of, that they gave in and raised their wages.

The use of the English word "strike" first appeared in 1768, when sailors, in support of demonstrations in London, "struck" or removed the topgallant sails of merchant ships at port, thus crippling the ships. Official publications have typically used the more neutral words "work stoppage" or "industrial dispute".

In 1917, the Mexican Constitution was the first national constitution that constitutionally guaranteed the right to strike.

In 1937 there were 4,740 strikes in the United States. This was the greatest strike wave in American history. This outburst of strikes occurred during a period of deep depression and massive unemployment.

A list of strikes of historic significance may be found here.

Categories of Strikes

Most strikes are undertaken by labour unions during collective bargaining. The object of collective bargaining is to obtain a contract (an agreement between the union and the company) which may include a no-strike clause which prevents strikes, or penalizes the union and/or the workers if they walk out while the contract is in force. The strike is typically reserved as a threat of last resort during negotiations between the company and the union, which may occur just before, or immediately after, the contract expires.

Sometimes a union will strike rather than sign an agreement with a no-strike clause. Such an action was documented in *Harlan County, USA*, a video about a United Mine Workers strike.

In some industrial unions, the no-strike clause is considered controversial.

Generally, strikes are rare: according to the News Media Guild, 98% of union contracts in the United States are settled each year without a strike. Occasionally, workers decide to strike without the sanction of a labour union, either because the union refuses to endorse such a tactic, or because the workers concerned are not unionized. Such strikes are often described as *unofficial*. Strikes without formal union authorization are also known as wildcat strikes.

In many countries, wildcat strikes do not enjoy the same legal protections as recognized union strikes, and may result in penalties for the union members who participate or their union. The same often applies in the case of strikes conducted without an official ballot of the union membership, as is required in some countries such as the United Kingdom.

A strike may consist of workers refusing to attend work or picketing outside the workplace to prevent or dissuade people from working in their place or conducting business with their employer. Less frequently workers may occupy the workplace, but refuse either to do their jobs or to leave. This is known as a sit-down strike (also known as an *Italian strike*, in Italian *Sciopero bianco*). A similar tactic is the work-in, where employees occupy the workplace but still continue work, often without pay, which to attempts to show they are still useful, or that worker self-management can be successful. This occurred for instance with factory occupations in the *Bienno Rossi* strikes- the "two red years" of Italy from 1919-1920.

Another unconventional tactic is work-to-rule, in which workers perform their tasks exactly as they are required to but no better. For example, workers might follow all safety regulations in such a way that it impedes their productivity or they might refuse to work overtime. Such strikes may in some cases be a form of "partial strike" or "slowdown".

During the development boom of the 1970s in Australia, the Green ban was developed by certain more socially conscious unions. This is a form of strike action taken by a trade union or other organised labour group for environmentalist or conservationist purposes. This developed from the black ban, strike action taken against a particular job or employer in order to protect the economic interests of the strikers.

United States labour law also draws a distinction, in the case of private sector employers covered by the National Labour Relations Act, between "economic" and "unfair labour practice" strikes. An employer may not fire, but may permanently replace, workers who engage in a strike over economic issues. On the other hand, employers who commit unfair labour practices (ULPs) may not replace employees who strike over ULPs, and must fire any strikebreakers they have hired as replacements in order to reinstate the striking workers.

Strikes may be specific to a particular workplace, employer, or unit within a workplace, or they may encompass an entire industry, or every worker within a city or country. Strikes that involve all workers, or a number of large and important groups of workers, in a particular community or region are known as general strikes. Under some circumstances, strikes may take place in order to put pressure on the State or other authorities or may be a response to unsafe conditions in the workplace.

A sympathy strike is, in a way, a small scale version of a general strike in which one group of workers refuses to cross a picket line established by another as a means of supporting the striking workers. Sympathy strikes, once the norm in the construction industry in the United States, have been made much more difficult to conduct due to decisions of the National Labour Relations Board permitting employers to establish separate or "reserved" gates for particular trades, making it an unlawful secondary boycott for a union to establish a picket line at any gate other than the one reserved for the employer it is picketing. Sympathy strikes may be undertaken by a union as an organization or by individual union members choosing not to cross a picket line. A jurisdictional strike in United States labour law refers to a concerted refusal to work undertaken by a union to assert its members' right to particular job assignments and to protest the assignment of disputed work to members of another union or to unorganized workers.

A student strike has the students (sometimes supported by faculty) not attending schools. In some cases, the strike is intended to draw media attention to the institution so that the grievances that are causing the students to "strike" can be aired before the public; this usually damages the institution's (or government's) public image. In other cases, especially in government-supported institutions, the student strike can cause a budgetary imbalance and have actual economic repercussions for the institution.

A hunger strike is a deliberate refusal to eat. Hunger strikes are often used in prisons as a form of political protest. Like student strikes, a hunger strike aims to worsen the public image of the target.

A "sickout", or (especially by uniformed police officers) "blue flu", is a type of strike action in which the strikers call in sick. This is used in cases where laws prohibit certain employees from declaring a strike. Police, firefighters, and air traffic controllers are among the groups commonly barred from striking: usually by state and federal laws meant to ensure the safety and/or security of the general public. So are teachers in some U.S. states. Workers have sometimes circumvented these restrictions by falsely claiming inability to work due to illness.

Newspaper writers may withhold their names from their stories as a way to protest actions of their employer.

Legal Prohibitions on Strikes

In the People's Republic of China and the Former Soviet Union

In some "Marxist-Leninist" regimes, such as the former USSR or the People's Republic of China, striking is illegal and viewed as counter-revolutionary see Trade unions in the Soviet Union, All-China Federation of Trade Unions. Since the government in such systems claims to represent the working class, it has been argued that unions and strikes were not necessary. In 1976, China signed the International Covenant on Economic, Social and Cultural Rights, which guaranteed the right to unions and striking, but Chinese officials declared that they had no interest in allowing these liberties. (In June 2008, however, the municipal government in Shenzhen in southern China introduced draft labour regulations, which labour rights advocacy groups say would, if implemented, virtually restore Chinese workers' right to strike.). Trade unions in the Soviet Union served in part as a means to educate workers about the country's economic system. Lenin referred to trade unions as "Schools of Communism." They were essentially state propaganda and control organs to regulate the workforce, also providing them with social activities.

In France

A "minimum service" during strikes in public transport was a promise of Nicolas Sarkozy during his campaign for the French presidential election. A law "on social dialogue and continuity of public service in regular terrestrial transports of passengers" was adopted on August 12, 2007, and it took effect on 1 January 2008.

This law, amongst other measures, forces certain categories of public transport workers (such as train and bus drivers) to declare to their employer 48 hours in advance if they intend to go on strike. Should they go on strike without having declared their intention to do so beforehand, they leave themselves open to sanctions.

The unions did and still do oppose this law and argue these 48 hours are used not only to pressure the workers but also to keep files on the more militant workers, who will more easily be undermined in their careers by the employers. Most importantly, they argue this law prevents the more hesitant workers from making the decision to join the strike the day before, once they've been convinced to do so by their colleagues and more particularly the union militants, who maximise their efforts in building the strike (by handing out leaflets, organising meetings, discussing the demands with their colleagues) in the last few days preceding the strike. This law makes it also more difficult for the strike to spread rapidly to other workers, as they are required to wait at least 48 hours before joining the strike.

This law also makes it easier for the employers to organise the production as it may use its human resources more effectively, knowing beforehand who is going to be at work and not, thus undermining, albeit not that much, the effects of the strike. However, this law has not had much effect as strikes in public transports still occur in France and at times, the workers refuse to comply by the rules of this law. The public transport industry-public or privately owned-remains very militant in France and keen on taking strike action when their interests are threatened by the employers or the government.

The public transport workers in France, in particular the "Cheminots" (employees of the national French railway company) are often seen as the most radical "vanguard" of the French working class. This law has not, in the eyes of many, changed this fact.

In the United Kingdom

The Industrial Relations Act 1971 was repealed through the Trade Union and Labour Relations Act 1974, sections of which were repealed by the Employment Act 1982.

The Code of Practice on Industrial Action Ballots and Notices, and sections 22 and 25 of the Employment Relations Act 2004, which concern industrial action notices, commenced on 1 October 2005.

Legislation was enacted in the aftermath of the 1919 police strikes, forbidding British police from both taking industrial action, and discussing the possibility with colleagues. The Police Federation which was created at the time to deal with employment grievances, and provide representation to police officers, has increasingly put pressure on the government, and repeatedly threatened strike action.

In the United States

The Railway Labour Act bans strikes by United States airline and railroad employees except in narrowly defined circumstances. The National Labour Relations Act generally permits strikes, but provides a mechanism to enjoin strikes in industries in which a strike would create a national emergency. The federal government most recently invoked these statutory provisions to obtain an injunction requiring the International Longshore and Warehouse Union return to work in 2002 after having been locked out by the employer group, the Pacific Maritime Association. Some jurisdictions prohibit all strikes by public employees, under laws such as the "Taylor Law" in New York. Other jurisdictions impose strike bans only on certain categories of workers, particularly those regarded as critical to society: police and firefighters are among the groups commonly barred from striking in these jurisdictions. Some states, such as Michigan, Iowa or Florida, do not allow teachers in public schools to strike. Workers have sometimes circumvented these restrictions by falsely claiming inability to work due to illness—this is sometimes called a "sickout" or "blue flu", the latter receiving its name from the uniforms worn by police officers, who are traditionally prohibited from striking. The term "red flu" has sometimes been used to describe this action when undertaken by firefighters.

Postal workers involved in 1978 wildcat strikes in Jersey City, Kearny, New Jersey, San Francisco, and Washington, D.C. were fired under the presidency of Jimmy Carter, and President Ronald Reagan fired air traffic controllers and the PATCO union after the air traffic controllers' strike of 1981.

Strikebreakers

A *strikebreaker* is someone who continues to work during strike action by trade unionists or temporary and permanent replacement workers hired to take the place of those on strike. Strikebreakers are commonly given derogatory terms like *scab* and *blackleg*. The act of working during a strike – whether by strikebreakers, management personnel, non-unionized employees or members of other unions not on strike – is known as *crossing the picket line*, regardless of whether it involves actually physically crossing a line of picketing strikers. Crossing a picket line can result in passive and/or active retaliation against that working person.

The classic example from United Kingdom industrial history is that of the miners from Nottinghamshire, who during the 1984-85 miners' strike did not support strike action by fellow mineworkers in other parts of the country. Those who supported the strike claimed that this was because they enjoyed more favourable mining conditions and thus better wages. However, the Nottinghamshire miners argued that they did not participate because the law required a ballot for a national strike and their area vote had seen around 75% vote against a strike.

Irwin, Jones, McGovern (2008) believe that the term 'scab' is part of a larger metaphor involving strikes. They argue that the picket line is symbolic of a wound and those who break its borders to return to work are the scabs who bond that wound. Others have argued that the word is not a part of a larger metaphor but, rather, originates from the old-fashioned English insult, "scab." The OED gives the etymology of 'scab' in this sense as a term of abuse or depreciation derived from the MDu. *schabbe*, applied to women with the senses 'slut' and 'scold' and 'scurvy'.

"Blackleg" is an older word and is found in the late-nineteenth/early-twentieth century folk song from Northumberland, *Blackleg Miner*. The term does not necessarily owe its origins to this tune of unknown origin. The song is, however, notable for its lyrics that encourage violent acts against strikebreakers.

Union Strikebreaking

The concept of *union strikebreaking* or *union scabbing* refers to any circumstance in which union workers, who normally might be expected to honor picket lines established by fellow working folk during a strike, are inclined or compelled to cross those picket lines or, in some manner, otherwise engage in workplace activity which may prove injurious to the strike.

Unionized workers are sometimes required to cross the picket lines established by other unions due to their organizations having signed contracts which include no-strike clauses. The no-strike clause typically requires that members of the union not conduct any strike action for the duration of the contract; such actions are called *sympathy* or *secondary strikes*. Members who honor the picket line in spite of the contract frequently face discipline, for their action may be viewed as a violation of provisions of the contract. Therefore, any union conducting a strike action typically seeks to include a provision of amnesty for all who honored the picket line in the agreement that settles the strike.

No-strike clauses may also prevent unionized workers from engaging in solidarity actions for other workers even when no picket line is crossed. For example, striking workers in manufacturing or mining produce a product which must be transported. In a situation where the factory or mine owners have replaced the strikers, unionized transport workers may feel inclined to refuse to haul any product that is produced by strikebreakers, yet their own contract obligates them to do so.

Historically the practice of union strikebreaking has been a contentious issue in the union movement, and a point of contention between adherents of different union philosophies. For example, supporters of industrial unions, which have sought to organize entire workplaces without regard to individual skills, have criticized craft unions for organizing workplaces into separate unions according to skill, a circumstance that makes union strikebreaking more common. Union strikebreaking is not, however, unique to craft unions.

Methods used by Employers to Deal with Strikes

Most strikes called by unions are somewhat predictable; they typically occur after the contract has expired. However, not all strikes are called by union organizations — some strikes have been called in an effort to pressure employers to recognize unions. Other strikes may be spontaneous actions by working people. Spontaneous strikes are sometimes called "wildcat strikes"; they were the key fighting point in May '68; most commonly, they are responses to serious (often life-threatening) safety hazards in the workplace rather than wage or hour disputes, etc.

Whatever the cause of the strike, employers are generally motivated to take measures to prevent them, mitigate the impact, or to undermine strikes when they do occur.

Strike Preparation

Companies which produce products for sale will frequently increase inventories prior to a strike. Salaried employees may be called upon to take the place of strikers, which may entail advance training. If the company has multiple locations, personnel may be redeployed to meet the needs of reduced staff.

Companies may also take out *strike insurance* prior to an anticipated strike, to help offset the losses which the strike would cause.

Strike Breaking

Some companies negotiate with the union during a strike; other companies may see a strike as an opportunity to eliminate the union. This is sometimes accomplished by the importation of replacement workers, strikebreakers or "scabs". Historically, strike breaking has often coincided with union busting. It was also called 'Black legging' in the early 20th century, during the Russian socialist movement.

Union Busting

One method of inhibiting a strike is elimination of the union that may launch it, which is sometimes accomplished through union busting. Union busting campaigns may be orchestrated by labour relations consultants, and may utilize the services of labour spies, or asset protection services. Similar services may be engaged during attempts to defeat organizing drives. A modern example of a union buster is The Burke Group.

Lockout

Another counter to a strike is a lockout, the form of work stoppage in which an employer refuses to allow employees to work. Two of the three employers involved in the Caravan park grocery workers strike of 2003-2004 locked out their employees in response to a strike against the third member of the employer bargaining group. Lockouts are, with certain exceptions, lawful under United States labour law.

Violence

Historically, some employers have attempted to break union strikes by force. One of the most famous examples of this occurred during the Homestead Strike of 1892. Industrialist Henry Clay Frick sent private security agents from the Pinkerton National Detective Agency to break the Amalgamated Association of Iron and Steel Workers strike at a Homestead, Pennsylvania steel mill. Two strikers were killed, twelve wounded, along with two Pinkertons killed and eleven wounded. In the aftermath, Frick was shot in the neck and then stabbed by Alexander Berkman, surviving the attack, while Berkman was sentenced to 22 years in prison.

Salary

A salary is a form of periodic payment from an employer to an employee, which may be specified in an employment contract. It is contrasted with piece wages, where each job, hour or other unit is paid separately, rather than on a periodic basis. From the point of a business, salary can also be viewed as the cost of acquiring human resources for running operations, and is then termed personnel expense or salary expense. In accounting, salaries are recorded in payroll accounts.

History

First Paid Salary

While there is no first pay stub for the first work-for-pay

exchange, the first salaried work would have required a human society advanced enough to have a barter system to allow work to be exchanged for goods or other work. More significantly, it presupposes the existence of organized employers—perhaps a government or a religious body—that would facilitate work-for-hire exchanges on a regular enough basis to constitute salaried work. From this, most infer that the first salary would have been paid in a village or city during the Neolithic Revolution, sometime between 10,000 BC and 6,000 BC.

By the time of the Hebrew Book of Ezra (550 BC to 450 BC), accepting salt from a person was synonymous with drawing sustenance, taking pay, or being in that person's service. At that time salt production was strictly controlled by the monarchy or ruling elite. Depending on the translation of Ezra 4:14, the servants of King Artaxerxes I of Persia explain their loyalty variously as "because we are salted with the salt of the palace" or "because we have maintenance from the king" or "because we are responsible to the king."

The Roman Word Salarium

Similarly, the Roman word *salarium* linked employment, salt and soldiers, but the exact link is unclear. The least common theory is that the word soldier itself comes from the Latin *sal dare* (to give salt). Alternatively, the Roman historian Pliny the Elder stated as an aside in his Natural History's discussion of sea water, that "[I]n Rome...the soldier's pay was originally salt and the word salary derives from it..." *Plinius Naturalis Historia XXXI*. Others note that *soldier* more likely derives from the gold solidus, with which soldiers were known to have been paid, and maintain instead that the *salarium* was either an allowance for the purchase of salt or the price of having soldiers conquer salt supplies and guard the Salt Roads (*Via Salarium*) that led to Rome.

Payment in the Roman Empire and Medieval and Pre-industrial Europe

Regardless of the exact connection, the *salarium* paid to Roman soldiers has defined a form of work-for-hire ever since in the Western world, and gave rise to such expressions as "being worth one's salt." Yet within the Roman Empire or (later) medieval and pre-industrial Europe and its mercantile colonies, salaried employment appears to have been relatively rare and mostly limited to servants and higher status roles, especially in government service. Such roles were largely remunerated by the provision of lodging and food, and livery clothes, but cash was also paid. Many courtiers, such as valets de chambre in late medieval courts were paid annual amounts, sometimes supplemented by large if unpredictable extra payments. At the other end of the social scale, those in many forms of employment either received no pay, as with slavery (though many slaves were paid some money at least), serfdom, and indentured servitude, or received only a fraction of what was produced, as with sharecropping. Other common alternative models of work included self-or co-operative employment, as with masters in artisan guilds, who often had salaried assistants, or corporate work and ownership, as with medieval universities and monasteries.

Payment During the Commercial Revolution

Even many of the jobs initially created by the Commercial Revolution in the years from 1520 to 1650 and later during Industrialisation in the 18th and 19th centuries would not have been salaried, but, to the extent they were paid as employees, probably paid an hourly or daily wage or paid per unit produced (also called piece work).

Share in Earnings as Payment

In corporations of this time, such as the several East India Companies, many managers would have been remunerated as owner-shareholders. Such a remuneration scheme is still common today in accounting, investment, and law firm partnerships where the leading professionals are equity partners, and do not technically receive a salary, but rather make a periodic "draw" against their share of annual earnings.

The Second Industrial Revolution and Salaried Payment

From 1870 to 1930, the Second Industrial Revolution gave

rise to the modern business corporation powered by railroads, electricity and the telegraph and telephone. This era saw the widespread emergence of a class of salaried executives and administrators who served the new, large-scale enterprises being created.

New managerial jobs lent themselves to salaried employment, in part because the effort and output of "office work" were hard to measure hourly or piecewise, and in part because they did not necessarily draw remuneration from share ownership.

As Japan rapidly industrialized in the 20th century, the idea of office work was novel enough that a new Japanese word (salaryman), was coined to describe those who performed it, and their remuneration.

Salaried Employment in the 20th Century

In the 20th century, the rise of the service economy made salaried employment even more common in developed countries, where the relative share of industrial production jobs declined, and the share of executive, administrative, computer, marketing, and creative jobs—all of which tended to be salaried—increased.

Salary and other Forms of Payment Today

Today, the idea of a salary continues to evolve as part of a system of all the combined rewards that employers offer to employees. Salary is coming to be seen as part of a "total rewards" system which includes bonuses, incentive pay, and commissions), benefits and perquisites (or perks), and various other tools which help employers link rewards to an employee's measured performance.

Salaries in the U.S.

In the United States, the distinction between periodic salaries (which are normally paid regardless of hours worked) and hourly wages (meeting a minimum wage test and providing for overtime) was first codified by the Fair Labour Standards Act of 1938. At that time, five categories were identified as being "exempt" from minimum wage and overtime protections, and therefore salariable. In 1991, some computer workers were added as a sixth category but effective August 23, 2004 the categories were revised and reduced back down to five (Executive, Administrative, Professional, Computer, and Outside Sales Employees). Salary is generally set on a yearly basis.

"The FLSA requires that most employees in the United States be paid at least the federal minimum wage for all hours worked and overtime pay at time and one-half the regular rate of pay for all hours worked over 40 hours in a workweek.

However, Section 13(a)(1) of the FLSA provides an exemption from both minimum wage and overtime pay for employees employed as bona fide executive, administrative, professional and outside sales employees. Section 13(a)(1) and Section 13(a)(17) also exempt certain computer employees. To qualify for exemption, employees generally must meet certain tests regarding their job duties *and* be paid on a salary basis at not less than $455 per week."

Of these five categories only Computer Employees has an hourly wage-based exemption ($27.63 per hour) while Outside Sales Employee is the only main category not to have the minimum salary ($455 per week) test though some sub categories under Professional (like teachers and practitioners of law or medicine) also do not have the minimum salary test.

A general rule for comparing periodic salaries to hourly wages is based on a standard 40 hour work week with 50 weeks per year (minus two weeks for vacation). (Example: $40,000/ year periodic salary divided by 50 weeks equals $800/week. Divide $800/week by 40 standard hours equals $20/hour). Real median household income in the United States climbed 1.3 percent between 2006 and 2007, reaching $50,233 according to a report released by the U.S. census bureau. This is the third annual increase in real median household income.

Salaries in Japan

In Japan, owners would notify employees of salary increases through "jirei". The concept still exists and has been replaced with an electronic form, or email in larger companies.

Salaries in India

In India, Salaries are generally paid on the 7th of every month. The minimum wages in India are governed by the Minimum Wages Act, 1948.

Training

The term *training* refers to the acquisition of knowledge, skills, and competencies as a result of the teaching of vocational or practical skills and knowledge that relate to specific useful competencies. It forms the core of apprenticeships and provides the backbone of content at institutes of technology (also known as technical colleges or polytechnics). In addition to the basic training required for a trade, occupation or profession, observers of the labour-market recognize today the need to continue training beyond initial qualifications: to maintain, upgrade and update skills throughout working life. People within many professions and occupations may refer to this sort of training as professional development.

Some commentators use a similar term for workplace learning to improve performance: training and development. One can generally categorize such training as *on-the-job* or *off-the-job*:

- On-the-job training takes place in a normal working situation, using the actual tools, equipment, documents or materials that trainees will use when fully trained. On-the-job training has a general reputation as most effective for vocational work.
- Off-the-job training takes place away from normal work situations — implying that the employee does not count as a directly productive worker while such training takes place. Off-the-job training has the advantage that it allows people to get away from work and concentrate more thoroughly on the training itself. This type of training has proven more effective in inculcating concepts and ideas.

Training differs from exercise in that people may dabble in exercise as an occasional activity for fun. Training has specific goals of improving one's capability, capacity, and performance.

Compare:

- Education
- Learning.

Types of Training

Physical Training

Physical training concentrates on mechanistic goals: training-programs in this area develop specific skills or muscles, often with a view to peaking at a particular time. Some physical training programs focus on raising overall physical fitness.

In military use, training means gaining the physical ability to perform and survive in combat, and learning the many skills needed in a time of war. These include how to use a variety of weapons, outdoor survival skills, and how to survive capture by the enemy, among others.

For psychological or physiological reasons, people who believe it may be beneficial to them can choose to practice relaxation training, or autogenic training, in an attempt to increase their ability to relax or deal with stress. While some studies have indicated relaxation training is useful for some medical conditions, autogenic training has limited results or has been the result of few studies.

Religion and Spirituality

In religious and spiritual use, training may refer to the purification of the mind, heart, understanding and actions to obtain a variety of spiritual goals such as closeness to God or freedom from suffering. Note for example the institutionalized spiritual training of Threefold Training in Buddhism, or discipleship in Christianity.

Artificial-intelligence Feedback

Researchers have developed training-methods for artificial-intelligence devices as well. Evolutionary algorithms, including genetic programming and other methods of machine learning, use a system of feedback based on "fitness functions" to allow computer programs to determine how well an entity performs a task. The methods construct a series of programs, known as a "population" of programs, and then automatically test them for "fitness", observing how well they perform the intended task. The system automatically generates new programs based on members of the population that perform the best. These new members replace programs that perform the worst. The procedure repeats until the achievement of optimum performance. In robotics, such a system can continue to run in real-time after initial training, allowing robots to adapt to new situations and to changes in themselves, for example, due to wear or damage. Researchers have also developed robots that can appear to mimic simple human behaviour as a starting point for training.

Apprenticeship

Apprenticeship is a system of training a new generation of practitioners of a skill. Apprentices (or in early modern usage "prentices") or protégés build their careers from apprenticeships. Most of their training is done on the job while working for an employer who helps the apprentices learn their trade, in exchange for their continuing labour for an agreed period after they become skilled. Theoretical education may also be involved, informally via the workplace and/or by attending vocational schools while still being paid by the employer.

Development

The system of apprenticeship first developed in the later Middle Ages and came to be supervised by craft guilds and town governments. A master craftsman was entitled to employ young people as an inexpensive form of labour in exchange for providing food, lodging and formal training in the craft.

Most apprentices were males, but female apprentices were found in crafts such as seamstress, tailor, cordwainer, baker and stationer. Apprentices usually began at ten to fifteen years of age, and would live in the master craftsman's household. Most apprentices aspired to becoming master craftsmen themselves on completion of their contract (usually a term of seven years), but some would spend time as a journeyman and a significant proportion would never acquire their own workshop.

Subsequently governmental regulation and the licensing of polytechnics and vocational education formalized and bureaucratized the details of apprenticeship.

Analogs at Universities and Professional Development

The modern concept of an internship is similar to an apprenticeship. Universities still use apprenticeship schemes in their production of scholars: bachelors are promoted to masters and then produce a thesis under the oversight of a supervisor before the corporate body of the university recognises the achievement of the standard of a doctorate. Another view of this system is of graduate students in the role of apprentices, post-docs as journeymen, and professors as masters.

Also similar to apprenticeships are the professional development arrangements for new graduates in the professions of accountancy and the law. A British example was training contracts known as 'articles of clerkship'. The learning curve in modern professional service firms, such as law firms or accountancies, generally resembles the traditional master-apprentice model: the newcomer to the firm is assigned to one or several more experienced colleagues (ideally partners in the firm) and learns his skills on the job.

Australia

Australian Apprenticeships is the new name for the scheme formerly known as 'New Apprenticeships'. Under the scheme, involving 400,000 people in 500 occupations, the Australian Government incentives and personal benefits programme are still the same. Australian Apprenticeships still encompass all apprenticeships and traineeships. They combine time at work with training and can be full-time, part-time or school-based. Youth can become apprentices starting as early as age 14 if there are willing employers.

As part of its policy paper-Skilling Australia for the Future, the Australian Government announced that it will expand the role of existing Australian Apprenticeships Centres to establish the Skills and Training Information Centres (STICs), providing information and advice skills & training.

Australian Apprenticeships is the generic term for apprentices and trainees. The distinction between the two lies mainly around traditional trades and the time it takes to gain a qualification. The Australian government uses Australian Apprenticeships Centres such as BUSY At Work or MEGT (Australia) to administer and facilitate the Australian Apprenticeships so that funding can be disseminated to eligible businesses and apprentices and trainees and to support the whole process as it underpins the future skills of Australian industry. Australia also has a fairly unique safety net in place for businesses and Australian Apprentices with its Group Training scheme. This is where businesses that are not able to employ the Australian Apprentice for the full period until they qualify, are able to lease or hire the Australian Apprentice from a Group Training Organisation. It's a safety net because the Group Training Organisation is the employer and provides continuity of employment and training for the Australian Apprentice.

Austria

Apprenticeship Training in Austria is organized in a Dual education system: company-based training of apprentices is complemented by compulsory attendance of a part-time vocational school for apprentices (Berufsschule). It lasts two to four years-the duration varies between the 250 different legally recognized apprenticeship trades.

About 40 percent of all Austrian teenagers enter apprenticeship training upon completion of compulsory education (at age 15). This number has been stable since the 1950s.

The five most popular trades are: Retail Salesperson (5,000 people complete this apprenticeship per year), Clerk (3,500/year), Car Mechanic (2,000/year), Hairdresser (1,700/year), Cook (1,600/year). There are many smaller trades with small numbers of apprentices, like "EDV-Systemtechniker" (Sysadmin) which is completed by less than 100 people a year.

The Apprenticeship Leave Certificate provides the apprentice with access to two different vocational careers. On the one hand, it is a prerequisite for the admission to the Master Craftsman Exam and for qualification tests, and on the other hand it gives access to higher education via the TVE-Exam or the Higher Education Entrance Exam which are prerequisites for taking up studies at colleges, universities, "Fachhochschulen", post-secondary courses and post-secondary colleges.

The person responsible for overseeing the training inside the company is called "Lehrherr" or "Ausbilder". An Ausbilder must prove he has the professional qualifications needed to educate another person. The "Ausbilder" must also prove he does not have a criminal record and is an otherwise respectable person. According to the laws: *the person wanting to educate a young apprentice must prove that he has an ethical way of living and the civic qualities of a good citizen.*

France

In France, apprenticeships also developed between the ninth and thirteenth centuries, with guilds structured around apprentices, journeymen and master craftsmen, continuing in this way until 1791, when the guilds were suppressed.

In 1851 the first law on apprenticeships came into force because people would kill other people. From 1919, young people had to take 150 hours of theory and general lessons in their subject a year. This minimum training time rose to 360 hours a year in 1961, then 400 in 1986.

The first training centres for apprentices (*centres de formation d'apprentis*, CFAs) appeared in 1961, and in 1971 apprenticeships were legally made part of professional training. In 1986 the age limit for beginning an apprenticeship was raised from 20 to 25. From 1987 the range of qualifications achieveable through an apprenticeship was widened to include the *brevet professionnel* (certificate of vocational aptitude), the *bac professionnel* (vocational baccalaureate diploma), the *brevet de technicien supérieur*(advanced technician's certificate), engineering diplomas, masters degree and more.

On January 18, 2005, President Jacques Chirac announced the introduction of a law on a programme for social cohesion comprising the three pillars of employment, housing and equal opportunities. The French government pledged to further develop apprenticeship as a path to success at school and to employment, based on its success: in 2005, 80% of young French people who had completed an apprenticeship entered employment. In France, the term apprenticeship often denotes manual labour but it also include other jobs like secretary, manager, engineer, shop assistant... The plan aimed to raise the number of apprentices from 365,000 in 2005 to 500,000 in 2009. To achieve this aim, the government is, for example, granting tax relief for companies when they take on apprentices. (Since 1925 a tax has been levied to pay for apprenticeships.) The minister in charge of the campaign, Jean-Louis Borloo, also hoped to improve the image of apprenticeships with an information campaign, as they are often connected with academic failure at school and an ability to grasp only practical skills and not theory. After the civil unrest end of 2005, the government, led by prime minister Dominique de Villepin, announced a new law. Dubbed "law on equality of chances", it created the First Employment Contract as well as manual apprenticeship from as early as 14 years of age. From this age, students are allowed to quit the compulsory school system in order to quickly learn a vocation. This measure has long been a policy of conservative French political parties, and was met by tough opposition from trade unions and students.

Germany

Apprenticeships are part of Germany's dual education system, and as such form an integral part of many people's working life. Finding employment without having completed an apprenticeship is almost impossible. For some particular technical university professions, such as food technology, a completed apprenticeship is often recommended; for some, such as marine engineering it may even be mandatory.

In Germany, there are 342 recognized trades (*Ausbildungsberufe*) where an apprenticeship can be completed. They include for example doctor's assistant, banker, dispensing optician, plumber or oven builder. The dual system means that apprentices spend about 50-70% of their time in companies and the rest in formal education. Depending on the profession, they may work for three to four days a week in the company and then spend one or two days at a vocational school (*Berufsschule*). This is usually the case for trade and craftspeople. For other professions, usually which require more theoretical learning, the working and school times take place blockwise e.g. in a 12–18 weeks interval. These *Berufsschulen* have been part of the education system since the 19th century.

In 2001, two thirds of young people aged under 22 began an apprenticeship, and 78% of them completed it, meaning that approximately 51% of all young people under 22 have completed an apprenticeship. One in three companies offered apprenticeships in 2003, in 2004 the government signed a pledge with industrial unions that all companies except very small ones must take on apprentices.

The latent decrease of the German population due to low birth rates is now causing a lack of young people available to start an apprenticeship.

Apprenticeship after General Education

After graduation from school at the age of fifteen to nineteen (depending on type of school), students start an apprenticeship in their chosen professions. Realschule and Gymnasium graduates usually have better chances for being accepted as an apprentice for sophisticated craft professions or apprenticeships in white-collar jobs in finance or administration.

An apprenticeship takes between 2,5 and 3,5 years. Originally, at the beginning of the 20th century, less than 1% of German students attended the Gymnasium (the 8-9 year university-preparatory school) to obtain the Abitur graduation which was the only way to university back then. In the 1950 still only 5% of German youngsters entered university and in 1960 only 6% did. Due to the risen social wealth and the increased demand for academic professionals in Germany, about 24% of the youngsters entered college/university in 2000. Of those, who did not enter university many started an apprenticeship. The apprenticeships usually end a person's education by age 18-20, but also older apprentices are accepted by the employers under certain conditions. This is frequently the case for immigrants from countries without an compatible professional training system. In the U.S. apprenticeships could occur at any age.

History

In 1969, a law (the *Berufsbildungsgesetz*) was passed which regulated and unified the vocational training system and codified the shared responsibility of the state, the unions, associations and the chambers of trade and industry. The dual system was successful in both parts of the divided Germany. In the GDR, three quarters of the working population had completed apprenticeships.

Business and Administrative Professions

The precise skills and theory taught on German apprenticeships are strictly regulated. The employer is responsible for the entire education programme coordinated by the german chamber of commerce. Apprentices obtain a special apprenticeship contract until the end of the education programme.

During the programme it is not allowed to assign the apprentice to a regularly employment and he is well protected from abrupt dismissal until the programme ends. The defined content and skillset of the apprentice profession must be fully provided and taught by the employer. The time taken is also regulated. Each profession takes a different time, usually between 24 and 36 months.

Thus, everyone who had e.g. completed an apprenticeship as an industrial manager (*Industriekaufmann*) has learned the same skills and has attended the same courses in procurement and stocking up, controlling, staffing, accounting procedures, production planning, terms of trade and transport logistics and various other subjects. Someone who has not taken this apprenticeship or did not pass the final examinations at the chamber of industry and commerce is not allowed to call himself an *Industriekaufmann*. Most job titles are legally standardized and restricted. An employment in such function in any company would require this completed degree.

Trade and Craft Professions

The rules and laws for the trade and craftswork apprentices such as mechanics, bakers, joiners, etc. are as strict as and even broader than for the business professions. The involved procedures, titles and traditions still strongly reflect the medieval origin of the system. Here, the average duration is about 36 months, some specialized crafts even take up to 42 months. After completion of the dual education, e.g. a baker is allowed to call himself a bakery journeyman (*Bäckereigeselle*). After the apprenticeship the journeyman can enter the master's school (*Meisterschule*) and continue his education at evening courses for 3–4 years or full-time for about one year. The graduation from the master's school leads to the title of a master craftsman (*Meister*) of his profession, so e.g. a bakery master is entitled as *Bäckermeister*. A master is officially entered in the local trade register, the craftspeople's roll (*Handwerksrolle*). A master craftsman is allowed to employ and to train new apprentices. In some mostly safety-related professions, e.g. that of electricians only a master is allowed to found his own company.

License for Educating Apprentices

To employ and to educate apprentices requires a specific license. The AdA-*Ausbildung der Ausbilder*-"Education of the Educators" license needs to be acquired by a training at the chamber of industry and commerce.

The masters complete this license course within their own master's coursework. The training and examination of new masters is only possible for masters who have been working several years in their profession and who have been accepted by the chambers as a trainer and examiner.

Academic professionals, e.g. engineers, seeking this license need to complete the AdA during or after their university studies, usually by a one-year evening course.

The holder of the license is only allowed to train apprentices within his own field of expertise. For example a mechanical engineer would be able to educate industrial mechanics, but not e.g. laboratory assistants or civil builders.

After the Apprenticeship of Trade and Craft Professions

When the apprenticeship is ended, the former apprentice now is considered a journeyman. He may choose to go on his journeyman years-travels.

India

In India, the Apprentices Act was enacted in 1961. It regulates the programme of training of apprentices in the industry so as to conform to the syllabi, period of training etc. as laid down by the Central Apprenticeship Council and to utilise fully the facilities available in industry for imparting practical training with a view to meeting the requirements of skilled manpower for industry.

The Apprentices Act enacted in 1961 and was implemented effectively in 1962. Initially the Act envisaged training of trade apprentices. The Act was amended in 1973 to include training of graduate and diploma engineers as "Graduate" & "Technician" Apprentices. The Act was further amended in 1986 to bring within its purview the training of the 10+2 vocational stream as "Technician (Vocational)" Apprentices.

Overall responsibility is with the Directorate General of Employment & Training (DGE&T) in the Union Ministry of Labour.

DGE&T is also responsible for implementation of the Act in respect of Trade Apprentices in the Central Govt. Undertakings & Departments. This is done through six Regional Directorates of Apprenticeship Training located at Kolkata, Mumbai, Chennai, Hyderabad, Kanpur & Faridabad.

State Apprenticeship Advisers are responsible for implementation of the Act in respect of Trade Apprentices in State Government Undertakings/Departments and Private Establishments. Department of Education in the Ministry of HRD is responsible for implementation of the Act in respect of Graduate, Technician & Technician (Vocational) Apprentices. This is done through four Boards of Apprenticeship Training located at Kanpur, Kolkata, Mumbai & Chennai.

Pakistan

In Pakistan, special apprenticeship programs running to fulfill the needs of IT industry in the coming years. So, for this purpose Pakistan Software Export Board formerly PSEB has launched a very attractive program for young IT graduates.

Under the IT Industry Apprenticeship Program, PSEB offers financial subsidy for the companies to recruit graduates possessing the basic skills and knowledge in Information Technology and other related disciplines to provide IT/ITeS services.

These recruits, generally graduates with some experience rather than traditional apprentices, are hired by companies as full-time employees and put through a 12-month program, consisting of in-company training, on-the-job training and mentoring. Since its launch, the IT Industry Apprenticeship Program has been awarded to 7 companies, approved by PSEB and ICT R&D Fund's Project Committee, which will result in the creation of over 700 job opportunities in the IT industry.

Turkey

In Turkey, apprenticeship has been part of the small business culture for centuries since the time of Seljuk Turks who claimed Anatolia as their homeland in 11th century.

There are three levels of apprenticeship. First level is the apprentice, i.e. the "cirak" in Turkish. The second level is pre-master which is called, "kalfa" in Turkish. The mastery level is called as "usta" and is the highest level of achievement. An 'usta' is eligible to take in and accept new 'ciraks' to train and bring them up. The training process usually starts when the small boy is of age 10-11 and becomes a full grown master at the age of 20-25. Many years of hard work and disciplining under the authority of the master is the key to the young apprentice's education and learning process.

In Turkey today there are many vocational schools that train children to gain skills to learn a new profession. The student after graduation looks for a job at the nearest local marketplace usually under the authority of a master.

United Kingdom

Apprenticeships have a long tradition in the United Kingdom, dating back to around the 12th century and flourishing by the 14th century. The parents or guardians of a minor would agree with a Guild's Master craftsman the conditions for an apprenticeship which would bind the minor for 5–9 years. They would pay a premium to the craftsman and the contract would be recorded in an indenture. In 1563, the Statute of Artificers and Apprentices was passed to regulate and protect the apprenticeship system, forbidding anyone from practising a trade or craft without first serving a 7-year period as an apprentice to a master (though in practice Freemen's sons could negotiate shorter terms).

From 1601, 'parish' apprenticeships under the Elizabethan Poor Law came to be used as a way of providing for poor, illegitimate and orphaned children of both sexes alongside the regular system of skilled apprenticeships, which tended to provide for boys from slightly more affluent backgrounds. These parish apprenticeships, which could be created with the assent of two Justices of the Peace, supplied apprentices for occupations of lower status such as farm labouring, brickmaking and menial household service.

In the early years of the Industrial Revolution entrepreneurs began to resist the restrictions of the apprenticeship system, and a legal ruling established that the Statute of Apprentices did not apply to trades that were not in existence when it was passed in 1563, thus excluding many new 18th century industries. In 1814 compulsory apprenticeship by indenture was abolished.

In modern times, apprenticeship became less important, especially as employment in heavy industry and artisan trades declined. Traditional apprenticeships reached their lowest point in the 1970s: by that time, training programmes were rare and people who were apprentices learned mainly by example. In 1986, National Vocational Qualifications (NVQs) were introduced, in an attempt to revitalise vocational training. Still, by 1990, apprenticeship took up only two-thirds of one percent of total employment.

In 1994, the Government introduced Modern Apprenticeships (since renamed 'Apprenticeships' in England, Wales and Northern Ireland; Scotland has retained Modern Apprenticeship), based on frameworks that are now devised by Sector Skills Councils. Apprenticeship frameworks contain a number of separately-certified elements:

- a knowledge-based element, typically certified through a qualification known as a 'Technical Certificate' (this component is not mandatory in the Scottish Modern Apprenticeship);
- a competence-based element, typically certified through an NVQ (in Scotland this can be through an SVQ or an alternative Competence Based Qualification); and
- Key Skills (in Scotland, Core Skills).

In Scotland, Modern Apprenticeship Frameworks are approved by the Modern Apprenticeship Group (MAG) and it, with the support of the Scottish Government, has determined that from January 2010, all Frameworks submitted to it for approval, must have the mandatory elements credit rated for the Scottish Credit and Qualifications Framework (SCQF).

As of 2009 there are over 180 apprenticeship frameworks. Unlike traditional apprenticeships, the current scheme extends beyond craft and skilled trades to parts of the service sector with no apprenticeship tradition. The Department for Children, Schools and Families has stated its intention to make apprenticeships a "mainstream" part of England's education system.

Employers who offer apprenticeship places have an employment contract with their apprentices, but off-the-job training and assessment is wholly funded by the state for apprentices aged between 16 and 18. In England, Government only contributes 50% of the cost of training for apprentices aged 19 and over.

Government funding agencies (in England, the Learning and Skills Council) contract with 'learning providers' to deliver apprenticeships, and may accredit them as a Centre of Vocational Excellence or National Skills Academy. These organisations provide off-the-job tuition and manage the bureaucratic workload associated with the apprenticeships. Providers are usually private training companies but might also be Further Education colleges, voluntary sector organisations, Chambers of Commerce or employers themselves.

United States

Apprenticeship programs in the United States are regulated by the National Apprenticeship Act, also known as the "Fitzgerald Act."

American Apprenticeship Educational Regime

In the United States, education officials and nonprofit organizations who seek to emulate the apprenticeship system in other nations have created school to work education reforms. They seek to link academic education to careers. Some programs include job shadowing, watching a real worker for a short period of time, or actually spending significant time at a job at no or reduced pay that would otherwise be spent in academic classes or working at a local business. Some legislators raised the issue of child labour laws for unpaid labour or jobs with hazards.

In the United States, school to work programs usually occur only in high school. American high schools were introduced in the early 20th century to educate students of all ability and interests in one learning community rather than prepare a small number for college. Traditionally, American students are tracked within a wide choice of courses based on ability, with vocational courses (such as auto repair and carpentry) tending to be at the lower end of academic ability and trigonometry and pre-calculus at the upper end.

American education reformers have sought to end such tracking, which is seen as a barrier to opportunity. By contrast, the system studied by the NCEE actually relies much more heavily on tracking. Education officials in the U.S., based largely on school redesign proposals by NCEE and other organizations, have chosen to use criterion-referenced tests that define one high standard that must be achieved by all students to receive a uniform diploma. American education policy under the "No

Child Left Behind Act" has as an official goal the elimination of the achievement gap between populations. This has often led to the need for remedial classes in college.

Many U.S. states now requiring passing a high school graduation examination to ensure that students across all ethnic, gender and income groups possess the same skills. In states such as Washington, critics have questioned whether this ensures success for all or just creates massive failure (as only half of all 10th graders have demonstrated they can meet the standards).

There is a movement in the U.S. to revive vocational education. For example, the International Union of Painters and Allied Trades (IUPAT) has opened the Finishing Trades Institute (FTI). The FTI is working towards national accreditation so that it may offer associate and bachelor degrees that integrate academics with a more traditional apprentice programs. The IUPAT has joined forces with the Professional Decorative Painters Association (PDPA) to build educational standards using a model of apprenticeship created by the PDPA.

Example of a U.S. Apprenticeship Program

Persons interested in learning to become electricians can join one of several apprenticeship programs offered jointly by the International Brotherhood of Electrical Workers and the National Electrical Contractors Association. No background in electrical work is required. A minimum age of 18 is required. There is no maximum age. Men and women are equally invited to participate. The organization in charge of the program is called the National Joint Apprenticeship and Training Committee.

Apprentice electricians work 37 to 40 hours per week at the trade under the supervision of a journeyman electrician and receive pay and benefits. They spend an additional 6 hours per week in classroom training. At the conclusion of training (five years for commercial and industrial construction, less for residential construction), apprentices become journeymen (and women). All of this is offered at no charge, except for the cost of books (which is approximately $200 per year). Persons completing this program are considered highly skilled by employers and command high pay and benefits. Other unions such as the Ironworkers, Sheet Metal Workers, Plasterers, Bricklayers and others offer similar programs.

Trade associations such as the Independent Electrical Contractors and Associated Builders and Contractors also offer a variety of apprentice training programs.

Professional Development

Professional development refers to skills and knowledge attained for both personal development and career advancement. Professional development encompasses all types of facilitated learning opportunities, ranging from college degrees to formal coursework, conferences and informal learning opportunities situated in practice. It has been described as intensive and collaborative, ideally incorporating an evaluative stage There are a variety of approaches to professional development, including consultation, coaching, communities of practice, lesson study, mentoring, reflective supervision and technical assistance.

Who Participates and Why

A wide variety of people, such as teachers, military officers and non-commissioned officers, health care professionals, lawyers, accountants and engineers engage in professional development. Individuals may participate in professional development because of an interest in lifelong learning, a sense of moral obligation, to maintain and improve professional competence, enhance career progression, keep abreast of new technology and practice, or to comply with professional regulatory organizations. Many American states have professional development requirements for school teachers. For example, Arkansas teachers must complete 60 hours of documented professional development activities annually. Professional development credits are named differently from state to state. For example, teachers: in Indiana are required to earn 90 Continuing Renewal Units (CRUs) per year; in Massachusetts, need 150 Professional Development Points (PDPs); and in Georgia, must earn 10 Professional Learning

Units (PLUs). American and Canadian nurses, as well as those in the United Kingdom, are required to participate in formal and informal professional development (earning Continuing education units, or CEUs) in order to maintain professional registration. Other groups such as engineering and geoscience regulatory bodies also have mandatory professional development requirements.

Approaches to Professional Development

In a broad sense, professional development may include *formal* types of vocational education, typically post-secondary or poly-technical training leading to qualification or credential required to obtain or retain employment. Professional development may also come in the form of pre-service or in-service professional development programs. These programs may be formal, or informal, group or individualized. Individuals may pursue professional development independently, or programs may be offered by human resource departments. Professional development on the job may develop or enhance process skills, sometimes referred to as leadership skills, as well as task skills. Some examples for process skills are 'effectiveness skills', 'team functioning skills', and 'systems thinking skills'. Professional development opportunities can range from a single workshop to a semester-long academic course, to services offered by a medley of different professional development providers and varying widely with respect to the philosophy, content, and format of the learning experiences. Some examples of approaches to professional development include:

- Case Study Method-The case method is a teaching approach that consists in presenting the students with a case, putting them in the role of a decision maker facing a problem (Hammond 1976).
- Consultation-to assist an individual or group of individuals to clarify and address immediate concerns by following a systematic problem-solving process.
- Coaching-to enhance a person's competencies in a specific skill area by providing a process of observation, reflection, and action.

- Communities of Practice-to improve professional practice by engaging in shared inquiry and learning with people who have a common goal
- Lesson Study-to solve practical dilemmas related to intervention or instruction through participation with other professionals in systematically examining practice
- Mentoring-to promote an individual's awareness and refinement of his or her own professional development by providing and recommending structured opportunities for reflection and observation
- Reflective Supervision-to support, develop, and ultimately evaluate the performance of employees through a process of inquiry that encourages their understanding and articulation of the rationale for their own practices
- Technical Assistance-to assist individuals and their organization to improve by offering resources and information, supporting networking and change efforts

Professional development is a broad term, encompassing a range of people, interests and approaches. Those who engage in professional development share a common purpose of enhancing their ability to do their work. At the heart of professional development is the individual's interest in lifelong learning and increasing their own skills and knowledge. The 21st century has seen a significant growth in online professional development. Content providers incorporate collaborative platforms such as discussion boards and wikis, thereby encouraging and facilitating interaction, and optimizing training effectiveness.

Affirmative Action

Affirmative action refers to policies that take factors including "race, color, religion, sex or national origin" into consideration in order to benefit an underrepresented group, usually as a means to counter the effects of a history of discrimination. The focus of such policies ranges from employment and education to public contracting and health programs. "Affirmative action" is action taken to increase the representation of women and minorities in areas of employment, education, and business from which they have been historically excluded.

Origins

The term "affirmative action" originated in the United States, and first appeared in President John F. Kennedy's Executive Order 10925. The term was used to refer to measures to achieve non-discrimination. In 1965, President Lyndon Johnson issued Executive Order 11246 which required federal contractors to take "affirmative action" to hire without regard to race, religion and national origin. In 1968, gender was added to the anti-discrimination list. Matching procedures in other countries are also known as reservation in India, positive discrimination in the United Kingdom and employment equity in Canada.

Purpose

Affirmative action is an attempt to promote equal opportunity. It is often instituted in government and educational settings to ensure that minority groups within a society are included in all programs. The justification for affirmative action is to compensate for past discrimination, persecution or exploitation by the ruling class of a culture, or to address existing discrimination.

International Policies

The International Convention on the Elimination of All Forms of Racial Discrimination stipulates that affirmative action programs may be required of countries that have ratified the convention, in order to rectify systematic discrimination. It states, however, that such programs "shall in no case entail as a consequence the maintenance of unequal or separate rights for different racial groups after the objectives for which they were taken have been achieved." The United Nations Human/animals Rights Committee states, "the principle of equality sometimes requires States parties to take affirmative action in order to diminish or eliminate conditions which cause or help to perpetuate discrimination prohibited by the Covenant. For example, in a State where the general conditions of a certain part of the population prevent or impair their enjoyment of human rights, the State should take specific action to correct those conditions. Such action may involve granting for a time to the part of the population concerned certain preferential treatment in specific matters as compared with the rest of the population. However, as long as such action is needed to correct discrimination, in fact, it is a case of legitimate differentiation under the Covenant."

National Approaches

In some countries which have laws on racial equality, affirmative action is rendered illegal because it doesn't treat all races equally. This approach of equal treatment is sometimes described as being "color blind", in hopes that it is effective against discrimination without engaging in reverse discrimination.

In such countries, the focus tends to be on ensuring equal opportunity and, for example, targeted advertising campaigns to encourage ethnic minority candidates to join the police force. This is sometimes described as "positive action."

The Americas

- Brazil. Some Brazilian Universities (State and Federal) have created systems of preferred admissions (quotas) for racial minorities (blacks and native Brazilians), the poor and people with disabilities. There are already quotas of up to 20% of vacancies reserved for the disabled in the civil public services. The Democrats party, accusing the board of directors of University of Brasília of "nazism", questioned the constitutionality of the quotas the University reserves to minorities on the Supreme Federal Court.
- Canada. The equality section of the Canadian Charter of Rights and Freedoms explicitly permits affirmative action type legislation, although the Charter does not *require* legislation that gives preferential treatment. Subsection 2 of Section 15 states that the equality provisions do "not preclude any law, program or activity

that has as its object the amelioration of conditions of disadvantaged individuals or groups including those that are disadvantaged because of race, national or ethnic origin, colour, religion, sex, age or mental or physical disability." The Canadian Employment Equity Act requires employers in federally-regulated industries to give preferential treatment to four designated groups: Women, people with disabilities, aboriginal people, and visible minorities. In most Canadian Universities, people of Aboriginal background normally have lower entrance requirements and are eligible to receive exclusive scholarships. Some provinces and territories also have affirmative action-type polices. For example, in Northwest Territories in the Canadian north, aboriginal people are given preference for jobs and education and are considered to have P1 status. Non-aboriginal people who were born in the NWT or have resided half of their life there are considered a P2, as well as women and disabled people.

- United States. Affirmative action was first established in Executive Order 10925, which was signed by President John F. Kennedy on March 6, 1961 and required government contractors to "not discriminate against any employee or applicant for employment because of race, creed, color, or national origin" as well as to "take affirmative action to ensure that applicants are employed, and that employees are treated during employment, without regard to their race, creed, color, or national origin". This executive order was superseded by Executive Order 11246, which was signed by President Lyndon B. Johnson on September 24, 1965 and affirmed the Federal Government's commitment "to promote the full realization of equal employment opportunity through a positive, continuing program in each executive department and agency". It is notable that affirmative action was not extended to women until Executive Order 11375 amended Executive Order 11246 on October 13, 1967, expanding the definition to include "sex." As it currently stands, affirmative action through Executive Order 11246 applies to "race, color, religion, sex, or national origin." In the U.S., affirmative action's original purpose was to pressure institutions into compliance with the nondiscrimination mandate of the Civil Rights Act of 1964. The Civil Rights Acts do not cover veterans, people with disabilities, or people over 40. These groups are protected from discrimination under different laws. Affirmative action has been the subject of numerous court cases, and has been contested on constitutional grounds. In 2003, a Supreme Court decision concerning affirmative action in universities allowed educational institutions to consider race as a factor in admitting students, but ruled that strict point systems are unconstitutional. Conservatives say that state officials have widely disobeyed it. Alternatively, some colleges use financial criteria to attract racial groups that have typically been under represented and typically have lower living conditions. Some states such as California (California Civil Rights Initiative) and Michigan have passed constitutional amendments banning affirmative action within their respective states. A study conducted at the University of Chicago in 2003 found that people with "black-sounding" names such as Lakisha and Jamal are 50 percent less likely to be interviewed for a job compared to people with "white-sounding" names such as Emily or Greg.

South Asia

- India
- Sri Lanka: In 1971 the Standardization policy of Sri Lankan universities was introduced as an affirmative action program for students from areas which had poor educational facilities due to 200 years purposeful discrimination by British colonialists. The British had practised communal favoritism towards Christians and the minority Tamil community for the entire 200 years they had controlled Sri Lanka, as part of a policy of divide and conquer.

East Asia

- Japan: Admission to universities as well as all government positions (including teachers) are determined by the entrance exam, which is extremely competitive at the top level. It is illegal to include sex, ethnicity or other social background (but not nationality) in criteria; however, there are informal policies to provide employment and long term welfare (which is usually not available to general public) to Burakumin at municipality level.
- People's Republic of China: "Preferential policies" required some of the top positions in governments be distributed to ethnic minorities and women. Also, many universities are required by government to give preferred admissions to ethnic minorities.
- South Korea: Admission to universities is also determined by the strict entrance exam, which is extremely competitive at the top level. But most of all Korean universities at the top level are adapting some affirmative actions in cases of Chinese ethnic minority, North Korean refugees, etc. in their recruiting new students. Besides, national universities have been pressed by the Korean government, so now they are trying to meet the governmental goal which is to recruit a proportion of female professors.

South East Asia and Oceania

- Malaysia: The Malaysian New Economic Policy or NEP serves as a form of affirmative action. Malaysia is the only other country (other one being South Africa) in the world which provides affirmative action to the majority because in general, the Malays have lower income than the Chinese who have traditionally been involved businesses and industries. Malaysia is a multiethnic country, with Malays making up the majority of close to 52% of the population. About 30% of the population are Malaysians of Chinese descent, while Malaysians of Indian descent comprise about 8% of the population.

Government policy provides preferential placement for ethnic Malays, and 95% of all new intakes for the army, hospital nurses, police, and other government institutions are Malays. As of 2004, only 7% of all government servants are ethnic Chinese, a drop from 30% in 1960. All eight of the directors of the national petroleum company, Petronas, are Malays, and only 3% of Petronas employees are Chinese. Additionally, 95% of all government contracts are awarded to ethnic Malays. The mean income for Malays, Chinese and Indians in 1957/58 were 134, 288 and 228 respectively. In 1967/68 it was 154, 329 and 245, and in 1970 it was 170, 390 and 300. Mean income disparity ratio for Chinese/Malays rose from 2.1 in 1957/58 to 2.3 in 1970, whereas for Indians/Malays the disparity ratio also rose from 1.7 to 1.8 in the same period. The Malays viewed Independence as restoring their proper place in their own country's socioeconomic order while the non-Malays were opposing government efforts to advance Malay political primacy and economic welfare. The rising tension and resentment of the Malays for the Chinese and vice versa culminated in the vicious riots of 13 May 1969.

- New Zealand: Individuals of Mâori or other Polynesian descent are often afforded improved access to university courses, or have scholarships earmarked specifically for them.

Europe

- Finland: In certain university education programs, including legal and medical education, there are quotas for Swedish-speaking applicants. The aim of the quotas is to guarantee that a sufficient number of Swedish speaking professionals are educated, thus safeguarding the linguistic rights of the Swedish-speaking Finns. The quota system has met with criticism from the Finnish speaking majority, some of whom consider the system unfair. In addition to these linguistic quotas, women may get preferential treatment in recruitment for certain public sector jobs if there is a gender imbalance in the field.

- France: No distinctions based on race, religion or sex are allowed under the 1958 French Constitution. Since the 1980s, a French version of affirmative action based on neighbourhood is in place for primary and secondary education. Some schools, in neighborhoods labeled "Prioritary Education Zones", are granted more funds than the others. Students from these schools also benefit from special policies in certain institutions (such as Sciences Po). The French Ministry of Defence tried in 1990 to give more easily higher ranks and driving licenses to young French soldiers with North-African ancestry. After a strong protest by a young French lieutenant in the Ministry of Defence newspaper ("Armées d'aujourd'hui"), this driving license and rank project was cancelled. After the Sarkozy election, a new attempt in favour of Arabian-French students was made but Sarkozy did not gain enough political support to change the French constitution. However, highly ranked French schools do implement affirmative action in that they are obligated to take a certain amount of students from impoverished families.
- Germany: Article 3 of the German basic law provides for equal rights of all people regardless of sex, race or social background. There are programs stating that if men and women have equal qualifications, women have to be preferred for a job; moreover, the handicapped should be preferred to healthy people. This is typical for all positions in state and university service as of 2007, typically using the phrase "We try to increase diversity in this line of work". In recent years, there has been a long public debate about whether to issue programs that would grant women a privileged access to jobs in order to fight discrimination. Germany's *Left Party* brought up the discussion about affirmative action in Germany's school system. According to Stefan Zillich, quotas should be "a possibility" to help working class children who did not do well in school gain access to

a *Gymnasium* (University-preparatory school). Headmasters of *Gymnasien* have objected, saying that this type of policy would "be a disservice" to poor children.

In 2009 the Berlin Senate decided that Berlin's Gymnasium should no longer be allowed to handpick all of their students. It was ruled that while Gymnasien should be able to pick 70 % to 65 % of their students, the other places at the Gymnasien are to be allocated by lottery. Every child will be able to enter the lottery, no matter how he or she performed in primary school. It is hoped that this policy will increase the number of working class students attending a Gymnasium. The Left proposed that Berlin Gymnasien should no longer be allowed to expel students who perform poorly so that the students who won a Gymnasium place in the lottery have a fair chance of graduating from that school. It is not clear yet if Berlin's senate will decide in favour of The Lefts proposal. There is also a discussion going on if affirmative action should be employed to help the children and grandchildren of the so called Gastarbeiter gain better access to German universities. One prominent proponent of this was Lord Ralf Dahrendorf It is argued that the Gastarbeiter willingly came to Germany to help build the industry and this should be honored.

- Norway: In all public limited companies (PCL) boards, either gender should be represented by 40%. This affects roughly 400 companies.
- Republic of Macedonia: Minorities, most notably Albanians, are allocated quotas for access to state universities, as well as in civil public services.
- Romania: Roma people (gipsy) are allocated quotas for access to state universities.
- Slovakia: The Constitutional Court declared in October 2005 that affirmative action i.e. "providing advantages for people of an ethnic or racial minority group" as being against its Constitution.
- Sweden: Special treatments of certain groups are commonplace in Sweden. Leveraging of the opportunities of these groups is encouraged by the state.

One example is the police, who give women and people from other cultural and ethnic backgrounds concessions when it comes to testing for entrance to the police academy.

- United Kingdom: In the UK, any discrimination, quotas or favouritism on the grounds of sex, race and ethnicity is generally illegal in both education and employment. Specific exceptions include:
  - The 1998 Good Friday Agreement required that the Police Service of Northern Ireland recruit equal numbers of Catholics and Protestants in order to eliminate the service's perceived bias towards Protestants.
  - The Labour Party passed the Sex Discrimination (Election Candidates) Act 2002, allowing them to use all-women shortlists to select more women as election candidates.

South Africa

The Apartheid government favoured white-owned companies and as a result, the majority of companies in South Africa were, and still are owned by white people. The aforementioned policies achieved the desired results, but in the process they marginalised and excluded black people. A notable exception is the high number of businesses owned and operated by people of Indian descent-keen business people who thrived even under Apartheid laws due to their entrepreneurship and the political difficulties faced by them. Many people of Chinese ancestry in South Africa, also classified as "black" under the Apartheid government, also thrived through owning and operating their own businesses.

When the new majority government came to power in 1994, led by the ANC, they decided to implement an affirmative action campaign to correct previous imbalances. As such, the previously disenfranchised majority and minority groups are being supported by forcing the formerly privileged white minority group to implement certain policies. These policies include quotas regarding how much of the procurement is from non-white companies, how much of the equity is owned by non-whites, how many employees are non-white and what position the non-whites have.

The Employment Equity Act and the Broad Based Black Economic Empowerment Act aim to promote and achieve equality in the workplace (in South Africa termed "equity"), by not only advancing people from designated groups but also specifically dis-advancing the others. Those specifically hindered are the white minority. By legal definition, the designated groups who are to be advanced in society include all people of color, white women, people with disabilities, and people from rural areas. The term "black economic empowerment" is somewhat of a misnomer, therefore, because the acts cover empowerment of any member of the designated groups, regardless of race. However, government's employment legislation reserves 80% of new jobs for black people and favours black-owned companies. It is quota-based, with specific required outcomes. By a relatively complex scoring system, which allows for some flexibility in the manner in which each company meets its legal commitments, each company is required to meet minimum requirements in terms of representation by previously disadvantaged groups. The matters covered include equity ownership, representation at employee and management level (up to board of director level), procurement from black-owned businesses and social investment programs, amongst others. In 2008, the High Court in South Africa has ruled that Chinese South Africans are to be reclassified as black people. As a result of this ruling, ethnically Chinese citizens will be able to benefit from government Black Economic Empowerment (BEE) policies.

There is growing discontent in South Africa that the Broad Based Black Economic Empowerment Act has only enriched a select few black people in the country, generally those who were well-connected within the ANC so as to benefit from smart BEE deals and tender awarding, often thought to border on corruption. The same black people appear further enriched in each large BEE deal made in South Africa.

9

Performance Appraisal

A performance appraisal, employee appraisal, performance review, or (career) development discussion is a method by which the job performance of an employee is evaluated (generally in terms of quality, quantity, cost, and time) typically by the corresponding manager or supervisor.

A performance appraisal is a part of guiding and managing career development. It is the process of obtaining, analysing, and recording information about the relative worth of an employee to the organization. Performance appraisal is an analysis of an employee's recent successes and failures, personal strengths and weaknesses, and suitability for promotion or further training. It is also the judgement of an employee's performance in a job based on considerations other than productivity alone.

Aims

Generally, the aims of a performance appraisal are to:

- Give employees feedback on performance
- Identify employee training needs
- Document criteria used to allocate organizational rewards
- Form a basis for personnel decisions: salary increases, promotions, disciplinary actions, bonuses, etc.
- Provide the opportunity for organizational diagnosis and development

- Facilitate communication between employee and administration
- Validate selection techniques and human resource policies to meet federal Equal Employment Opportunity requirements.
- To improve performance through counselling, coaching and development.

Methods

A common approach to assessing performance is to use a numerical or scalar rating system whereby managers are asked to score an individual against a number of objectives/ attributes.

In some companies, employees receive assessments from their manager, peers, subordinates, and customers, while also performing a self assessment. This is known as a *360-degree appraisal* and forms good communication patterns. The most popular methods used in the performance appraisal process include the following:

- Management by objectives
- 360-degree appraisal
- Behavioural observation scale
- Behaviourally anchored rating scales.

Trait-based systems, which rely on factors such as integrity and conscientiousness, are also commonly used by businesses. The scientific literature on the subject provides evidence that assessing employees on factors such as these should be avoided.

The reasons for this are twofold:

1) Because trait-based systems are by definition based on personality traits, they make it difficult for a manager to provide feedback that can cause positive change in employee performance. This is caused by the fact that personality dimensions are for the most part static, and while an employee can change a specific behaviour they cannot change their personality. For example, a person who lacks integrity may stop lying to a manager because they have been caught, but they still have low integrity

and are likely to lie again when the threat of being caught is gone.

2) Trait-based systems, because they are vague, are more easily influenced by office politics, causing them to be less reliable as a source of information on an employee's true performance. The vagueness of these instruments allows managers to fill them out based on who they want to/feel should get a raise, rather than basing scores on specific behaviours employees should/should not be engaging in. These systems are also more likely to leave a company open to discrimination claims because a manager can make biased decisions without having to back them up with specific behavioural information.

Employment Integrity Testing

Integrity as defined by Webster's Dictionary is a firm adherence to a code of especially moral or artistic values. Some synonyms are uprightness, honesty, probity, rectitude, truthfulness, veracity, trustworthiness, fairness, honor, moral fiber, principle, soundness, wholeness, and oneness. All of these words describe the type of employee one would like to hire.

Integrity testing, pre employment screening, pre-employment screening tests, employee assessments, credibility testing and employment testing are all synonyms for the analyses used in detecting employee concealment. These tests are supplemental to background checks and can also be administered after candidates have started to work. With today's technology a well trained organization can objectively evaluate a candidate's potential both positive and negative. Industrial espionage is one of the most important security issues in the business world today and regular integrity testing can assist in the reduction of negligent hiring liability.

These supplemental tests can augment the requirement by all US states that require employers to complete criminal background checks for certain jobs, which may include teaching, childcare and healthcare professions that involve contact with vulnerable segments of our society. The advantage of the integrity test is that it does not require the access to a candidate's criminal records, it gives pertinent information about how that person measures up to the company's code of conduct. According to ADP and the United States Department of Justice (DOJ) pre employment screening has become commonplace and has gained popularity of the last 25 years.

US Laws

The US laws can be interpreted differently and privacy advocates are quick to point out what can and cannot be accessed by companies. However, by using a test that evaluates the candidate on the spot and does not require outside involvement eliminates those issues. Integrity tests evaluate the integrity of the candidate not whether the information on the resume is correct. For that reason this type of test is invaluable.

Pre Employment Screening Tests

Pre-employment screening tests are an invaluable tool to Human Resource Professionals. They enable the company to verify the veracity of the information provided to them by the potential employee. However, these background tests and credit checks require authorizations and may not create a correct profile of the candidate. Supplemental tests that can verify the characteristics. These tests are called Integrity Tests.

Periodic Employment Testing

This type of reusable testing enables employers to verify that the employees that are currently working are performing to the company's code of conduct. In addition it enables companies to obtain an accurate assessment of its' workforce.

Workplace Diversity

Cultural diversity includes the range of ways in which people experience a unique group identity, which includes gender, sexual orientation, race, ethnic and age. An organization's culture tends to determine the extent to which it is culturally diverse.

While diversity in the workplace brings about many benefits to an organization, it can also lead to many challenges. It is the responsibility of managers within organizations to use diversity as an influential resource in order to enhance organizational effectiveness. In the *Journal of Applied Behavioural Science,* C.L. Walck defines managing diversity in the workplace as "Negotiating interaction across culturally diverse groups, and contriving to get along in an environment characterized by cultural diversity".

In a journal entitled *The multicultural organization*, by Taylor Cox, Jr., Cox talks about three organization types which focus on the development on cultural diversity. The three organization types are: the monolithic organization, the plural organization, and the multicultural organization. In the monolithic organization, the amount of structural integration (the presence of persons from different cultural groups in a single organization) is very minimal. "In the United States, this organization usually represents white male majorities in the overall employee population with few women and minority men in management jobs". "The plural organization has a more heterogeneous membership than the monolithic organization and takes steps to be more inclusive of persons from cultural backgrounds that differ from the dominant group". The multicultural organization not only contains many different cultural groups, but it values this diversity.

Benefits of Diversity in the Workplace

Diversity is beneficial to both the organization and the members. Diversity brings substantial potential benefits such as better decision making and improved problem solving, greater creativity and innovation, which leads to enhanced product development, and more successful marketing to different types of customers. Simply recognizing diversity in a corporation helps link the variety of talents within the organization. The act of recognizing diversity also allows for those employees with these talents to feel needed and have a sense of belonging, which in turn increases their commitment to the company and allows each of them to contribute in a unique way. Diversity also provides organizations with the ability to compete in global markets. Diverse organizations will be successful as long as there is a sufficient amount of communication within them.

Because people from different cultures perceive messages in different ways, communication is vital to the performance of an organization. Miscommunication within a diverse workplace will lead to a great deal of challenges. Diversity is not only about preventing unfair discrimination and improving equality but also valuing differences and inclusion, spanning such areas as ethnicity, age, race, culture, sexual orientation, physical disability and religious belief.

Scott Page's (2007) mathematical modeling research of team work supports this view. He demonstrated that heterogeneous teams consistently out-performed homogeneous teams on a variety of tasks. Page points out that diversity in teamwork is not so simple in the messy real world. Too often the cultural differences create problems. The goal is to manage diversity to take full advantage of it.

Challenges of Diversity in the Workplace

There are challenges to managing a diverse work population. Managing diversity is more than simply acknowledging differences in people.

Many organizational theorists have suggested reasons that work-teams highly diverse in work-relevant characteristics can be difficult to motivate and manage. There are many challenges which face culturally diverse workplaces, and a major challenge is miscommunication within an organization. In an article entitled *Developing Receiver-Centered Communication in Diverse Organizations,* written by Judi Brownell, she explains that meanings of messages can never be completely shared because no two individuals experience events in exactly the same way. Even when native and non-native speakers are exposed to the same messages, they may interpret the information differently. It is necessary for employees who are less familiar with the primary language spoken within the organization to receive special attention in meeting their communication requirements. "In high context cultures, communicators share an experiential base that can be used to assign meanings to messages. Low context cultures, on the other hand, provide little information on which to base common understandings and so communicators must be explicit". Because of this fact, it is better to view all diverse organizational environments as low-context cultures.

Cultural bias is an additional factor which challenges culturally diverse work environments. Cultural bias includes both prejudice and discrimination. "Prejudice refers to negative attitudes toward an organization member based on his/her culture group identity, and discrimination refers to observable adverse behaviour for the same reason".

Another challenge faced by culturally diverse organizational environments is assimilation. According to the journal *Cultural Diversity in the Workplace: The State of the Field,* Marlene G. Fine explains that "Assimilation into the dominant organizational culture is a strategy that has had serious negative consequences for individuals in organizations and the organizations themselves. Those who assimilate are denied the ability to express their genuine selves in the workplace; they are forced to repress significant parts of their lives within a social context that frames a large part of their daily encounters with other people." She goes on to mention that "People who spend significant amounts of energy coping with an alien environment have less energy left to do their jobs. Assimilation does not just create a situation in which people who are different are likely to fail, it also decreases the productivity of organizations".

Creating the Multicultural Organization

"The key to managing a diverse workforce is increasing individual awareness of and sensitivity to differences of race, gender, social class, sexual orientation, physical ability, and age". There are several ways to go about creating the multicultural organization that performs extremely well.

In her article, Judi Brownell identifies three skills which help to develop effective communication in diverse organizational environments. These skills include self-monitoring, empathy, and strategic decision-making. Self-monitoring refers to a communicator's awareness of how his or her behaviour affects another person, and his or her willingness to modify this behaviour based on knowledge of its impact. Empathy enables the receiver to go beyond the literal meaning of a message and consider the communicator's feelings, values, assumptions, and needs. Strategic decision-making implies that the communication sources and channels used to reach organization members, as well as the substance of the messages conveyed, are mindfully selected.

Managing Diversity Tools

Managing diversity goes far beyond the limits of equal employment opportunity and affirmative action. High performing diversity managers recognize that specialized skills are necessary for creating a productive, diverse workforce. They seek out continuous learning opportunities and some go as far as acquiring certification. Managers must be willing to work towards changing the organization in order to create a culture of diversity and inclusion. Assessment skills and diversity education are key elements of culture change. However, the leadership's support of the change cannot be understated.

Implementation

Diversity issues change over time, depending on local historical and dynamic conditions. Overt "diversity programs" are usually limited to large employers, government agencies and businesses facing rapid demographic changes in their local labour pool and help people work and understand each other. The implementation of diversity is often limited to the Human resources department when there is also a good economic case for UK companies to use it as a tool to reach new market shares.

Legal Frameworks

US anti-discrimination laws prohibit employers giving any consideration to customers' preferences for being served by employees of a given gender, ethnic group, or color. In general, the laws also prevent consideration based on religion, although the law allows major exceptions of this provision for religious organizations. Many countries are also introducing anti-discrimination laws (for example the DDA in the UK) forcing companies to be more aware of diversity. The law student organization Building a Better Legal Profession generated significant controversy in October 2007 for reporting data suggesting that most private law firms themselves lacked demographic diversity.

Affirmative Action

Affirmative action refers to policies that take factors including "race, color, religion, sex or national origin" into consideration in order to benefit an underrepresented group, usually as a means to counter the effects of a history of discrimination. The focus of such policies ranges from employment and education to public contracting and health programs. "Affirmative action" is action taken to increase the representation of women and minorities in areas of employment, education, and business from which they have been historically excluded.

Origins

The term "affirmative action" originated in the United States, and first appeared in President John F. Kennedy's Executive Order 10925. The term was used to refer to measures to achieve non-discrimination. In 1965, President Lyndon Johnson issued Executive Order 11246 which required federal contractors to take "affirmative action" to hire without regard to race, religion and national origin. In 1968, gender was added to the anti-discrimination list. Matching procedures in other countries are also known as reservation in India, positive discrimination in the United Kingdom and employment equity in Canada.

Purpose

Affirmative action is an attempt to promote equal opportunity. It is often instituted in government and educational settings to ensure that minority groups within a society are included in all programs. The justification for affirmative action is to compensate for past discrimination, persecution or exploitation by the ruling class of a culture, or to address existing discrimination.

International Policies

The International Convention on the Elimination of All Forms of Racial Discrimination stipulates that affirmative action programs may be required of countries that have ratified the convention, in order to rectify systematic discrimination. It states, however, that such programs "shall in no case entail as a consequence the maintenance of unequal or separate rights for different racial groups after the objectives for which they were taken have been achieved." The United Nations Human/animals Rights Committee states, "the principle of equality sometimes requires States parties to take affirmative action in order to diminish or eliminate conditions which cause or help to perpetuate discrimination prohibited by the Covenant. For example, in a State where the general conditions of a certain part of the population prevent or impair their enjoyment of human rights, the State should take specific action to correct those conditions. Such action may involve granting for a time to the part of the population concerned certain preferential treatment in specific matters as compared with the rest of the population. However, as long as such action is needed to correct discrimination, in fact, it is a case of legitimate differentiation under the Covenant."

National Approaches

In some countries which have laws on racial equality, affirmative action is rendered illegal because it doesn't treat all races equally. This approach of equal treatment is sometimes described as being "color blind", in hopes that it is effective against discrimination without engaging in reverse discrimination.

In such countries, the focus tends to be on ensuring equal opportunity and, for example, targeted advertising campaigns to encourage ethnic minority candidates to join the police force. This is sometimes described as "positive action."

The Americas

- Brazil. Some Brazilian Universities (State and Federal) have created systems of preferred admissions (quotas) for racial minorities (blacks and native Brazilians), the poor and people with disabilities. There are already quotas of up to 20% of vacancies reserved for the disabled in the civil public services. The Democrats party, accusing the board of directors of University of Brasília of "nazism", questioned the constitutionality of the quotas the University reserves to minorities on the Supreme Federal Court.

- Canada. The equality section of the Canadian Charter of Rights and Freedoms explicitly permits affirmative action type legislation, although the Charter does not *require* legislation that gives preferential treatment. Subsection 2 of Section 15 states that the equality provisions do "not preclude any law, program or activity that has as its object the amelioration of conditions of disadvantaged individuals or groups including those that are disadvantaged because of race, national or ethnic origin, colour, religion, sex, age or mental or physical disability." The Canadian Employment Equity Act requires employers in federally-regulated industries to give preferential treatment to four designated groups: Women, people with disabilities, aboriginal people, and visible minorities. In most Canadian Universities, people of Aboriginal background normally have lower entrance requirements and are eligible to receive exclusive scholarships. Some provinces and territories also have affirmative action-type polices. For example, in Northwest Territories in the Canadian north, aboriginal people are given preference for jobs and education and are considered to have P1 status. Non-aboriginal people who were born in the NWT or have resided half of their life there are considered a P2, as well as women and disabled people.
- United States. Affirmative action was first established in Executive Order 10925, which was signed by President John F. Kennedy on March 6, 1961 and required government contractors to "not discriminate against any employee or applicant for employment because of race, creed, color, or national origin" as well

as to "take affirmative action to ensure that applicants are employed, and that employees are treated during employment, without regard to their race, creed, color, or national origin". This executive order was superseded by Executive Order 11246, which was signed by President Lyndon B. Johnson on September 24, 1965 and affirmed the Federal Government's commitment "to promote the full realization of equal employment opportunity through a positive, continuing program in each executive department and agency". It is notable that affirmative action was not extended to women until Executive Order 11375 amended Executive Order 11246 on October 13, 1967, expanding the definition to include "sex." As it currently stands, affirmative action through Executive Order 11246 applies to "race, color, religion, sex, or national origin." In the U.S., affirmative action's original purpose was to pressure institutions into compliance with the nondiscrimination mandate of the Civil Rights Act of 1964. The Civil Rights Acts do not cover veterans, people with disabilities, or people over 40. These groups are protected from discrimination under different laws. Affirmative action has been the subject of numerous court cases, and has been contested on constitutional grounds. In 2003, a Supreme Court decision concerning affirmative action in universities allowed educational institutions to consider race as a factor in admitting students, but ruled that strict point systems are unconstitutional. Conservatives say that state officials have widely disobeyed it. Alternatively, some colleges use financial criteria to attract racial groups that have typically been under represented and typically have lower living conditions. Some states such as California (California Civil Rights Initiative) and Michigan have passed constitutional amendments banning affirmative action within their respective states. A study conducted at the University of Chicago in 2003 found that people with "black-sounding" names such as Lakisha and Jamal are 50 percent less likely to be interviewed for a job compared to people with "white-sounding" names such as Emily or Greg.

South Asia

Reservation in India

Indian Government now Indian law provides for a quota system whereby a percentage of posts are reserved in employment in Government and in the public sector units, and in all public and private educational institutions, except in the religious/linguistic minority educational institutions, in order to mitigate backwardness of the socially and educationally backward communities and the Scheduled Castes and Tribes who do not have adequate representation in these services and institutions. The reservation policy is also extended to the Scheduled Castes and Scheduled Tribes for representation in the Parliament of India. The central government of India reserves 27% of higher education, and individual states may legislate further reservations. Reservation cannot be exceeded 50%, as per the rulings given by the supreme court, but certain Indian states like Rajasthan have proposed a 68 % reservation which includes a 14% reservation for forward castes.

Reservations are intended to increase the social diversity in campuses and workplaces by lowering the entry criteria for certain identifiable groups that are grossly under-represented in proportion to their numbers in the general population. Caste is the most used criteria to identify under-represented groups. However there are other identifiable criteria for under-representation—gender (women are under represented), state of domicile (North Eastern States, as Bihar and Uttar Pradesh are under-represented), rural people, etc. — as revealed by the Government of India sponsored National Family Health and National Sample surveys.

The underlying theory is that the under-representation of the identifiable groups is a legacy of the Indian caste system. After India gained independence, the Constitution of India listed some erstwhile groups as Scheduled Castes (SC) and Scheduled Tribes (ST). The framers of the Constitution believed that, due to the caste system, SCs and the STs were historically oppressed and denied respect and equal opportunity in Indian society and were thus under-represented in nation-building activities. The Constitution laid down 15% and 7.5% of vacancies to government aided educational institutes and for jobs in the government/public sector, as reserved quota for the SC and ST candidates respectively for a period of five years, after which the situation was to be reviewed. This period was routinely extended by the succeeding governments.

Later, reservations were introduced for other sections as well. The Supreme Court ruling that reservations cannot exceed 50% (which it judged would violate equal access guaranteed by the Constitution) has put a cap on reservations. However, there are state laws that exceed this 50% limit and these are under litigation in the Supreme Court. For example, the caste-based reservation fraction stands at 69% and is applicable to about 87% of the population in the state of Tamil Nadu.

Types of Reservation

Seats in educational institutions and jobs are reserved based on a variety of criteria. The quota system sets aside a proportion of all possible positions for members of a specific group. Those not belonging to the designated communities can compete only for the remaining positions, while members of the designated communities can compete for all positions (reserved and open). For example, when 2 out of 10 clerical positions in railways are reserved for ex-servicemen, those who have served in the Army can compete both in the General Category as well as in the specific quota.

Caste based

Seats are reserved for Schedules Castes, Scheduled Tribes, and Other Backward Castes (based chiefly on caste at birth) in varying ratio by the central government and state government. This caste is decided based on birth, and can never be changed. While a person can change his religion, and his economic status can fluctuate, the caste is permanent.

In central government funded higher education institutions, 22.5% of available seats are reserved for Scheduled Caste (Dalit) and Scheduled Tribe (Adivasi) students (15% for SCs, 7.5% for STs). This reservation percentage has been raised to 49.5%, by including an additional 27% reservation for OBCs 10. In AIIMS

14% of seats are reserved for SCs, 8% for STs. In addition, SC/ ST students with only 50% scores are eligible. This ratio is followed even in Parliament and all elections where a few constituencies are earmarked for those from certain communities. In a few states like Tamil Nadu, the percentage of reservation is 18% for SCs and 1% for STs, being based on local demographics. In Andhra Pradesh, 25% of educational institutes and government jobs for BCs, 15% for SCs, 6% for STs and 4% for Muslims.

Management Quota

Most controversial quota is the Management quota according to the advocaters of Pro-caste reservation people. It is also been seriously criticised by leading educationalists as it is a quota based on economic status irrespective of caste, race and religion as anybody who has money can buy his seat. It reserves about 15 % seats in private colleges for the students who are decided by the college management's own criteria. The criteria involves the colleges own entrance exam or minimum %age of 10+2 legally.

Gender Based

Women's reservations Women get 33% reservation in gram panchayat (meaning village assembly, which is a form of local village government) and municipal elections. There is a long-term plan to extend this reservation to parliament and legislative assemblies. In addition, women in India get reservation or preferential treatments in education and jobs. Certain men consider this preferential treatment of women in India as discrimination against them in admissions to schools, colleges, and universities. For instance, several law schools in India have a 30% reservation for females. Progressive political opinion in India is strongly in favour of providing preferential treatment to women in order to create a level playing field for all of its citizens.

The Women's reservation Bill was passed by the Rajya Sabha on 9 March 2010 by a majority vote of 186 members in favour and 1 against. It will now go to the Lok Sabha, and if passed there, would be implemented.

Religion Based

The Tamil Nadu government has allotted 3.5% of seats each to Muslims and Christians, thereby altering the OBC reservation to 23% from 30% since it excludes persons belonging to Other Backward Castes who are either Muslims or Christians. The government's argument is that this sub-quota is based on the backwardness of the religious communities and not on the religions themselves. Andhra Pradesh's administration has introduced a law enabling 4% reservations for Muslims. This has been contested in court. Kerala Public Service Commission has a quota of 12% for Muslims. Religious minority status educational institutes also have 50% reservation for their particular religions. The Central government has listed a number of Muslim communities as backward Muslims, making them eligible for reservation.

State of Domiciles

With few exceptions, all jobs under state government are reserved to those who are domiciles under that government. In PEC Chandigarh, earlier 80% of seats were reserved for Chandigarh domiciles and now it is 50%.

Undergraduate Colleges

Institutes like JIPMER have a policy of reserving postgraduate seats for those who completed their MBBS in JIPMER. [AIIMS] used to reserve 33% of its 120 postgraduate seats for the 40 undergraduate students (meaning everyone who had completed MBBS in AIIMS was assured a postgraduate seat, which was judged illegal by a Court.

Other Criteria

Some reservations are also made for:

- Sons/Daughters/Grandsons/Grand daughters of Freedom Fighters.
- Physically handicapped.
- Sports personalities.
- Non-Resident Indians (NRIs) have a small fracton of reserved seats in educational institutions. They have to pay more fees and pay in foreign currency.

- Candidates sponsored by various organizations.
- Those who have served in the armed forces (ex-serviceman quota).
- Dependants of armed forces personnel killed in action.
- Repatriates.
- Those born from inter-caste marriages.
- Reservation in special schools of Government Undertakings/PSUs meant for the children of their employees (e.g. Army schools, PSU schools, etc.).
- Paid pathway reservations in places of worship (e.g. Tirupathi Balaji Temple, Tiruthani Murugan (Balaji) temple).
- Seat reservation for Senior citizens/PH in Public Bus transport.

Relaxations

In view of the fact that several of the top undergraduate and graduate institutions in India, such as the IITs, the IIMs are among the most selective in the world, it is not surprising that most reservation criteria are applied at the stage of entrance examinations for these institutions. Some of the criteria are relaxed for reserved categories, while others are completely eliminated. Examples include:

1. The minimum high school marks criteria are relaxed for reserved seats.
2. Age
3. Fees, Hostel Room Rent etc.

It is important to note, however, that the criteria required to graduate from an institution are never relaxed, although some institutions provide reduced load programs (such as the ones at IITs) to meet the special needs of these students.

- Sri Lanka. In 1971 the Standardization policy of Sri Lankan universities was introduced as an affirmative action program for students from areas which had poor educational facilities due to 200 years purposeful discrimination by British colonialists. The British had practised communal favoritism towards Christians and the minority Tamil community for the entire 200 years they had controlled Sri Lanka, as part of a policy of divide and conquer.

East Asia

- Japan. Admission to universities as well as all government positions (including teachers) are determined by the entrance exam, which is extremely competitive at the top level. It is illegal to include sex, ethnicity or other social background (but not nationality) in criteria; however, there are informal policies to provide employment and long term welfare (which is usually not available to general public) to Burakumin at municipality level.
- People's Republic of China. "Preferential policies" required some of the top positions in governments be distributed to ethnic minorities and women. Also, many universities are required by government to give preferred admissions to ethnic minorities.
- South Korea. Admission to universities is also determined by the strict entrance exam, which is extremely competitive at the top level. But most of all Korean universities at the top level are adapting some affirmative actions in cases of Chinese ethnic minority, North Korean refugees, etc. in their recruiting new students. Besides, national universities have been pressed by the Korean government, so now they are trying to meet the governmental goal which is to recruit a proportion of female professors.

South East Asia and Oceania

- Malaysia. The Malaysian New Economic Policy or NEP serves as a form of affirmative action. Malaysia is the only other country (other one being South Africa) in the world which provides affirmative action to the majority because in general, the Malays have lower income than the Chinese who have traditionally been involved businesses and industries. Malaysia is a multiethnic country, with Malays making up the majority of close to 52% of the population. About 30% of the population are Malaysians of Chinese descent, while Malaysians of Indian descent comprise about 8% of the population. Government policy provides preferential placement for ethnic Malays, and 95% of all new intakes for the army, hospital nurses, police, and other government institutions are Malays. As of 2004, only 7% of all government servants are ethnic Chinese, a drop from 30% in 1960. All eight of the directors of the national petroleum company, Petronas, are Malays, and only 3% of Petronas employees are Chinese. Additionally, 95% of all government contracts are awarded to ethnic Malays. The mean income for Malays, Chinese and Indians in 1957/58 were 134, 288 and 228 respectively. In 1967/68 it was 154, 329 and 245, and in 1970 it was 170, 390 and 300. Mean income disparity ratio for Chinese/Malays rose from 2.1 in 1957/58 to 2.3 in 1970, whereas for Indians/Malays the disparity ratio also rose from 1.7 to 1.8 in the same period. The Malays viewed Independence as restoring their proper place in their own country's socioeconomic order while the non-Malays were opposing government efforts to advance Malay political primacy and economic welfare. The rising tension and resentment of the Malays for the Chinese and vice versa culminated in the vicious riots of 13 May 1969.

- New Zealand. Individuals of Mâori or other Polynesian descent are often afforded improved access to university courses, or have scholarships earmarked specifically for them.

Europe

- Finland. In certain university education programs, including legal and medical education, there are quotas for Swedish-speaking applicants. The aim of the quotas is to guarantee that a sufficient number of Swedish speaking professionals are educated, thus safeguarding the linguistic rights of the Swedish-speaking Finns.

The quota system has met with criticism from the Finnish speaking majority, some of whom consider the system unfair. In addition to these linguistic quotas, women may get preferential treatment in recruitment for certain public sector jobs if there is a gender imbalance in the field.

- France. No distinctions based on race, religion or sex are allowed under the 1958 French Constitution. Since the 1980s, a French version of affirmative action based on neighbourhood is in place for primary and secondary education. Some schools, in neighborhoods labeled "Prioritary Education Zones", are granted more funds than the others. Students from these schools also benefit from special policies in certain institutions (such as Sciences Po). The French Ministry of Defence tried in 1990 to give more easily higher ranks and driving licenses to young French soldiers with North-African ancestry. After a strong protest by a young French lieutenant in the Ministry of Defence newspaper ("Armées d'aujourd'hui"), this driving license and rank project was cancelled. After the Sarkozy election, a new attempt in favour of Arabian-French students was made but Sarkozy did not gain enough political support to change the French constitution. However, highly ranked French schools do implement affirmative action in that they are obligated to take a certain amount of students from impoverished families.
- Germany. Article 3 of the German basic law provides for equal rights of all people regardless of sex, race or social background. There are programs stating that if men and women have equal qualifications, women have to be preferred for a job; moreover, the handicapped should be preferred to healthy people. This is typical for all positions in state and university service as of 2007, typically using the phrase "We try to increase diversity in this line of work". In recent years, there has been a long public debate about whether to issue programs that would grant women a privileged access to jobs in order to fight discrimination. Germany's *Left*

Party brought up the discussion about affirmative action in Germany's school system. According to Stefan Zillich, quotas should be "a possibility" to help working class children who did not do well in school gain access to a *Gymnasium* (University-preparatory school). Headmasters of *Gymnasien* have objected, saying that this type of policy would "be a disservice" to poor children.

In 2009 the Berlin Senate decided that Berlin's Gymnasium should no longer be allowed to handpick all of their students. It was ruled that while Gymnasien should be able to pick 70 % to 65 % of their students, the other places at the Gymnasien are to be allocated by lottery. Every child will be able to enter the lottery, no matter how he or she performed in primary school.

It is hoped that this policy will increase the number of working class students attending a Gymnasium. The Left proposed that Berlin Gymnasien should no longer be allowed to expel students who perform poorly so that the students who won a Gymnasium place in the lottery have a fair chance of graduating from that school. It is not clear yet if Berlin's senate will decide in favour of The Lefts proposal. There is also a discussion going on if affirmative action should be employed to help the children and grandchildren of the so called Gastarbeiter gain better access to German universities. One prominent proponent of this was Lord Ralf Dahrendorf It is argued that the Gastarbeiter willingly came to Germany to help build the industry and this should be honored.

- Norway. In all public limited companies (PCL) boards, either gender should be represented by 40%. This affects roughly 400 companies.
- Republic of Macedonia. Minorities, most notably Albanians, are allocated quotas for access to state universities, as well as in civil public services.
- Romania. Roma people (gipsy) are allocated quotas for access to state universities.
- Slovakia. The Constitutional Court declared in October 2005 that affirmative action i.e. "providing advantages

for people of an ethnic or racial minority group" as being against its Constitution.

- Sweden. Special treatments of certain groups are commonplace in Sweden. Leveraging of the opportunities of these groups is encouraged by the state. One example is the police, who give women and people from other cultural and ethnic backgrounds concessions when it comes to testing for entrance to the police academy.
- United Kingdom. In the UK, any discrimination, quotas or favouritism on the grounds of sex, race and ethnicity is generally illegal in both education and employment. Specific exceptions include:
  - The 1998 Good Friday Agreement required that the Police Service of Northern Ireland recruit equal numbers of Catholics and Protestants in order to eliminate the service's perceived bias towards Protestants.
  - The Labour Party passed the Sex Discrimination (Election Candidates) Act 2002, allowing them to use all-women shortlists to select more women as election candidates.

South Africa

The Apartheid government favoured white-owned companies and as a result, the majority of companies in South Africa were, and still are owned by white people. The aforementioned policies achieved the desired results, but in the process they marginalised and excluded black people. A notable exception is the high number of businesses owned and operated by people of Indian descent-keen business people who thrived even under Apartheid laws due to their entrepreneurship and the political difficulties faced by them. Many people of Chinese ancestry in South Africa, also classified as "black" under the Apartheid government, also thrived through owning and operating their own businesses.

When the new majority government came to power in 1994, led by the ANC, they decided to implement an affirmative action campaign to correct previous imbalances. As such, the previously disenfranchised majority and minority groups are being supported by forcing the formerly privileged white minority group to implement certain policies. These policies include quotas regarding how much of the procurement is from non-white companies, how much of the equity is owned by non-whites, how many employees are non-white and what position the non-whites have.

The Employment Equity Act and the Broad Based Black Economic Empowerment Act aim to promote and achieve equality in the workplace (in South Africa termed "equity"), by not only advancing people from designated groups but also specifically dis-advancing the others. Those specifically hindered are the white minority. By legal definition, the designated groups who are to be advanced in society include all people of color, white women, people with disabilities, and people from rural areas. The term "black economic empowerment" is somewhat of a misnomer, therefore, because the acts cover empowerment of any member of the designated groups, regardless of race. However, government's employment legislation reserves 80% of new jobs for black people and favours black-owned companies. It is quota-based, with specific required outcomes. By a relatively complex scoring system, which allows for some flexibility in the manner in which each company meets its legal commitments, each company is required to meet minimum requirements in terms of representation by previously disadvantaged groups. The matters covered include equity ownership, representation at employee and management level (up to board of director level), procurement from black-owned businesses and social investment programs, amongst others. In 2008, the High Court in South Africa has ruled that Chinese South Africans are to be reclassified as black people. As a result of this ruling, ethnically Chinese citizens will be able to benefit from government Black Economic Empowerment (BEE) policies.

There is growing discontent in South Africa that the Broad Based Black Economic Empowerment Act has only enriched a select few black people in the country, generally those who were well-connected within the ANC so as to benefit from smart BEE deals and tender awarding, often thought to border on corruption. The same black people appear further enriched in each large BEE deal made in South Africa. Many articles have been written in this regard however the ruling ANC party has to date not altered this policy, with criticism of the policy being claimed to be a racist attack on black people becoming wealthier:

- Mail & Guardian
- MoneyWeb
- MoneyWeb
- Fin24
- Business Report
- Mail & Guardian.

A black author, Moeletsi Mbeki, published a book entitled 'Architects of Poverty' in which he describes how BEE has failed most South Africans by creating a small group of black elitist capitalists made up of ANC politicians, whilst hindering the emergence of black entrepreneurship.

Many South Africans believe that Affirmative Action is in its essence a racist policy, no different to those policies of the Apartheid government. Academic papers have been published on the topic, including how the perpetuation of racial identity in post-Apartheid South Africa is contrary to the building of a non-racial South Africa..

Professor Marinus Wiechers has written how affirmative action is a breeding ground for racism and racist sentiments.

Many white people are being marginalised through the government's affirmative action policies which see most large corporate companies forced to have a high percentage of their staff at all levels be black. This results in companies having policies in place to ensure that all new recruits are non-white and in many cases black only. White people, whether skilled or not, are excluded from many employment opportunities based purely on the color of their skin. This is seen by many to be racist in itself.

Israel

Israel has affirmative action for the Aliyah from Ethiopia (Jewish Ethiopians), with regard to housing, education and integration into employment. There are currently no significant affirmative action programs for Arabs in Israel, although some programs were fleetingly attempted by the Rabin government prior to Rabin's assassination.

Alternative Views

A 2009 Quinnipiac University survey found American voters opposed to the application of affirmative action to gay people, 65 over 27 percent. African-Americans were found to be in favour by 54 over 38 percent.

Debate

Support

The principle of affirmative action is to promote societal equality through the preferential treatment of socioeconomically disadvantaged people. Often, these people are disadvantaged for historical reasons, such as oppression or slavery. According to a poll taken by *USA Today*, most Americans support affirmative action for women; with minorities, it is more split. Men are only slightly more likely to support affirmative action for women; though a majority of both do. However, a slight majority of Americans do believe that affirmative action goes beyond ensuring access and goes into the realm of preferential treatment.

Opposition

Opponents of Affirmative Action such as George Sher believe that affirmative action devalues the accomplishments of people who are chosen based on the social group to which they belong rather than their qualifications. Opponents also contend that affirmative action devalues the accomplishments of all those who belong to groups it is intended to help, therefore making affirmative action counterproductive. Opponents, who sometimes say that affirmative action is "reverse discrimination", further claim that affirmative action has undesirable side-effects in addition to failing to achieve its goals. They argue that it hinders reconciliation, replaces old wrongs with new wrongs, undermines the achievements of minorities, and encourages individuals to identify themselves as disadvantaged, even if they are not. It may increase racial tension and benefit the more privileged people within minority groups at the expense of the least fortunate within majority groups (such as lower-class whites). American economist, social and political commentator, Dr. Thomas Sowell identified some negative results of race-based affirmative action in his book, *Affirmative Action Around the World: An Empirical Study.* Sowell writes that affirmative action policies encourage non-preferred groups to designate themselves as members of preferred groups (i.e., primary beneficiaries of affirmative action) to take advantage of group preference policies; that they tend to benefit primarily the most fortunate among the preferred group (e.g., upper and middle class blacks), often to the detriment of the least fortunate among the non-preferred groups (e.g., poor whites or Asians); that they reduce the incentives of both the preferred and non-preferred to perform at their best — the former because doing so is unnecessary and the latter because it can prove futile — thereby resulting in net losses for society as a whole; and that they increase animosity toward preferred groups.

Organization Development

Organization development (OD) is a planned, organization-wide effort to increase an organization's effectiveness and viability. Warren Bennis has referred to OD as a response to change, a complex educational strategy intended to change the beliefs, attitudes, values, and structure of organization so that they can better adapt to new technologies, marketing and challenges, and the dizzying rate of change itself. OD is neither "anything done to better an organization" nor is it "the training function of the organization"; it is a particular kind of change process designed to bring about a particular kind of end result. OD can involve interventions in the organization's "processes," using behavioural science knowledge as well as organizational reflection, system improvement, planning, and self-analysis.

The term "Organization Development" is often used interchangeably with Organizational effectiveness, especially when used as the name of a department within an organization. Organization development is a growing field that is responsive to many new approaches including Positive Adult Development. At the core of OD is the concept of organization, defined as two or more people working together toward one or more shared goal(s). Development in this context is the notion that an organization may become more effective over time at achieving its goals.

OD is a long range effort to improve organization's problem solving and renewal processes, particularly through more effective and collaborative management of organizational culture, often with the assistance of a change agent or catalyst and the use of the theory and technology of applied behavioural science. Although behavioural science has provided the basic foundation for the study and practice of organizational development, new and emerging fields of study have made their presence known.

Experts in systems thinking, leadership studies, organizational leadership, and organizational learning (to name a few) whose perspective is not steeped in just the behavioural sciences, but a much more multi-disciplinary and inter-disciplinary approach have emerged as OD catalysts. These emergent expert perspectives see the organization as the holistic interplay of a number of systems that impact the process and outputs of the entire organization. More importantly, the term change agent or catalyst is synonymous with the notion of a leader who is engaged in doing leadership, a transformative or effectiveness process as opposed to management, a more incremental or efficiency based change methodology.

Organization development is a "*contractual relationship* between a *change agent* and a *sponsoring organization* entered into for the purpose of *using applied behavioural science and or other organizational change perspectives* in a *systems context* to *improve organizational performance* and the *capacity of the organization to improve itself*".

Organization development is an ongoing, systematic process to implement effective change in an organization. Organization development is known as both a field of applied behavioural science focused on understanding and managing organizational change and as a field of scientific study and inquiry. It is interdisciplinary in nature and draws on sociology, psychology, and theories of motivation, learning, and personality.

Interventions

"Interventions" are principal learning processes in the "action" stage of organization development. Interventions are structured activities used individually or in combination by the members of a client system to improve their social or task performance.

They may be introduced by a change agent as part of an improvement program, or they may be used by the client following a program to check on the state of the organization's health, or to effect necessary changes in its own behaviour. "Structured activities" mean such diverse procedures as experiential exercises, questionnaires, attitude surveys, interviews, relevant group discussions, and even lunchtime meetings between the change agent and a member of the client organization. Every action that influences an organization's improvement program in a change agent-client system relationship can be said to be an intervention.

There are many possible intervention strategies from which to choose. Several assumptions about the nature and functioning of organizations are made in the choice of a particular strategy. Beckhard lists six such assumptions:

1. The basic building blocks of an organization are groups (teams). Therefore, the basic units of change are groups, not individuals.
2. An always relevant change goal is the reduction of inappropriate competition between parts of the organization and the development of a more collaborative condition.
3. Decision making in a healthy organization is located where the information sources are, rather than in a particular role or level of hierarchy.
4. Organizations, subunits of organizations, and individuals continuously manage their affairs against goals. Controls are interim measurements, not the basis of managerial strategy.

5. One goal of a healthy organization is to develop generally open communication, mutual trust, and confidence between and across levels.
6. People support what they help create. People affected by a change must be allowed active participation and a sense of ownership in the planning and conduct of the change.

Interventions range from those designed to improve the effectiveness of individuals through those designed to deal with teams and groups, intergroup relations, and the total organization. There are interventions that focus on task issues (what people do), and those that focus on process issues (how people go about doing it). Finally, interventions may be roughly classified according to which change mechanism they tend to emphasize: for example, feedback, awareness of changing cultural norms, interaction and communication, conflict, and education through either new knowledge or skill practice.

One of the most difficult tasks confronting the change agent is to help create in the client system a safe climate for learning and change. In a favorable climate, human learning builds on itself and continues indefinitely during man's lifetime. Out of new behaviour, new dilemmas and problems emerge as the spiral continues upward to new levels.

In an unfavorable climate, in contrast, learning is far less certain, and in an atmosphere of psychological threat, it often stops altogether. Unfreezing old ways can be inhibited in organizations because the climate makes employees feel that it is inappropriate to reveal true feelings, even though such revelations could be constructive.

In an inhibited atmosphere, therefore, necessary feedback is not available. Also, trying out new ways may be viewed as risky because it violates established norms. Such an organization may also be constrained because of the law of systems: If one part changes, other parts will become involved. Hence, it is easier to maintain the status quo. Hierarchical authority, specialization, span of control, and other characteristics of formal systems also discourage experimentation. The change agent must address himself to all of these hazards and obstacles. Some of the things which will help him are:

1. A real need in the client system to change
2. Genuine support from management
3. Setting a personal example: listening, supporting behaviour
4. A sound background in the behavioural sciences
5. A working knowledge of systems theory
6. A belief in man as a rational, self-educating being fully capable of learning better ways to do things.

A few examples of interventions include team building, coaching, Large Group Interventions, mentoring, performance appraisal, downsizing, TQM, and leadership development.

Workforce Planning

Strategic Workforce Planning is the business process for ensuring that an organization has suitable access to talent to ensure future business success. Access to talent includes considering all potential access sources (employment, contracting out, partnerships, changing business activities to modify the types of talent required, etc.). By talent is meant the skills, knowledge, predisposition and ability to undertake required activities including decisions making. Strategic Planning considers the business risks concerning insufficient, disrupted, mis-deployed talent on the organization's business priorities. Workforce planning is considered an iterative discipline. The cycle of workforce planning includes filling resource requests, analysing resource utilization, forecasting capacity, managing and identifying the resources (human) to fill that capacity, and then re-starting the cycle.

Strategic Workforce Planning is analogous to the treasurer role which is concerned with ensuring the organization has suitable access to working capital. This role also looks at multiple sources for access and similar risks to those mentioned above.

One of the more restrictive and potentially dangerous assumptions is that Strategic Planning is only about talent in the form of employees. Hiring is a strategy for accessing talent and will often be the superior one. However, the use of employees to meet talent needs carries with it unique risks that can be mitigated using alternative access sourcing arrangements. Regardless of the access source used, insightful assessment of the strategy's attendant business risk is prudent.

The process for starting out Strategic Workforce Planning is link with the organization's strategy. This means identifying the critical talent needs that if not met can materially adversely impact business success. Once the business risks are fully appreciated then attention turns to schedule and timing. Assessing current internal capability and assessing its relative position when it will be called upon in the future. Speculating on future sourcing options and identifying the preferred sourcing option. Implementation and execution follow. Attention to periodically reviewing the "sanity" of the current plan is prudent.

Workforce Analytics Approach

The focus is to analyse current and historical employee data to identify key relationships among variables and use this to provide insight into the workforce they need for the future. Workforce analysis usually includes reviewing employee recruitment, promotion and turnover patterns. In addition the analysis can also include reviewing the age and gender profiles of the workforce.

An analytical approach is important as it provides a fact based method of understanding workforce behaviours. Workforce analytics also provides further context to workforce planning efforts by ensuring perceived workforce behaviours are consistent with actual behaviours identified using a more quantitative approach.

Modeling Approach

This approach incorporates forecasting and scenario planning. Forecasting uses quantitative data to create forecasts incorporating multiple what-if and modeling the future. Scenario Planning being the more useful tool where there are uncertainties, therefore incorporating quantitative and qualitative.

Segmentation Approach

Breaking the workforce into segments along the lines of their jobs and determining relevance to strategic intent. Provides a technique for prioritizing.

Steps in Workforce Planning

Though there is no definitive 'Start here' activity for any of the approaches to Strategic Workforce Planning, there are five fundamentals activities that most Workforce Plan models have:

- Environment Scan
- Current Workforce Profile
- Future Workforce View
- Analysis and Targeted Future
- Closing the gaps.

Bibliography

Allen, J. : *Cultural Industries and the Production of Culture,* Taylor & Francis, 2007.

Arndt, William B. Jr. : *Theories of Personality*, Macmillan, New York, 1974.

Asch, M : *Abnormal and Developmental Psychology*, Ivy Pub, Delhi, 2003.

Bieber, I.: *Homosexuality: A Psychoanalytic Study of Male Homosexuals.* New York: Basic Books, 1962.

Boring, E.G.: *A History of Experimental Psychology*. New York: The Century Company, 1929.

Chaudhri, R.D. : *Herbal Drugs Industry : A Practical Approach to Industrial Pharmacognosy*, Eastern, Delhi, 1996.

Dibbern, Jens : *The Sourcing of Application Software Services, Empirical Evidence of Cultural, Industry and Functional Differences,* Physica Verlag Heidelberg, 2004.

Dicken, P. : *Wheels of Change, the Automobile Industry, Global shift, Mapping the Changing Contours of the World Economy*, London, 2007.

Dubey, K.C. : *Experimental and Developmental Psychology*, Omega Pub, Delhi, 2009.

Ellis, A. :*Humanistic Psychology, The Rational-emotive Approach,* Julian Press, New York, 1973.

Georgi, A. : *Psychology as a Human Science*, Harper & Row, New York, 1970.

Ginsburgh, Victor A. : *Economics of Art and Culture*, Contributions to Economic Analysis, Elsevier, 2004.

Grace, G. : *School Leadership: Beyond Educational Development*, London, Falmer, 1995.

Harold, L. : *Entertainment Industry Economics, A Guide for Financial Analysis,* Cambridge University Press, 2004.

Harvey, Francis : *A Primer of GIS, Fundamental Geographic and Cartographic Concepts,* The Guilford Press, 2008.

Jalan, P.K. : *Industrial Sector Reforms in Globalization Era*, Sarup, Delhi, 2004.

Kumar, Arvind : *Industrial Pollution and Management*, APH, Delhi, 2004.

Lee, Jeong-kyu : *Historic Factors Influencing Korean Higher Education,* Seoul, Jimoondang, 2000.

McDonnell, R.A. : *Principles of Geographical Information Systems*, Oxford University Press, Oxford, 1998.

Moustakas, S.: *Existential Psychotherapy and the Interpretation of Dreams,* J. Aronson, C., Northvale, NJ, 1994.

Pathak, Bachcha : *Industrial Policy of India : Changing Facets*, Deep and Deep, Delhi, 2007.

Rathod, P B : *Dynamics of Political Psychology*, ABD Pub, Delhi, 2008.

Sagar, G. Vidya : *Pharmaceutical Industrial Management*, Pharma Book Syndicate, Delhi, 2005.

Sharma, Ram Nath : *Advanced Industrial Psychology*, Atlantic, Delhi, 2004.

Strasser, S. *Phenomenology and the Human Science,* Duquesne University Press, Pittsburgh, PA, 1963.

Suri, R.K. : *Dynamics of Industrial Relations*, Pentagon Press, Delhi, 2007.

William, D. : *Social and Personality Development, Infancy through Adolescence,* New York: Norton, 1983.

Index

L

M

N

O

P

R

S

T

V

W